On the Global Waterfront

On the Global Waterfront

The Fight to Free the Charleston 5

MONTHLY REVIEW PRESS
NEW YORK, NY

C.I.P. data available from the publisher.

Design: Terry J. Allen

Monthly Review Press
146 West 29th Street, Suite 6W
New York, NY 10019

www.monthlyreview.org

10 9 8 7 6 5 4 3 2

Table of Contents

Acknowledgements

We thank Jodi Hortman and Glenn Justis in the Dorchester County Solicitor's office, the librarians at the Charleston Public Library, Fran Shuler at ILA Local 1422 and Greg Dropkin at Labournet for their help collecting documents, Marvin Dulaney and Harlan Greene at Avery Institute, and Jim Campbell for his informed understandings and good conversation. Special thanks to Armand Derfner and Peter Wilborn for helping us tell an important side of the story and to Donna Dewitt for her unending support.

Members of the business community who were particularly obliging include John Hassell III, Robert New, Howard Hunter, Larry Young, Lee Tigner, Bruce Miller and Perry Collins who spoke to us before the project had taken the shape it has today. Members of the South Carolina political arena who helped greatly include Gilda Cobb-Hunter, Robert Ford and David Mack. Others who gave us their time were former Gov. Jim Hodges, John Graham Altman and Chip Limehouse.

We thank the Rev. Joseph Darby, Rev. Don Flowers, Andy Brack, Blease Graham, Bill Moore and George Hopkins as well as Eli Poliakoff and Andrew Herod for their earlier research. We thank Samantha Clark for making the original connection, Rudy Feagin for his belief in us and Fred Whitehead for his access to hard-to-find histories.

For their kind hospitality we thank the members of Bibleway Baptist Church and Morris Brown A.M.E., the Liverpool dockers, Vancouver I.L.W.U. staffers Tim Footman and Steve Suttie, the Riley family and the members and staff of the South Carolina AFL-CIO. For their advice on how to propose, write, rewrite and promote the book, we thank David Prosten and

Sarah Flynn, Michael Yates, Kate Gleeson, Lynne Kirk, Steve Stallone, Jack Heyman, Will Moredock and Greg Palast. Thanks to Steve Zeltzer for his video support and to Martin Paddio for knowing this story had to be told. Any weaknesses are ours, but this book is stronger for the contributions of these good people.

We thank everyone we interviewed, whether quoted or not, for their knowledge and time. To the contributors large and small to this project, we thank you for making it happen.

And finally, to Ken Riley, the officers and the members of Local 1422, thank you for trusting us and helping us tell this story.

Dedicated to longshoremen everywhere. May you exercise your power to build a brighter future for us all.

Preface

by Greg Palast

WHO GIVES A FLYING FART about labor unions today? Only 7 percent, one in fourteen U.S. workers belongs to one. That's fewer than the number of Americans who believe that Elvis killed John Kennedy.

Even the label, "labor union," has something vaguely Thirties about it.

Think "longshoremen" and what comes to mind is *On the Waterfront*, with Marlon Brando, the good guy, beating up the evil union boss. The union bosses were the thugs, Mobbed-up bullies, the dockworkers' enemies.

The movie's director, Elia Kazan, perfectly picked up the anti-union zeitgeist of that era of red-baiting Joe McCarthy—which could go well today. After all, Senator Hillary Clinton was on the board of the number one union-busting corporation on the planet, Wal-Mart.

Elected labor leaders are, in our media, always "union bosses." But the *real* bosses, the CEOs, the guys who shutter factories and ship them to China . . . they're never "bosses," they're "entrepreneurs."

So what we have here is a *very unfashionable* book in which the main man, a hero who never meant to be a hero, is a union president.

His stage is on the waterfront. Not the one in the Brando movie. The real one where tough crews "shape up," hoping for a decent daily wage. Then even hope gets taken away one morning when a multi-continental shipping corporation tells them to go to Hell, there're beggars down the dock who will load the containers for peanuts.

This, then, is the story of globalization left out of Thomas Friedman's wonders-of-the-free-market fantasies. In Friedman's bestseller, *The World is Flat*, we begin with his uplifting game of golf with an Indian tycoon.

This book is *not* globalization in golf shoes, but globalization stripped down to its dirty underpants. Friedman makes the point that he flew business class to Bangalore on his way to the greens to meet his millionaire. Erem and Durrenberger go steerage class. And the people they write about don't go anywhere at all. These are the dockworkers who move the containers of Wal-Mart toys from Guatemala to sell to customers in Virginia who can't afford health insurance because they lost their job in the toy factory.

But there's a twist. The unexpected stand-up champion in the story is a dockworker in Barcelona, Spain. I won't give away more except to say that the book tells us about reaching across borders, not sealing them.

The entire story rides on a detective story. We open on a scene with six hundred police in riot gear facing a few dozen angry-as-hell workers on the docks of Charleston. In the darkness, rocks, clubs and blood fly. Five union men are arrested for conspiracy to riot. Four black and one white. The prosecutor: a white, Bible-thumping Attorney General running for Governor and a city ripped in half—union/non-union, white/black. The movers and shakers versus the moved and shaken.

Erem and Durrenberger ask themselves why they were so drawn to a story of five cargo-handlers from South Carolina, indicted a decade ago. Maybe it's because the fight to free the Charleston 5 shows how courage, heart, and solidarity can lead to victory in the midst of a mad march into globalization that threatens to turn us all into the Wal-Mart 5 Billion.

IN JANUARY 2000, South Carolina was on the tail end of a national public relations beating for flying the Confederate flag over its statehouse when the protest at the port of Charleston sparked an international campaign that would test how far South Carolina would go to jeopardize its image and its economy for the sake of its nineteenth-century ideals. The flag debate would subside within six months, but the confrontation at the port, which made only a short splash on the national media, would drag South Carolina and the Port of Charleston through a worldwide mud pit for the next twenty-two months.

Everyone would take a side. Everyone would take a risk. Everyone would feel the pain. This is that story.

1

The Provocation

[Longshoremen] like to see themselves as rough-and-ready individuals, and that is the image that they project both to outsiders and to one another. It would be a mistake not to take this seriously, for no image of self can be maintained unless one is willing and at least marginally able to demonstrate when challenged that he has the attributes that he advertises.

—Willie Pilcher, longshoreman and anthropologist[1]

JANUARY 2000 WAS A PRECARIOUS TIME in South Carolina. The state was perched on the edge of change while clutching tenaciously to history and tradition. It was a canary in the coalmine of our national political life. In spite of its reputation for backwardness, South Carolina pointed the way to unprecedented political divisiveness, economic inequities, and cultural cruelty for the rest of the nation, the way we willingly followed for the decade to come.

That January's critical events began on Martin Luther King Jr. Day with the biggest civil rights protest in four decades and certainly the biggest in South Carolina's history. After six months of escalating media coverage of the state's political polarization—not unlike the kind our entire country would soon suffer—more than 46,000 people converged on the state's capitol building to demand removal of the Confederate flag that had flown over the building since 1961.[2] It was raised then to signify defiance to federal civil rights laws.[3] Though Confederates had not been able to muster more than 7,000 for a counterprotest to the NAACP-sponsored march, they received equal if not more media time in the ongoing debate over "heritage" vs. "racism."

South Carolina's tiny organized labor force flexed its civil and labor rights muscle in support of the march. The most noticeable support came from the wealthiest and blackest union, Local 1422 of the International Longshoremen's Association (ILA) in Charleston. Ken Riley was the newly elected president of the small local with 600 permanent and 400 casual workers, almost all black. The master contract that covered all East Coast ports provided high wages and, therefore, healthy dues payments to the union. The local chartered buses to take protesters from Charleston to Columbia to attend the rally.

A week earlier, when Charleston's popular white mayor Joe Riley organized a protest march to Columbia, an enthusiastic group of some twenty ILA members with bright T-shirts and signs joined in. Twice the mayor's staff reminded them to move to the back of the line and quiet down because they were drawing attention away from the mayor.

After a second day of this treatment, union leader Ken Riley called off the union's participation in the march. With his usual aplomb, Riley let the insulting treatment of the mayor's staff roll off his back as just another one of those things that black people learn to tolerate in Charleston. With thirty years of successful service running Charleston—more than half the black union leader's life—the mayor and his staff knew the limits of what a politician could get away with among his own constituents, especially black ones.

The handful of buses the union paid for to provide transportation to the demonstration in Columbia was nothing compared to the construction project the union was undertaking. Riley's leadership team was in the middle of planning a $6.5 million building to replace the one down the street which the city was displacing with a new bridge. Such an expenditure was a financial leap of faith for the union, whose members decided to foot the cost of a substantial community hall and make it available for wedding receptions and other celebrations, meetings, and demonstrations. The union hall would become the center for progressive political action from the Democratic Party to grassroots community agitation for years to come and the space in which both the strongest promises and worst betrayals in modern South Carolina history would be forged.

But just days after the 46,000 protesters in Columbia dispersed to every corner of the country, Ken Riley and his local found themselves in the fight of their lives right in their own backyard: the Columbus Street Terminal in Charleston. This event would make the national and international news, too, but Riley didn't have the NAACP's media machine to back him up, so keeping it in the national eye would prove to be a challenge.

There had been forebodings. One was the State Law Enforcement Division's (SLED) Lt. Buster Edwards's visit to Ken Riley at the union hall. Edwards and Riley had developed a professional understanding during those tough times when the chicken companies tried to go nonunion at the port, as they were in their factories upstate.[4] SLED had agreed to make Edwards a liaison to the local, in no small part because he was black, he was personable, and he could build rapport quickly. Now, whenever the union was going to picket or demonstrate at any of the terminals, Riley would let Edwards know how many people would be there so SLED wouldn't have to turn out more police than necessary—which they both knew would just be a provocation—but there would be enough police presence to keep everything in order.

"I thought I ought to warn you of something," Edwards said, getting down to business.

"What's going on?" Riley asked.

"Well, I just got a call, and you're not going to believe this. . . . You know that Nordana trouble you guys've been having?"

"Sure, you know we've been picketing them every couple of weeks, ever since they went nonunion a few months ago," Riley responded. "But we'll get it worked out. We've been talking with the Ports Authority and the company."

"Yeah, but there's another ship coming in next week," Edwards said.

"Yep," Riley confirmed. "We'll have the usual thirty, maybe fifty folks out there with signs. We got the permits already. It'll be fine; no big deal."

"Well, it's gonna be a big deal," Edwards said.

"What are you talking about?"

"There's gonna be six hundred police out there to meet you guys," Edwards said slowly. "Not five hundred ninety-nine, but six hundred exactly."

"WHAT?" Riley said. "For *what*?"

"That's exactly what *I* said when I was told. I can't tell you what's going on, but there'll be six hundred police there when that ship comes to port."

Riley had a hard time believing Edwards. Maybe he had bad information. Maybe it was an intentional rumor meant to scare them off. It was so outrageous he didn't give it any more thought. Until the afternoon of January 19.

ON HIS WAY TO THE HALL THAT DAY, Riley stopped at the port's offices to endure another futile negotiating session with State Ports Authority officials, Stevedoring Services of America, known simply as SSA, the company that hires and supervises the work of the union longshoremen, and Nordana, the shipping line that until recently had always hired union companies to work their ships. SSA, one of the largest global logistics firms in the world, hired all of its longshoremen out of the Local 1422 hall. But Nordana was tiny compared to its mega-container ship competitors and was having trouble competing on their scale. To reduce its freight-handling costs Nordana had dropped SSA and contracted with a nonunion stevedoring firm owned by Georgetown businessman Perry Collins.

Collins promised Nordana that his company could hire nonunion longshoremen to unload its ships at the old navy yard in North Charleston, outside the jurisdiction of the State Ports Authority and the union, but Collins's plans had evaporated. Meanwhile, workers had been protesting every Nordana ship that came to port at the Columbus Street Terminal, and Nordana's clients were getting nervous.

That morning, sitting at the port's offices negotiating, Nordana officials weren't willing to change their minds and Collins's nonunion workers were still unloading the ships for half the wages. The union's three months of picketing and protesting had not changed the company's position. Riley walked out of the fruitless and frustrating talks.

As lunchtime approached, Riley ran some errands near his home in West Ashley and headed back across town to the union hall around 3 p.m. He saw buses passing the on-ramp as he approached I-26. At first he thought they were full of tourists, the stock and trade of the other mainstay of Charleston's economy besides the port. But as he caught up to the buses, he saw the gold state seals on their sides.

"Oh my *God*," he thought. "Those buses are coming for us!"

KEN RILEY AND HIS MEN were a small union in a rabidly antiunion state—generally less-educated black men making sometimes as much as $100,000 per year to perform what many perceive to be unskilled though dangerous work, in a state with an average wage of $8 per hour, in a country where unions had been on the decline for decades. Riley's charm and the respect he commanded from both blacks and whites couldn't change those facts, that friction, that grating truth that ran against the natural order of things and the proper place for black people in genteel South Carolina.

It didn't matter to the white establishment, many of whom made multiples of any longshoremen's salary without ever lifting a soft manicured finger, that those rugged, loud, rough black men and a handful of women kept the port machinery well greased and running smoothly. Lacking the "unskilled" workers' expert and hard-won understanding of the waterfront, many of these white "professionals" would have been crushed in a moment on the docks. It never occurred to the (mostly white) men and women who worked for the governor or the chamber of commerce or the State Ports Authority that the demands those black men and their fathers and grandfathers had made over a century and a half of backbreaking, sometimes humiliating, and always exhausting work was what created the reputation and the standards that by 1999 poured $63 million *per day* into Charleston's and South Carolina's economy. From the perspective of their air-conditioned offices, machines did the work, and the uneducated black men walking around on the waterfront could never merit a hundred-thousand-dollar annual income or anything close to it.

The privileged men at the top would never concede that those black men at the bottom, often working at two or three in the morning, in sleet and rain, as well as in the heat of high noon, had created the wealth that allowed the State Ports Authority to purchase, for example, $34 million worth of land in upstate South Carolina and then lease it to luxury car manufacturer BMW corporation for $1 per year to lure the company to the state.[5]

No, it was too much of a stretch for them to realize that a $22-per-hour base rate plus overtime, plus container royalties, plus benefits for brutish longshoremen was the base figure upon which every percentage of the immense wealth generated by the second-largest and most efficient port on the East Coast was calculated in the system of cost-plus contracting. Yet it was that basic standard, the prevailing wage at the Port of Charleston and everything that rested upon it, that would be at risk for the next twenty-two months. It could prove to be a foundation of stone or a house of cards—and it all depended on who prevailed.

BY 3:30 P.M. ON JANUARY 19, 2000, two City of Charleston Police Department (CCPD) coach buses and a CCPD school bus had pulled up to the intersection of Morrison and Immigration. Armored personnel carriers, the SWAT team's vehicle, and other menacing military-style trucks were pulling into the terminal.

Vehicles that looked like some cross between squad cars and armored personnel carriers, four officers in each, were parked at every telephone pole, and more were coming. Police lined up like infantry along eight blocks of Morrison Drive. Mounted officers commanded the cops by the hundreds who were drilling in the middle of a closed-off portion of the street. Police dogs tugged at their leashes. Police marched, boots stomping, not far from the union hall, their shields and batons at the ready, practicing for the night to come.

Still looking down the road at the military might amassing, Riley pulled into his parking space at the union hall. "Lord, what are we gonna do tonight?" he half thought, half prayed. And then he heard the answer loud and clear: *Nothing*. He looked down the road again and said, smiling to himself, "Yeah, that's right. We're not gonna do *nothing*!"

Riley walked into the hall looking for the presidents of the other waterfront unions, Johnny Alvanos of the white Clerks and Checkers union and Ben Parker of the black Mechanics union. The Nordana ship was due in at seven that night. Riley's brother Leonard had already put out the word to the usual twenty or thirty picketers. The attorneys had already submitted the city permits that optimistically provided for a picket up to the unlikely number of one hundred people.

The massive police presence changed everything.

At their briefing hall less than a mile from the port, the Charleston police force gathered to prepare for one of the biggest peacetime displays of force in South Carolina's history.[6] Captain Gary Tillman addressed the hundred and twenty or so black and white men and women in uniform that packed the room and stood along the walls to explain that the State Ports Authority's chief executive officer Bernie Groseclose had requested assistance from area police. Groseclose attributed recent vandalism, threats, and the stoppage of work on one ship to the longshoremen's protests.[7]

The captain explained that seven other law enforcement agencies, totaling five hundred and fifty officers, would be joining them that night. "We want to have such a show of force to project an image that we can't lose this battle tonight," he said. "And it has all the potential of being a battle."

The captain told his officers that police had received a tip that union people from Georgia, North Carolina, and Virginia would be coming to the protest. He warned the officers they would be wet and cold that night, and when it came time to instruct them on the use of two-way radios, he told them:

I'd like you to keep transmissions down to a minimum. If somebody's getting their ass kicked over at Immigration and Morrison Drive, we certainly don't want to hear that "Hey, I need a relief over at whatever location."

The police were ready for war.

RILEY KNEW THERE HAD BEEN SMALL SKIRMISHES on the docks the last few times a Nordana ship had docked and he expected a response, but this incredible military display was an assault on longshoremen, on their credibility, on a new reputation he had begun to build for the longshoremen. It was an effort to make them look like a bunch of thugs and it was uncalled for. A large part of him thought it was a setup, a provocation, to force the longshoremen to do something they'd regret for a long time to come.

If the police and the port were successful, it could kill everything the new leadership was trying to do in the community. Riley's father and his uncle had shown him how to build the connections and walk the invisible lines drawn all over Charleston. But this was like nothing his elders had ever faced, and these were longshoremen, not businessmen, the police were provoking.

Longshoremen were slowly gathering in the parking lot where they usually chatted before going into the hall for a hiring. Three or four times a day, men and a few women came by to see if a ship had docked, and how many gangs it would need to work its cargo. To "shape," as the old-timers called the hiring process each day, they'd stand waiting in groups divided by skills and seniority for the foremen to choose among them the quota of workers each ship needed. Regular workers plus scores of "casuals," less experienced but willing men and women, would hold out their cards for the foreman to take, hoping they'd make the union wages and benefits that day to count toward seniority and permanent membership. Each "gang" would head out in every kind of weather to one of four terminals in Charleston—the Columbus Street Terminal near the union hall, Wando Welch up the river, or the smaller North Charleston or Union Pier.

At the port, an operator in a crane towering above them would lift a trailer truck-sized container from the hold of a ship. Using hand signals, the longshoreman would guide the container to the trailer chassis where other longshoremen locked it down at each corner. Another longshoreman would drive the "yard dog" truck cab used for pulling the chassis through the container yard to its designated place where another crane would lift the container off the chassis and place it into its designated position in a stack of other containers.

The massive Rubber Tire Gantry cranes in the yard dwarfed any container hanging from between the standards of their tall square frames. A worker sitting in a tiny cab six stories up at the top of the giant machine controlled its precise movements as it lifted and lowered boxes containing several tons of freight within inches of their mark.

If they were loading instead of unloading a ship, the longshoreman would unlock a container from a chassis and guide the crane operator to lift and then lower it in to the hold or on to the deck of the ship where fellow longshoremen would lash the container into place for the voyage to its destination. Lashers attach long steel rods in X's across the ends of containers to secure them to each other top to bottom. They make their way gingerly between the containers, being sure of their footing, as a fall could be deadly.

The mostly white clerks and checkers, members of another union local, kept track of each container as it came or went, where it was stored, where it was from, and where it was bound.

In another part of the port, longshoremen "stuffed" and "stripped" containers that have mixed loads of goods to reorganize them so that the newly packed containers can be loaded onto trucks for shipment across the state or across the country.

That afternoon, there weren't any other ships coming in, but word of mouth had created a stir at the hall, and more workers than usual were hanging around waiting to see what would happen. The local union presidents discussed strategy in the upstairs boardroom. Downstairs, more and more men drifted in and out of the building, watching the show of force gathering on the road in front of their hall.

At 6 p.m. the presidents called the members together in the hall and announced their plan. By then, hundreds had assembled.

"Okay, everybody, we've discussed this, and we've decided there won't be any picketing tonight," Riley told the group. Alvanos nodded in agreement to the couple dozen white clerks in the crowd, and Parker looked through the crowd for the few mechanics who repair and maintain the thousands of chassis on the port. "Look, we could go down there, and you know what could happen," Riley warned the members. "We've come up with a better plan."

In the crowd were men Riley had grown up with, men who had supported him in his battle to reform the local. But also in the crowd were some of the old guard, supporters of the previous administration of Ben Flowers, who had served as president for almost twenty years. The new leaders thought Flowers would sacrifice the best interests of the union and the men to avoid any confrontations. He had gone along to get along, and members had paid the price for his compliance. Riley was convinced the old-timers had nothing like he and his men shared—a brotherhood that comes from taking risks together and building something better than their fathers had. The new leadership had changed the role of the union and taken it beyond the waterfront, into the community, all the way to Columbia and up the coast to New York. Riley wanted to change the way the International was being run, to distance the union from its not entirely unearned reputation of being linked with the Mob. That meant this black guy from the South had to be willing to ruffle some white feathers up north, too.

These new leaders, all of whom had graduated from college, set an example so that more longshoremen would send their children to college and buy their own homes, instead of spending their paychecks partying every week. The new slate didn't drink, didn't smoke, and didn't cuss, and banned all activity unrelated to the union from the hall's parking lot. Now, on payday, a time that always flushed the community with cash, the women looking for their men, the small businessmen, and the fellow partyers who used to cruise the lot had to find a new place to hook up with the newly paid longshoremen; the union hall was off-limits. The last three years had raised longshoremen's self-esteem and their image in the community, but it hadn't been easy to change old habits. Supporters of the old leadership could sabotage what these new guys had done, especially now, a week before the union election.

"Look, we are not going to go down there," Riley said. "We have nothing to gain. We can't get to the ship. We can't even get to the gate. It's dark so no one can read our signs." The men grumbled. "They are already spending this money," Riley continued, "and when the media reports what took place tonight, the police will be the ones to look like fools. They were down there and we were not."

That idea went over better, because this was a matter of respect more than anything else. Finally, Riley told the group to go home and come back to fill the parking lot by midnight. By then the police would have sent some officers home and when they saw the longshoremen reassembling, they would call them back. "At midnight, we'll decide whether to do it again. It's cold. It's wet. Let's keep them spending the money *all night*."

The men laughed nervously but wondered if it would do anything to save their jobs or make a strong enough statement about how wrong this all was— Nordana getting away with using a nonunion stevedore and sending six hundred cops to meet the union's picket. They sauntered out of the hall, snickering and winking at the reporters standing just outside the door.

"It's just a big chess game," one longshoreman said to a guy with a notebook.

"Be patient, you'll get your story," said another.

"It's going to be a long night," Riley told a reporter with Charleston's *Post and Courier*.

Some workers went home to talk with their families about what was happening. Others hovered in the parking lot, chatting and laughing.

WHEN LONGSHOREMEN BEGAN TO RETURN at 11:30 p.m., police were blockading the exit to Morrison Drive off the bridge. The workers had to detour almost ten blocks just to get to their union hall, fueling the resentment that had been growing all day. By the time they started gathering in the parking lot and entering the hall, the streets were cool and damp from an early rain but tempers were as hot as an August afternoon on the docks. The union officers were still upstairs talking. They had counted forty full patrol cars leaving the terminal at 9:30 p.m. and watched them, as predicted, heading right back as the hall began to fill at 11:30. Riley's phone rang.

"The guys are back, and they're saying they want to go down there," one of the union delegates reported from downstairs.

By the time Riley and the other officers got to the hiring hall, it was teeming with longshoremen talking and shouting to one another. The group greeted the three presidents respectfully by hushing up quickly.

Elijah Ford, one of the regular Nordana picketers and one of the men displaced by Nordana's decision to go nonunion, was the first to speak up from the floor.

"We know what you said, but we're going down to picket," he told the presidents. "That's where we always go, and we're going to stand up for our jobs tonight."

Riley was the key strategist. He had the largest local by far and the largest liability. Twenty years of political battles in the union had trained him to know when to let the men lead. But Riley had spent a lifetime learning about the power and brutality of the white establishment in Charleston. When he was eight, he and Leonard watched a white bus driver beat a black carpenter when the tired man refused to give up his seat to a white woman. When he was sixteen, white students spit at him in his newly integrated high school. He and other black students would meet under an oak tree every day to compare notes on how the white kids were treating them. They agreed that if a dangerous situation developed they'd pull the fire alarm to summon help.[8] At the College of Charleston, a professor set up tutoring for an entire class of failing students except the black ones. Other professors failed black students on essay tests, while the same students would ace the more objective math and science exams.

Every man in the union hall had stories like these that they never bothered to tell because they were so much a normal part of being black. Yet this, plus his many travels north as a child with his father, picking cucumbers and tomatoes in New York, had taught Riley to appreciate the power of the prejudice his men were up against when they walked out to face that army. Reuben Greenberg, Charleston's black Jewish police chief, had proven he would not use excessive force; Riley had seen him permit reasonable protests on the docks before. But what was assembled out there was much bigger than Greenberg. Besides, the chief was out of the country.

"Okay, for those of you who want to go, go ahead," Riley said. "But please be careful; please do *not* engage those officers." A number of delegates, elected leaders Riley could trust, went with the group.

The men picked up signs, some showing signs of wear from the last picket, and headed out the door. Outside, a handful of community activists who had seen the events unfold on the evening news, joined the picketers as they headed down the road, chanting. The presidents stayed back—for now.

The one-lane blacktop road called Immigration Street leads to the Columbus Street Terminal and intersects Morrison Drive at nearly ninety degrees. Facing the port, along the left side of the road, is a chain-link fence to protect the yard covered with stacks of massive, colorful containers stretching all the way to Morrison and back to the terminal. On the other side, an open barren field waits for the next temporary industrial building to go up. Spartina, or cordgrass, had spread from the nearby wetlands and taken over the open space.

About seventy yards from Morrison Drive, railroad tracks cross Immigration. To the left, the tracks pass inland through the yard of blue, red, green, and metallic containers. To the right, the tracks curve away slowly through the weedy field. Like all railroad tracks, these are spiked into ties set in gravel, and old leftover railroad ties, some rotten or splintered, lay in the gravel alongside the tracks.

The tracks end at the terminal, near the ships, where men load and unload cargo from trains to trucks to ships any time of day or night. Past where the tracks intersect it, the blacktop road ends at the gated chain-link fence and a guard shack. Four hundred yards past the tracks sits the terminal gate, and out of sight of the road or the tracks and behind that are the docks and the ships: the $23-billion-per-year industry on which the Charleston waterfront prides itself, the engine of its economy.[9]

ONE OF THE LONGSHOREMEN who filed out of the hall that second time on January 19 said there were six hundred to seven hundred of them there; someone else said it was closer to three hundred or four hundred people, and about half of those walked to Immigration Street while the rest "hung back."[10] They were shouting and cussing, chanting, and waving their arms.

Reporters from the newspapers and television stations stood to the side, taking in what they could in the light from generator-powered construction lamps the police had erected high over the road. One television cameraman ran forward to the police line and turned around to shoot footage of the approaching longshoremen from the vantage point of the front row of the police.

Three longshoremen, one holding a sign, led the men out of the union hall parking lot, down Morrison Drive for two hundred yards to Immigration Street. Two took the sides of the road. Leonard, the senior of the three and Riley's older brother, headed down the center, later swinging to the right. They knew what they had to do: protect their men from harm, but make their point.

As they turned the corner to Immigration Street, they saw the front lines of the police force gathered and waiting for them. About halfway down that narrow road, squeezed between the railroad tracks and the port gate and bulging off the blacktop into the field, were police officers as far back as they could see. The helicopter spotlight swung across the scene from above and the wind from the rotors twisted the protest signs. Lighting the front lines of the police were temporary lights hung from tall poles at the corner and on the right, near the railroad tracks, the designated "no entry point" police would defend.[11]

THE LAWMEN AND WOMEN had come from all across South Carolina to assemble at the Columbus Street Terminal that night. The State Law Enforcement Division, the South Carolina Highway Patrol, and officers from the sheriff's office of nearby Mt. Pleasant, and every other law enforcement agency in the metro area were there. K-9 dogs paced among the ranks. The thumping of a police helicopter hovering overhead added to the combat atmosphere as its spotlight scanned the scene. A sniper lay on his stomach on the roof of an ambulance, his elbows resting just behind the flashing bar of lights, his sight trained on the space just ahead of the front police line.

The marching longshoremen met the police a few yards in front of the railroad tracks. A couple of longshoremen walked right past the first officer and into the line, which gave way slightly until an officer pushed back, almost bear-hugging one longshoreman from behind.[12]

The police yielded, stepping back slowly until the longshoremen's front line reached the tracks. One officer put up his baton with straight arms then twisted it in a half swing. In response a longshoreman yanked the baton out of the officer's hands and ran back into the crowd. The officer followed and for a moment was surrounded by onlooking longshoremen, most unaware of what was happening. Another officer stepped in, the longshoremen stepped away, and the first officer stepped back into line.[13]

Then the two lines formed up, an invisible buffer of air between them. The generic chanting turned to specific charges aimed directly at individual officers. "Why you doin' this? These are our *jobs*, man!" But only the words of the men in front could land on any officer, so the ones in back picked up gravel instead. Bits of rock and gravel made "clacking" sounds as they hit and bounced off the plastic riot shields and helmets.

Then protesters in the back began to aim higher and much more forcefully at the light, trying to put it out. Union delegates walked up and down the front of the line, waving their arms at members, encouraging them to stop throwing rocks. Most heeded the delegates, but others, when they thought no one was looking, continued to toss pieces of railroad ties, rocks, and sticks onto the police in the front lines. Longshoremen at the front continued to confront police officers directly and forcefully, asking how they could do this, telling them this was about their jobs and their port.[14]

The police had stopped moving backwards. Throngs of longshoremen, many of whom could not see to the front, were still pushing from behind, forcing Leonard and the others into the line of police shields.[15] The officers began to push back. People on both sides were calling for calm, but as one longshoreman put it, "There's only so far I can let someone push me."

The longshoremen backed up briefly, and Leonard shouted that some of them should head down the tracks. He hoped at least some police would follow them, and he would divide the troops and diffuse the tension at the front line. As he headed down the tracks, too far to turn back, he realized he was alone. Behind him, at a distance he couldn't quite see clearly, the shoving continued. He kept going. He knew that terminal better than his own backyard on Savage Road and was pretty sure he could get through the fence where it crossed the tracks.

At the fence, Leonard felt around low for a gap and found it, but decided it was easier to jump over. He carefully grabbed hold of two smooth sections of barbed wire, and leapt over the fence. He walked onto the terminal without a plan in his head. He kept near the train cars and thought maybe he could pull some police from the back lines and distract them. Before that thought went far he heard some officers talking and their boots crunching on the gravel.

A State Ports Authority sergeant was walking near the north railroad gate with two other SPA officers and two police dogs when he saw someone standing about 50 feet away, next to a container.[16] It was Leonard.

They walked up to him and asked him if he was a longshoreman. Leonard came out with his hands up, worried that the police might be trigger-happy that night. The dogs evoked an old and familiar threat as well. They arrested him for trespassing and put him in a bus at the back of the massed police force, near the terminal gate.

AT THE RAILROAD TRACKS, the shoving continued. A longshoreman grabbed a baton. Another baton went up and landed on another longshoreman's head and he fell to the ground. A baton swung down on some police helmets as well.

Among the feet and legs of two front lines of officers at the north end, a baton came down so hard it made a *whack!* sound. Longshoreman Charles Brave, the Union's deacon, was on the ground behind the police line. He yelled as the baton came down on him hard. Then another *whack!* Another yell. "Why you got me layin' on the ground?" Brave asked. Another *whack!* "Aaaaggh!" *Whack!* "Aaaagggh! What you beatin' me for man? What you beatin' me for? Why you hittin' a man on the ground?" There were muffled sounds as the officers stood him up. As he walked away he was breathing heavily. "It's all right," he said.

From behind them another officer barked orders. "Third line! Third line! Give me a fucking third line here!"[17]

RILEY AND THE OTHER PRESIDENTS had just sat down in Riley's office to wait. "We got the call within twelve minutes of when they walked out of here," Riley said later. "One of our guys, a checker, had his head busted open. I dropped the phone and ran out that front door and never stopped till I got to the front line. I could hear the clacking and firing of guns, helicopters—there were bright lights in my face. I've never been to war but I know what it's like now. The first guy I jumped over was lying on the road with his head busted open."

A black longshoreman was standing near the checker, making repeated 911 calls from his cell phone and not getting any help for the man on the ground who was holding his head. A television cameraman and a police videographer were filming the caller's attempt to get help for the downed man. The caller told the 911 operator that they had a man down at the Columbus Street Terminal and he had been waiting twenty minutes for an ambulance.[18] When would medical help arrive?

CHARLESTON POLICE CHIEF REUBEN GREENBERG had just returned from giving a police academy training in Bulgaria and was behind the police line, watching. The chief was a short but imposingly stocky black man who commanded the respect of law enforcement experts across the country. In his thirty years commanding Charleston's police force, he had built a reputation for firm law enforcement wrapped in a thick layer of genuine community relations. The chief described himself an old civil rights demonstrator from Berkeley,[19] but one port business owner referred to him as to "the right of Attila the Hun."[20] Needless to say, he received mixed reviews from the community during his tenure as chief.

The chief was known for his ability to control crowds through negotiating. But he hadn't built one of the most well-educated yet notorious police forces in the country by giving way to violence. He believed the situation had escalated to this point because of the ineffectiveness of the acting chief of the State Ports Authority police, Lindy Rinaldi.

"You might find [a police force] that was more unprofessional in Sparta, Mississippi, but I doubt it," he said later.

To Greenberg, the ILA was a bunch of rough, drunken, and violent long-shoremen going up against Greenberg's "college cops." He considered their whole effort doomed from the start but admitted they had leadership to be reckoned with in Ken Riley. He could see Riley run to the front of the crowd from where he was standing, but Riley didn't see him.

Riley and the delegates were able to put some space between the long-shoremen and the police. There were only two men left confronting each other—a state trooper and a longshoreman, each holding one end of the trooper's nightstick. Riley pushed his own man hard in the chest to break the impasse, and as he turned back to the trooper Riley never saw what hit him.[21]

Dazed, he reached up to feel his forehead through his cap. There was a dent. He pulled off his hat and felt blood pouring into his eyes. His head was ringing as he wiped blood out of his eyes. He could hear his cousin yelling at the trooper who had hit Riley as the trooper fell back into the mass of shields and uniforms.

"You didn't have to do that! You didn't have to do that!"

Seeing their president hit, the longshoremen let loose again. Men who had been lobbing gravel at the light now began to pelt the police. Three men pulled down the temporary light pole while others confronted a cameraman with a local television station and told him to stop shooting.[22] They pushed his camera lens down so it recorded a jumpy montage of images and then the pavement before it cut to black. The soundtrack recorded the cameraman's and the reporter's annoyance. (Longshoremen assumed the cameramen were working for the police, who had filmed every picket, and that any footage would be used selectively against them.[23])

Demonstrators grabbed the still cameras of the *Post and Courier* photographer who had come too close, but they were secured by the straps around his neck. Police hoisted the photographer behind their line. Far in the back, some longshoremen pushed over a television station van parked along Immigration and it crunched onto its side. An occasional shard of rotten railroad tie from the roadbed and a steady stream of airborne gravel flew in the direction of the police. The projectiles bounced harmlessly off their shields.

Two longshoremen saw Riley stagger, and supporting him under both arms, walked him back to the corner of Morrison and Immigration and returned to the protest. Georgette Carr, one of the women members, took him from there, walking him to his car in the parking lot of the union hall. Carr wrapped a shirt she'd found around Riley's head for a bandage and Riley drove himself to the hospital.

AN UNMARKED STATE TROOPER SUBURBAN with lights and a siren followed by an unmarked state trooper Crown Victoria approached the crowd from the rear and forced its way through.[24] When troopers in the Suburban threw a concussion grenade and tear gas canisters out both windows toward the front of the car, it sounded like war had broken out. The crowd cleared, except for one longshoreman who was looking to see what had caused the smoke. The front car slammed into at least one worker, rolling him over the hood where he athletically jumped up and walked over the roof and off the back. Longshoremen surrounded a third car, which quickly shifted into gear and followed the other cars through the crowd. Anything longshoremen could lay their hands on busted through the windows, dented doors, glanced off the lights flashing on the car's roof. Once the cars were behind the police line, the crowd, reduced to half by the tear gas, calmed down again. Delegates once again worked to move the longshoremen backward.

"'This has been declared to be an unlawful assembly. You will be given time to remove yourself from the area. In the name of the people of the state of South Carolina you are commanded to disperse. There will be no innocent parties."[25] The words from the police bullhorn became a repetitive chant and bounced off the brick walls of the low-rise housing project across Morrison behind the longshoremen.

The clouds of smoke, tear gas, and explosions of the concussion grenades were enough to drive the cameramen and reporters back to safer vantage points from which to chronicle what was happening beyond the obscuring miasma.

Local 1422 Delegate James Freeman and Recording Secretary Anthony Shine were at the front, closest to the police line, had calmed people down again and were talking with law enforcement officers. Seeing they were getting nowhere in their discussion and that most of their men were heading back to the hall, the leaders decided it was time to go and waved off of any further conversation. They had made their point.

Ken Riley would know what to do about the arrested workers. The last few men turned their backs on the police line and began walking away, the rest of the longshoremen a good thirty feet or more in front of them on the way to Morrison Drive and the union hall. In a good faith gesture to the officers behind them, the delegates, now walking away, waved their arms at their sides as if to herd the men forward, away from the dark line defending the railroad tracks, but there was no one to herd. The gap between the small group of workers and the police widened to sixty, seventy, a hundred feet. The demonstration was over.

Then Greenberg gave the order to disperse the crowd.[26] The remaining reporters stood at such a distance, looking through clouds of smoke in the dark, that they couldn't see what was happening between the police line and the longshoremen. It was clear that whatever the police did to break up "the riot" was justified given the overturned television van, the rock throwing, the downing of the construction light, and the intimidation of newspeople. They had their stories, they had film and pictures and they had deadlines. What they saw, woven with their own fears and suppositions, is what they filed as news that night. There had been a riot. Every headline, every newscast shouted "riot!"

CAPTAIN TOM ROBERTSON ARRIVED at the hospital just minutes before Ken Riley. The two men knew and respected each other from the many picket lines the union had organized and the police officer had monitored. The policeman stood at the admissions desk with one hand at the back of his head, and the longshoreman stood behind him with one hand at the front of his.

After they were treated, they were put in neighboring beds. Riley looked over at Robertson.

"We have to stop meeting like this," he said wryly. They chuckled, but the stitches both of them had received were still throbbing.

Shine, a childhood friend of the Riley brothers, found Ken Riley at the hospital, still lying in bed.

"It got worse after you left," he told him. "You're not going to believe it, but the worst is that we can't find Pompey." Pompey was Leonard Riley's childhood nickname.

"*What?*" Riley said, sitting up. "Where's Pompey?"

"We don't know," Shine told him. "We called his cell phone. Nobody's seen him."

"We've got to find him," Riley said. That single thought overrode all others. Ignoring his splitting headache, forgetting the skirmish he had just witnessed, Ken Riley left the hospital in search of his brother. Shine never did tell Riley the rest of the story, of what happened after Riley had left, after the longshoremen had withdrawn, after Greenberg gave the order. . . . It all blurred together into one dim, dark, and violent night they had all escaped still alive.

EVERYONE AT THE PORT THAT NIGHT had a different story to tell: how many longshoremen were there, whether anyone was drinking, what they hurled and what they didn't, who called in such a massive police force and why, and what difference those details made in the long run. But everyone agreed that it was a miracle no one got killed.

This was no understatement. To be black *and* a union member in South Carolina facing a sea of well-armed, exhausted, law enforcement officers from multiple units across the state, police primed for "battle," was a very dangerous thing. People knew all too well how such confrontations had played out in the past. In 1968, at the South Carolina State University in Orangeburg seven lawmen killed three and wounded twenty-seven demonstrators. In 1969, black hospital workers in Charleston tried to organize and faced off against the National Guard. In 1979, in Greensboro, North Carolina, Klansmen infiltrated by police who knew of their plans killed five marchers trying to organize textile workers. The time had come again for workers to face off against police and the state, but at least this time they left no corpses in the streets.

Around 7 a.m. the state police dismantled their forces. Ten people were treated at the hospital (Riley received twelve stitches for the blow to his head, Robertson received seven) and eight people were arrested: Charles Brave, Jason Edgerton, Elijah Ford Jr., William Grant, Joseph McPherson, Leonard Riley, John Scrughan, and Ricky Simmons. Ultimately, a different combination of five workers would head for trial.

IN A RARE LATE-NIGHT SESSION, a local magistrate viewed the police and television videotape. The men were charged with misdemeanor trespassing, a signal from the police that despite the sensational TV news reports of "riot on the waterfront," local law enforcement did not consider this a riot. The court moved quickly, knowing that if longshoremen were wrongfully jailed it wouldn't bode well for port operations. The rumor was already spreading that the union threatened to walk off the job on a ship coming in that morning.[27] The local vice president of SSA put a call in to Mayor Joe Riley to report the rumor that if the men weren't set free no one would shape the next day.[28] It took only minutes for the veteran judge to decide that the situation had just gotten out of hand and to release the men on bond.

Attorney General Charlie Condon got word of the "riot" almost immediately. A second-term attorney general from an old Charleston family, Condon was a man with his sights on higher office and his feet firmly rooted in the religiously and politically conservative landscape of South Carolina, a landscape becoming popular in the North and West as well.[29]

He would act quickly and decisively. Within a day, he would take action against this Mafia-influenced union from the North. It was one more way he could continue to build the public image of his personal values, his desire to build a government that knows right from wrong, punishes evil-doers swiftly, and declares itself for all good reasons an optimal business climate unencumbered by unions.[30]

Many in Charleston say the events so many people witnessed and participated in on January 19, 2000, should have dropped by the wayside within weeks, an ugly blip, but only a blip, on the radar screen of Southern race, police and working-class relations.

Instead, Charlie Condon and those who believed in him and worked for him would turn that blip into an open sore that the biggest players in world commerce would watch carefully. The brutal sounds of domestic warfare from the Charleston waterfront that night would not be remembered by most *Good Morning America* and CNN viewers who saw sixty seconds of dramatic footage the next day. Yet they echoed throughout South Carolina politics and world trade for almost two years, unfurling the flag of the new Confederacy—neoconservativism—over the Civil War tourist attraction known as the prosperous Port of Charleston. This one warlike night at the port would lead, eventually, to a new dynamic between one local community, the most powerful transportation workers in the world and the new global economy.

2

Storm Rising

*Without efficient access to world markets, South Carolina would lose its chief
asset in attracting and keeping companies that bring high-paying jobs,
increased tax revenues, and economic prosperity to the state.*
> —Bernard Groseclose Jr., South Carolina Ports Authority[1]

EVENTS LIKE THIS DON'T JUST HAPPEN. The incidents that culminated that
rainy January night had remained invisible to most of the press and the attorney
general. With an eye on the bottom line, a small Danish shipping company
tried to cut costs by ending their twenty-seven-year relationship with their
stevedoring firm in Charleston. It was that decision and the responses in
Charleston over the next four months that led to the massing of police, the
longshoremen's protest, and the lives of five of their fellow workers resting in
the hands of South Carolina's white, conservative, and ambitious Attorney
General Charlie Condon.

Nordana was a small, family-owned shipping line based in Denmark.
Their seventy ships traveled from the Mediterranean to the Caribbean,
then to Central America, stopped at various ports along the U.S. East
Coast, and then returned to Europe. It was a tiny shipping line compared
to the massive Maersk and Holland line carriers, and to maximize their
effectiveness, Nordana's ships combined container cargo with "ro-ro"—
roll-on, roll-off—cargo such as Caterpillar tractors and Sea Ray boats that

were put on flats with wheels and rolled up a ramp that opened to the back of the ship.

In early to mid-1999, Claes Rechnitzer, Nordana's executive vice president, went to Charleston to negotiate with Stevedoring Services of America, Nordana's current stevedore and the largest stevedoring firm in the United States. He would either negotiate substantial cost savings or shut down shipping to the United States and lay off more than a hundred people.

Lee Tigner and Larry Young of SSA told him there was no way the stevedore could substantially reduce its costs. Stevedore firms contract with shippers like Nordana to manage the movement of their cargo. The majority of a stevedore's costs were in the labor, the wages of the longshoremen who worked the ships. SSA, like all major East Coast stevedoring firms, belonged to USMX, the shipping association that negotiates those wages with the International Longshoremen's Association. Because all union stevedores worked within the limits of the ILA contract, wages were standard across the eastern United States. Tigner and Young explained to the Nordana representative that SSA and all of its clients were bound by that union contract. These arrangements provided a predictable and stable environment for business.[2] The wage rate was standard for all stevedoring firms, and their ability to compete depended on factors such as efficiency, because time in port is a major cost for shippers; how well the ships were loaded, because badly loaded container ships could present all manner of hazards and delays; and on the flexibility a stevedore was willing to risk in its profit margin.

When shipping companies hired union stevedoring firms, they were paying for both expertise and labor peace. They could expect the right combination of workers at the docks to most efficiently and safely handle the shipper's cargo, and for those workers to know what they were doing to get the job done right. They were also paying for the stevedore's expertise in managing the longshoremen, whom the shipping companies never spoke to directly. Stevedoring services, which have expanded over the years to include warehousing and other logistics services, provide a well-oiled machine operating on local relationships with longshoremen that keep the port running smoothly and quietly.

THIS PEACE, QUIET, AND EFFICIENCY could not be expected for a shipping company that decided to work outside of that arrangement. Nordana wasn't bound to any agreement with the union because it had never signed on as a member of the shippers' association. So when the price got too high and the competition too steep, Nordana went shopping. That's when Rechnitzer met Perry Collins, the Georgetown, South Carolina, businessman with stevedoring experience who was looking to create some nonunion container stevedoring competition. That fall, four months before January 19, 2000, Nordana sealed the deal with Collins, and his company, WSI. Collins promised Nordana the 40 percent in savings the company desperately needed to maintain its U.S. operations and additional port services his expanding company was just beginning to provide. Rechnitzer left the details to Nordana's agent in Charleston, Christy Hunt, who would represent the company's interests on the ground and make sure everything ran smoothly.

The only obstacle was the International Longshoremen's Association, Local 1422. USMX was an association of container carriers, and the union's agreement was for all container cargo. Container ships were the last bastion of union work on the ports. The union had lost its lock on conventional cargo, such as break bulk (steel, wood pulp, paper) and bulk (grain, woodchips, cement) years ago, though local unions in individual ports could sometimes negotiate for the work.

Much of the estimated $63 million of commerce per day that came through the Port of Charleston was in the 37,000 containers the longshoremen moved.[3] No one could afford to have the men who unload the boats stop work in protest, even for an hour. Of course, the men couldn't stop work if they weren't on the ships to begin with, and the Nordana/WSI deal took care of that. Plus, as Collins had told Nordana, South Carolina was a right-to-work state, meaning that no worker was bound to belong to a union to do a particular job. The union couldn't force WSI workers to join, and Collins made sure his people wouldn't want to.

Still, the port is a small workplace when it comes to longshoremen who have access to every corner of every terminal at all hours of the day and night, so it would be better for a company attempting to operate nonunion to maintain some distance. Collins had the solution: WSI would do an end-run around the union and the ports authority and lease the old navy yard at Pier Juliet in North Charleston, which had much of the infrastructure he would need to load and unload Nordana's ships.

For a new company, there was more room to breathe at the navy yard. WSI would be able to provide not only stevedoring services, but terminal services

—such as container storage and crane operations—to Nordana. Collins would kill two birds with one stone: no more ILA contract and no more State Ports Authority employees. He could have complete control, and that translated into lower stevedoring costs and lower terminal fees for Nordana. It would be a win-win situation for both parties, and a system the biggest shipping lines in the world had been developing with union stevedores for years. Nordana, a small shipping line, had found WSI, a small stevedoring firm, and it looked like a match made in heaven. If Collins could make it work, maybe others would break away from USMX and come looking for him, too.

THE HONEYMOON WAS SHORT. Immediate opposition came from the State Ports Authority, much more powerful than any Southern union, which was not about to watch the work move just out of reach and lose the millions in fees and taxes generated by Nordana ships and others that might follow suit. The SPA's opposition came in the form of Southern-style, good ol' boy subterfuge and it blindsided the Danish shipping company. SPA officials began pummeling Nordana's Christy Hunt with phone calls, threatening the company not to pull out of the port and warning her that what WSI and Nordana wanted to do was against the law.[4]

Collins hadn't mentioned any such trouble so Nordana officials paid no attention to the ports authority, assuming the administrators were just upset over lost business and were doing what they could to keep Nordana.

But when Hunt got a call from the city of North Charleston, where the navy yard is located, confirming what she'd heard from port officials, she realized the navy yard plans were permanently off the table.[5] The City of North Charleston, in an apparent attempt to limit the SPA's power to expand into their city limits, had passed an ordinance banning containers. The good people of North Charleston had already grown restless with containers stacked high and close to their homes and trucks roaring up and down their narrow roads.[6]

It was clear to Rechnitzer that the SPA was behind these roadblocks. His frustration with the port grew.

"[The] S.C. SPA really acts as one of the heavy-handed monopolists of the past," he told Hunt. "They tried to corner the market but found gaps, which make them desperate and unpredictable."[7]

The port may have been desperate and unpredictable, but it was also quite powerful, as the indefatigable Collins would find out. He attempted another end run around the SPA, purchasing a nearby Shipyard Creek property in North Charleston with water access and zoning laws that would permit Nordana to dock.[8] But the SPA was already operating a break bulk terminal at the old navy yard just north of the location, and didn't look favorably on competition downriver. Since the property would have required dredging to accommodate a Nordana ship and the SPA is the local sponsor for all dredging projects, the project was dead in the water.

Nordana grudgingly came to the table with the State Ports Authority in mid-October. They negotiated a new three-year agreement, but Rechnitzer was not happy.[9]

"I did not personally expect that a government or quasi-government entity like the port of Charleston would interfere or be active in trying to block a private entity's purchase of land outside the port," he said. "They were very active out there and it was my definite opinion that they were active in pushing the difficulties the right way."[10]

So in October 1999, Nordana found itself in a tough spot. The only place it could dock its ships was at a State Ports Authority terminal, where until now union longshoremen loaded and unloaded every container, but its contract was with WSI, a decidedly nonunion company. Using WSI would put the company in the black, but it would also put Nordana on a collision course with the ILA. Nordana would be the first company to attempt to unload containers with nonunion labor in two decades. The Danes left it to Christy Hunt to deal with the situation in Charleston. As far as Rechnitzer was concerned, despite its reputation for trouble, the ILA could do little or nothing about the situation. This was South Carolina, after all, not New York.

"Everyone in Charleston with knowledge about union matters expects that the most radical reaction would be a picket line outside the terminal area for a few days," he explained to his colleagues. "As South Carolina is a right-to-work state, any such picket line, however can not physically prevent nonunion workers/cargo to enter the terminal."[11] Rechnitzer, who had never met a union longshoreman in person, had no reason to doubt this information. The first ship to dock after November 18, 1999, would be covered by the new agreement.

News spreads fast and at a conference in New Orleans in late September, Johnny Alvanos told Riley that Nordana was going nonunion. Nordana had canceled its contract with SSA.

Although none of Nordana's ships were entirely container cargo, Riley couldn't afford to let one container land in Charleston with nonunion labor. He'd seen his predecessors and his national union leaders let the industry pick away at the union's strength, and he wasn't about to let that happen on his watch.

Riley and Alvanos went looking for Benny Holland and the other southeastern U.S. district union officials to discuss it with them.

"Benny, we just got word Nordana's going nonunion," Riley told the district president, whose office was based in Houston.[12]

Holland turned to Clyde Fitzgerald, his vice president. "Well, they're still union in Houston, right?"

"Yeah," Fitzgerald answered, and that was the extent of the conversation.

A TALL DANE WHO WORKED FOR NORDANA happened to be staying on the same floor of the hotel where Riley was staying. Riley saw him walking down the hall one day and walked with him.

"You're with Nordana, right?" Riley asked.

"Yes," the man answered with a heavy Danish accent.

"I'm the president of the ILA in Charleston," Riley said. "Are you going nonunion in Charleston?"

"Yes," the man answered.

"We need to talk," Riley said.

"It's too late," the man said. "We need to cut costs on the East Coast. That decision has already been made." Riley never even got his name.

Back in Charleston, Riley started writing letters to the New York headquarters of the union to alert John Bowers, ILA's national president. Bowers was a longtime ILA boss in the old "gangs of New York" kind of way. His administration's long-standing ties to well-known Mafia families such as Gambino and Genovese were the stuff of legend up and down the East Coast.[13] The eighty-year-old leader was a union man through and through, but of the same generation, and some would say cut of the same cloth, as the infamous Jimmy Hoffa of the Teamsters. This was a generation of union man who understood power politics, appreciated the strength of the right political connections and called on the darker side of human nature when necessary to promote the interests of union members and their leadership.

But since September 1999, Ken Riley and Eddie McBride, president of the Savannah local, had been trying to reform the ILA from the inside through a group called the Longshore Workers Coalition. Bowers resented Riley's role in the group, which threatened the union he had helped build for more than forty years and had steered for the last twenty years. This "coalition," with tentacles into almost every local on the East Coast including Canada, caused discomfort if not outright rage among Bowers's executive board members and operated, as far as the president was concerned, like a "union within the union."[14] It was equivalent to treason. Now this young local leader from Charleston had to call on his international union president, alert him to the serious problems in Charleston and ask for his help.

So though he put in his calls and letters to Bowers, Riley didn't sit around waiting for a response. He took his case to his members at an October union meeting at which he explained that Nordana had gone nonunion. On the surface the job affected fewer than a few dozen longshoremen, the gangs that usually worked the boat. But, Riley explained, it affected every single one of them. If Nordana got away with this, every other shipping line would try it, too. Then say good-bye to a decent living, good benefits and a secure future. Even with this plea, he and the other leaders were only able to convince a few dozen people to picket Nordana ships when they came in. At stake was the very future of this 150-year-old Charleston union built by former slaves and their children. Riley had grown up in the age of containerization, and his own father had watched thousands of fellow longshoremen leave the waterfront when the labor-intensive dock work dried up, replaced by neat, simple containers moved by massive machinery. Only the lucky ones could survive better away from the waterfront than on it. But there was more to it than that. The union represented much more than the economic future of a thousand black men. The union was the product of a power struggle that black workers had lost more often than they ever had won, and it was a symbol that standing together and taking risks, getting beaten down but standing back up, can make life better for regular guys on the street and their families. The union was bigger than any one fight with an employer. The union was hope, and Ken Riley couldn't let that hope die.

Nordana's decision couldn't go unanswered, but Riley was ill equipped to stop it. He called on his friends elsewhere in the labor movement, such as it was in South Carolina. The Charleston Federation of Labor included all the unions of the AFL-CIO that operated in Charleston. But at the time, the federation was largely made up of building trades unions and like many small local labor federations, was largely inoperative.

Then Riley called Donna Dewitt, the president of the state federation of labor, and asked her advice and support. But Donna was based in Columbia, and most of her days were spent fighting an uphill battle in the legislature to protect what few rights union workers had left in South Carolina.

Other small community groups could turn out a few volunteers to picket—Carolina Alliance for Fair Employment (CAFÉ) and others. A handful of ILA retirees and some other local union activists would show up at times. So between a few hard-core community members and the dozen or so longshoremen who regularly worked Nordana ships but now would not, ILA Local 1422 could have a presence amounting to a couple of dozen people at the Columbus Street gates when the ship came in.

It wouldn't be enough, but it was all the union president, just coming to the end of his first term, knew to do, and it was everything that was legally available to a union in South Carolina in 1999.

THERE WAS NO IMMEDIATE ACTIVE SUPPORT coming from New York or Houston, and Nordana wasn't budging. The local might lose Nordana, but there was only so much Riley could juggle at once. The city was building a bridge through his union hall and offering $2.5 million for property appraised at almost twice that. He was facing reelection in January, and winning meant he could continue to implement the plans and programs his leadership team had developed for the local and be in a better place to demand reforms at the international union level. He was constantly negotiating with local stevedoring firms for better conditions for his members and working with Dewitt to fend off state-level legislative efforts to restrict the already limited power of South Carolina workers.

Riley sized up his possible statewide political allies. Gov. Jim Hodges, a Democrat, should have been an ally because the union supported his election campaign. But his support was unlikely. In 1999, the governor nominated Riley to sit on the State Ports Authority board, but withdrew the nomination when the state chamber of commerce threatened the governor's political future if he allowed any union representation on the SPA board. To justify the withdrawal, the governor whispered rumors about Riley's past to make it look as if he *had* to withdraw his name for the longshoreman's sake. The move was so reprehensible to Riley's friends and allies that Donna Dewitt resigned as chair of the Democratic Party in Orangeburg County in protest. Riley, disappointed but not surprised, shrugged it off as politics as usual in South Carolina.

Locally, the Democratic Party would support him, but it was small, not well organized, and not likely to cause problems with its statewide organization—or be effective for anything. And only for a moment did he consider the NAACP, which had escalated its pressure on the state by calling for a massive rally in January to protest the Confederate flag at the statehouse and a boycott of tourism in South Carolina, but there was no telling how that would turn out. From the days of the civil rights movement and before, the NAACP was known more for accommodation than for direct action, and if there were any resources to offer they were at the national level, not the local one. Riley realized that no other group had the kind of resources the union did. It would fall on him.

He decided to cash in on what the longshoremen's job performance meant to South Carolina, having built Charleston's reputation as the most efficient port on the East Coast. Riley met with Charleston's mayor, Joe Riley, who in the union leader's experience was a decent and fair man, but very savvy and not one to step into a fray he didn't start. This was definitely port business, and though the mayor listened politely and sounded sympathetic, he wasn't about to speak up publicly on the matter. Riley took his case to county officials, who were even less responsive. He then took it to John Hassell, director of the Maritime Association, a group of more than 150 port businesses, who was also sympathetic but at a loss at what to do. He even met with Bernard Groseclose, head of the State Ports Authority. He told everyone that this was not going to happen. The ILA was not going to watch its standards get rolled back forty years.

"We're going to take a stand," he told each one. "And it will impact other businesses on the port. It won't make good press for the port, when we've got other ports in the neighborhood. This is going to cause a disruption in the fastest, most efficient port in the country."

Everyone he met with was politically astute. They knew the damage longshoremen could do. But these men didn't know Riley like they knew his predecessor, Ben Flowers, a man who may have made threats like these in his sixteen years in office but never followed through. Still, Riley was reaching out to South Carolinians, powerbrokers who would certainly make things happen for local citizens sooner than they would for some no-name shipping company from Denmark. He was depending on it.

Yet the legal deck was effectively and thoroughly stacked against the union. What could they do besides gather a few picketers at the terminal gate? So every time a ship came in, Local 1422's attorney Peter Wilborn filed another permit request with the Charleston Police Department. Sometimes he filed for fifty people, sometimes for a hundred, though seldom did more than thirty show up. The police never turned him down. It looked as though everyone was in for the long haul. Nordana became one more crisis in a series of crises. The union would try to make each picket bigger and more effective. That was the best Riley could hope for.

Every two weeks or so, another Nordana ship docked at the Columbus Street Terminal, and each time longshoremen picketed the ship. First they put up pickets on Immigration Street, the road leading into the terminal, but they soon realized that wouldn't be enough. The ship's captain couldn't even see the pickets and the workers just kept working the ship. City and port police monitored the pickets but didn't get in their way.

By the end of November, the picketers turned up the heat.[15] They walked through the terminal gates and climbed onto some yard dogs. When the SPA police approached them, they ran between the containers. They played this cat and mouse game for about an hour, letting the nonunion workers see them, and then left.[16]

A few days later, protest and incompetence combined to complicate a Nordana shipment. About twenty-five protesters were on the docks again to greet Nordana. At 5 p.m., the WSI foreman and two other nonunion workers arrived, but police noticed that the foreman smelled as if he'd been drinking. The ship wasn't due till 11 p.m. The three workers left the berth an hour later and, according to police reports, a "busload" of union people followed them around the terminal. An hour after that, port police discovered that the tires on three yard dogs were slashed.

When the ship arrived at eleven, there were no line handlers to take the lines to tie the ship up to the dock. When the nonunion line handlers finally arrived, they tied the ship up improperly, causing problems for another ship that was about to leave the terminal. The Nordana crew had to rework the lines before the second ship could sail.[17] Meanwhile, about a dozen protesters stood behind a concrete barricade the police had erected, watching the circus.

A half hour later, a port police officer found roofing nails on a ro-ro barge docked at the berth. [18] If they hadn't been discovered, the roll-on roll-off cargo coming on and off the ship that night would not have rolled very far.

In the meantime, after several calls from Riley, Benny Holland, the ILA district president in Houston, agreed to try to get Nordana to meet with the Charleston leaders in Baltimore in December. The local port authority facilitated the meeting and the port director attended. Rechnitzer and Brodersen from Nordana met with Holland and Riley, Alvanos and Richard Hughes, whose home port was Baltimore, from the ILA. No one from ILA's New York office came to the meeting.

"We have financial problems and we need to cut costs," the executives from Nordana explained. [19]

"We can look at some things," Holland said. "We can do something. If we had known about this . . . but SSA didn't tell us there was a problem."

"Well, all this is good," the Nordana people responded politely, "but it's a bit too late. We've already signed a five-year contract. Maybe in five years we can look at the ILA again."

Once they said that, Riley was ready to leave. His mind was already back in Charleston, mapping out his next move. He was the first one out the door when the meeting ended.

By the time the next ship arrived in mid-December, longshoremen were turning up the heat through more creative civil disobedience. This kind of action increased interest among the longshoremen, and 150 of them greeted Nordana's ship Stjernborg, ignoring two-dozen city and port police and running into the terminal. Three longshoremen jumped on a yard dog a nonunion WSI worker was operating, pulled out the keys, and yanked the hoses to disable the machine, but they didn't lay a hand on the worker.

To separate union from nonunion longshoremen on the dock, port police had erected low barricades between the two ships being worked side by side, one by ILA members and the other by WSI workers. Some longshoremen jumped into yard dogs and raced them up to the barricades and back, blasting their ear-splitting horns at the nonunion longshoremen working the Nordana ship just yards away. [20]

Activists had no way of knowing if their antics would have any impact, and dared not hope they did. In fact, Nordana was feeling the pain. The day after the Stjernborg disruption, Rechnitzer contacted the State Ports Authority, trying to negotiate a discount for the delays caused by the protesters during the last two calls to port. The unanticipated costs were cutting into the savings Nordana had hoped to enjoy with its lower-paid stevedore and longshoremen. In his letter, Rechnitzer referred to "outstanding" issues from an earlier meeting in Charleston with the SPA. This was one of many proposals Rechnitzer made to get the SPA to bear at least some of the increased costs the delays incurred.[21]

But SPA marketing director George Young was at his limit. A man whose job it was to keep all shipping lines happy and returning to the port, Young realized that Nordana's decision to go nonunion was jeopardizing more than its one small contract was worth to the SPA.

"I do not think this is so much a matter of communication as it is a matter that you are unable to accept 'no' as an answer to any request," Young wrote in response to Rechnitzer. "As regards reductions in charges for whatever services . . . we are not prepared to make any whatsoever."

Young had never experienced such disruption at the Port of Charleston. He was in charge of maintaining the port's excellent reputation, a reputation he saw sliding steadily into the sludge thanks to Nordana. He turned the tables on Nordana:

"Would that you could indemnify me against this pox caused by your actions in my house, which could jeopardize multi-millions in multi-year contract renewals with some major existing clients due in 2000, if there is a perception of labor discord," Young wrote.[22]

By the third week of December, the local union had secured promises from trucking companies not to pull Nordana containers and contacted a number of Nordana's biggest clients, and union leaders had offered Nordana a 46 percent reduction in costs if it would give the work back to a union stevedore, but the company hadn't changed course. Riley told local members that Benny Holland in Houston had been very supportive but he also let them know that New York (that is, Bowers and the other international leadership) wasn't providing any assistance at all.

January 2000 brought the arrival of another Nordana ship and a new level of problems for the State Ports Authority. On January 2, 2000, as the rest of the country was recovering from Y2K mania, an SPA police officer was reporting extra black stripes down the sides of five Sea Ray boats waiting for Nordana shipment.[23] There were more anomalies on the port: a container missing because its identifying numbers had been painted over, busted Start and Stop buttons on a gantry crane, and more. None of these incidents were ever successfully pinned to the longshoremen, but it was clear to port authorities that the protest wasn't going to die down and, worse, somebody was willing to stoop to sabotage to win this war.

Then, on January 3, 2000, Nordana's ship *Surveyor* docked at the Columbus Street Terminal. Some twenty to forty union longshoremen walked past police into the terminal again, successfully boarded the ship through its ro-ro ramp, stood in the hold for a few minutes to make their point, and walked off. They hovered dockside for another half hour, some riding around in yard dogs and others standing under the giant gantry crane. The protest so shook up the nonunion longshoremen and the captain that the ship pulled out of port before completing the work, leaving some cargo sitting on the dock and causing the company significant customs problems and expenses for months to come. The pattern of protest was not lost on the acting chief of the SPA police, Lindy Rinaldi. Two days after *Surveyor* left, Rinaldi told the chief public relations officer, Ann Moise, that it was time to take police enforcement to a new level.

"ILA protest activity surrounding the Nordana vessel using WSI labor continues to escalate with each additional vessel arrival," Rinaldi said. "Extreme measures must be implemented. . . . If faced with the same operational conditions as 1-3-2000, I feel that law enforcement may be faced with the possibility of having to use lethal action."[24] Rinaldi was willing to get ugly, very ugly, with the ILA.

By now, WSI's Collins was in court to get an injunction against the longshoremen. He failed to identify any specific longshoremen who had come onto the terminal or gone aboard the ship to disrupt his company's work. He had witnessed no violence or vandalism. The judge threw the case out but warned the longshoremen against any violence on the port.[25]

Rinaldi contacted every available law enforcement head from Charleston's chief of police Reuben Greenberg to the State Law Enforcement Division's chief, Robert Stewart. In a series of meetings in January, the group planned every detail for hundreds of officers from multiple agencies to protect the arrival of the next Nordana ship, scheduled for January 17, 2000. They negotiated which agency would pay for what, who would supply how many officers with what kind of gear, and even reserved a room with small chairs, crayons, and paper for the children of longshoremen they might arrest that night.[26] On Greenberg's request, SPA CEO Bernard Groseclose sent a written request for reinforcements to every law enforcement chief. Law enforcement agencies eventually committed more than six hundred officers to the event. Greenberg himself would line up four videographers, including one in the helicopter, and a still photographer to catch every possible angle that night.

But police were more concerned with how to control two major events on the same day: the NAACP rally in Columbia and the Nordana ship in Charleston. Greenberg had already anticipated this and had told Groseclose to hold the ship offshore for two days until law enforcement could regroup in Charleston. Rinaldi passed the message on to her boss, Moise.

"Waiting until all agencies are available before bringing in the Nordana vessel is what supporting law enforcement is insisting on," Rinaldi said.[27]

The days ticked by without change. The Nordana ship was now scheduled to arrive January 19, and talks among the union, the port, and the company had shown no progress.

The day the Nordana ship was scheduled to dock, SPA officials tensely watched last-minute negotiations between the union and Nordana and reported to other law enforcement agencies standing at the ready to come in. Rumors flew about a last-minute settlement, but none was in sight. The police would have to carry through with their plans.[28]

The Nordana ship *Skodsborg* would arrive at Charleston at 7 p.m. on January 19. That morning, in a last-ditch effort to regain peace at the port, Nordana's Rechnitzer and Brodersen met with the SPA's Groseclose and operations manager Bill McLean, 1422's Ken Riley, and SSA's Larry Young. Nordana made its best offer yet.

"Nordana indicated that it would be considered to allow its present stevedore in Charleston, WSI [Perry Collins], to enter a subcontract with another stevedoring company employing ILA longshoremen," Rechnitzer reported to his colleagues. The agreement would have to keep costs down, allow WSI to supervise, and not have any influence on WSI's other nonunion operations.[29]

Young was willing to negotiate, but Riley, having made repeated overtures, was done. He wasn't about to let WSI make a profit off of union longshoremen's wages. He demanded that a union stevedore work that night's ship. Rechnitzer refused and Riley walked out of the room.

That might have been the end of civil negotiations, but the company was confident its operations would not be interrupted by unruly longshoremen this time. The police were pouring in from around the state. Rechnitzer had retained a former governor's law firm to help his damaged relations in Charleston, and that firm had been talking with Greenberg, the head of SLED and, of course, Groseclose, who was in regular contact with the governor to confirm his support.[30] The Dane had enlisted his own South Carolina power-brokers. No one would slow down his ship that night, and he was there to make sure of it.

WHEN RILEY PULLED INTO THE UNION HALL parking lot that afternoon he saw what the night would bring—the hundreds of police with dogs, helicopters and more, waiting for a showdown. By daybreak, eight of his fellow union members would be in jail and others would be at the hospital. The nation's morning television news programs would show sixty seconds of Charleston 's dockworkers throwing rocks and railroad ties at riot police. What would become of these men? What could possibly become of them that hadn't played out a thousand times before in the Deep South Ken Riley knew so well? What could ever turn this around?

3

Condon and the "Christians"

In recent years, with the rise of the religious right, which is not religious and not very right, came an awareness of the way black churches used to do things. They've effectively co-opted that.

—Rev. Joseph Darby, Morris Brown A.M.E. Church[1]

SOUTH CAROLINA HAS ALWAYS been planted firmly in America's Christian tradition. It's said that H. L. Mencken once referred to Greenville, home of Bob Jones University, as the buckle on the Bible Belt. Thus it's no surprise that Christian religiosity has successfully incorporated itself into the economy and politics of South Carolina, enmeshing itself so that the two at times seem like one.

"It's hard to separate religion from politics in South Carolina," explained state representative Gilda Cobb-Hunter, a black social worker who has served as a legislator since 1992. "We open our sessions every day with prayer. Most meetings open with prayer. You hear this whole religious tone weaving through debate, depending on the issue. . . . Religion is still very vibrant and still a part of the political fabric."[2]

Attorney General Charlie Condon, the man who would prosecute the Charleston longshoremen with such a vengeance he would jeopardize the reputation of the port and the entire state, was the embodiment of this merging of religion and politics, the human result of a political process as old as the

South. While most people in the rest of the country would be shocked by George W. Bush's blatant exploitation of religion in the White House post-2000, what Cobb-Hunter and others experienced up close heading into the twenty-first century was built upon decades of careful planning and organizing by some of the sharpest political strategists of our time. South Carolina was not the sidelines for their success, it was their fertile seedbed.

The convergence of politics and religiosity formed the bedrock of assumptions and understandings on which every politician, every businessperson, every worker and every community leader in South Carolina had always operated.[3] Those who disagree with the assumptions, whether black or white, Democrat or Republican, had to adapt to them.[4] And in 1999, everyone from Attorney General Charlie Condon to a blossoming local mega-church was part and parcel of that ongoing adaptation, an evolution one might say (with irony) that would become the national norm within the first years of the oncoming century.

Ever since the Scopes "Monkey" Trial of 1925 when a high school biology teacher was convicted for illegally teaching Charles Darwin, a case that backfired and built a wave of popular support for evolution across the nation, the Christian Right had been planning its resurgence. It found root, finally, in the 1970s in the commercial ventures of Christian preachers like Billy Graham and Oral Roberts combined with the political maneuverings of Republican operatives like Paul Weyrich, all of whom built their fortunes on the previous decade's visions of impending "cultural decay." With the creation of the Heritage Foundation, which spawned dozens of other well-funded conservative think tanks, the Christian Right would lead a political and cultural revolution culminating in 1994 with the takeover of the U.S. Congress from Democrats for the first time in forty years.

Condon was right there, building his political career throughout the 1980s and 1990s by jumping from the Democratic to Republican parties in 1990, just in time to ride the tide of the 1994 "Republican Revolution" in a state central to the "Southern strategy" that helped Richard Nixon win the presidency more than twenty years earlier. That tide was still rising at the end of the century, about to come ashore like Hurricane Katrina with the success of a neo-conservative-driven presidential administration just as the millennium turned.

Condon had chaired Republican Bob Dole's 1995 campaign for president in South Carolina and was well positioned to aid the Bush family. His work for Dole led to his efforts on behalf of Elizabeth Dole in the 1999 Republican presidential primaries. It was a short step to become co-chairman of George W. Bush's campaign in South Carolina after that year's primaries.

In twenty-two years Condon had never lost an election, either as a solicitor or as the state's attorney general. He was living on exclusive Sullivan's Island near Charleston, hometown to his father and grandfathers who had built a department store dynasty that made Condon a household name in the area, at least until the big boys like Kmart and Wal-Mart put family-owned enterprises out of business. Because of his expansive Irish Catholic family, Condon could pick up the phone and connect with any sector of the community, and his last name alone would make the person on the other end take the call.[5]

He had the picture-perfect public service family as well: the steadfast wife who was a medical doctor and four kids. He avoided any personal scandal, though many in the media and across South Carolina found his frequent provocative pronouncements to the press and some of his legal opinions scandalous enough.

Condon had graduated *magna cum laude* from Catholic Notre Dame University and returned to the South for a law degree from Duke University before coming home to build his practice and political career. In 1980, at the age of twenty-seven, he was the youngest candidate ever elected solicitor in South Carolina, launching a successful public career he enjoyed for the next two decades. During his term as ninth circuit solicitor he instituted a mentoring program, created the South Carolina Father of the Year award, and remained an active member of the Stella Maris Catholic Church on Sullivan's Island.[6]

Such a sterling life and career would look good on a "Condon for U.S. Senate" or "Condon for Governor" brochure, and a run for higher office seemed likely.

"If one looks at other states, historically the attorney general's office has been the stepping stone to the governorship," said state senator John Courson. "This office has never been perceived in the past as a political office in South Carolina before. But it's a natural progression."[7]

Condon certainly did his best to use the attorney general's office for advocacy. His pro-Confederate flag position, for one, was unwelcome by civil rights activists, union activists, and businesses hurt by the subsequent boycott. But that position, combined with his enthusiastic attacks on the National Association for the Advancement of Colored People, made him friends among a key constituency in the state—neo-Confederates.

"I, as a life member of the Sons of Confederate Veterans, have sworn a solemn oath to see that the true story of our South is told, explained, and defended," local resident Bill Schleuning would post to the SCV website during Condon's 2001 gubernatorial campaign. "In so doing I can assure you that we could have no better friend in Columbia than the Attorney General [Condon] if he is elected governor."[8]

Unfortunately for Condon, even in South Carolina the attorney general's office was not designed for advocacy. The attorney general would push his role to the limit, and it eventually became an Achilles' heel in his case against the Charleston longshoremen.

As the state's lead prosecutor in the late 1990s, Condon had what some would consider the natural mean streak that comes with the job, but his positions were consistent with much of the Christian conservative ideology developing at the national level. This made him a man of principle among his supporters. He received national media coverage for prosecuting crack-addicted pregnant women for child abuse, a case he would lose in a unanimous U.S. Supreme Court decision in 2000.[9] He issued a statement that the sex education materials provided by the Centers for Disease Control (CDC) should not be used in public schools because they violated a 1988 state law mandating teachers to limit instruction to abstinence and relations between married heterosexuals. He said the CDC materials "repeatedly authorize or even encourage premarital sex."[10] And when in 1996 the U.S. Supreme Court ruled that Virginia Military Institute, and by extension South Carolina's Citadel, had to admit women, Condon announced, "We lost this case because we were defending single-gender, heterosexual education."[11]

Condon carefully honed his reputation and political career by echoing the conservative Christian community as he understood it. With the fundamentalists' disciplined takeover of the Republican Party on the march, Condon would have to make up for his Catholicism with a political and religious fervor Protestant Christian Coalition members would appreciate and trust.[12]

Condon may not have anticipated a national mainstream press and Democratic Party firestorm over Bush's campaign appearance (under Condon's chairmanship) at Bob Jones University, an institution known for its racist, even anti-Catholic, policies and extreme right-wing politics, but it would play well with that 35 percent of South Carolina Republicans who consider themselves Christians conservatives.[13] Indeed, he may have been counting on their approval and support for his own political ambitions.

They were the perfect fit. The Christian Coalition, claiming more than a million members nationally, had effectively taken over the Republican Party in 1994, which in turn had taken over the U.S. Congress. Within two years the Coalition would reach its height, raking in more than $26 million from supporters and leaving its mark on politics with its "Voters Guide" distributed from pulpits across the nation. And Christian Coalition members *voted*.

Meanwhile, after a dozen years of slowly and methodically gaining control of board seats, fundamentalists took over the Southern Baptist Convention and caused this powerful segment of this conservative Christian contingent to split.

"In many ways in the South you cannot really separate what happened in the Southern Baptist Convention and what happened in the Republican Party," explained pastor Don Flowers of Providence Baptist Church in Charleston. "I think they are in lockstep together. There was a theology that was a fundamentalist theology that took root in the late seventies, early eighties that did not like the ambiguity of life, that wanted everything to be black and white, right and wrong. There is no gray. In some ways it started theologically, [others] would say politically, I think they started together and one used the other."[14]

There was no doubt at the time that the Coalition was the future of the party. At a 1998 national Christian Coalition dinner, the group's president applauded members' work in taking over the party: "Ladies and gentlemen, you're the hidden army. And let me say, it is more than the Republican Party that is our target. Ladies and gentlemen, it is the United States of America; we are determined to change our culture."[15]

The Coalition's power and visions of its place in the right-wing groundswell that was polarizing the nation at the time cannot be overstated. This was the context within which Condon would prosecute the longshoremen and eventually run for office. At the height of the Coalition's power, during his second term as attorney general, South Carolina's Republican governor David Beasley, himself a born-again Christian who courted the Coalition, went to an appreciation dinner for then-director Ralph Reed. Speaker of the House Newt Gingrich and Senate Majority Leader Trent Lott attended the dinner, as did several other politicians. In his speech praising the Coalition leader, Beasley compared Reed to Jesus Christ.[16]

Conspicuously missing in all of this Christian political maneuvering were black Christians, who as a group stayed far away, largely because at every turn coalition members preached and organized against the civil rights movement.[17]

AT THE 1998 ANNUAL MEETING of the coalition, Charlton Heston praised Coalition supporters by stating: "Heaven help the God-fearing, law-abiding Caucasian middle class."[18] No room for black people in that vision, but that too worked in Condon's favor. He had little interest in appealing to the state's blacks. First, he could assume they were Democrats, as most blacks in South Carolina were. Second, they had an entirely different interpretation of basic moral values, one that clearly didn't rest on people keeping to their proscribed places in this world.[19]

The Christian Coalition came under allegations of racism when, in 2001, ten black employees of the organization sued it for discrimination, alleging that blacks were not allowed to use the front door and had to eat in segregated areas of the Coalition's Washington, D.C., headquarters. The Coalition would later send lawyers to prevent any correction of the controversial 2000 Florida vote that sent G. W. Bush to the White House. Most allegations of wrongdoing in that election were based on disparate treatment at the polls based on race.[20]

Charlie Condon may have been raised a good Catholic, but in the end it is most important in South Carolina politics to define oneself as a good Christian. One's political positions must be true and just by that test, and he made sure the Baptists in the voter pool knew where he stood.

"What I like to do is sort of imagine what these decisions are going to look like after you're gone. I do believe there's a Judgment Day," he would say later, during his gubernatorial campaign. "Once you center your life with God, it allows real freedom, enabling you to be salt and light. You're here to improve, to try and do God's will."[21]

So in January 2000, when the attorney general was briefed about the rioting black union workers at the port, Charlie Condon didn't have to hesitate about prosecuting. There was no ambiguity here. These men represented everything that was antithetical to a good Christian upbringing and South Carolina law—they had no respect for authority; they didn't know their place; they were an obstacle to American ingenuity as it is embodied in the corporate spirit; and they were lucky to have the jobs God blessed them with, which paid much more than any uneducated black man in South Carolina deserved.

Besides, it was a political no-brainer. South Carolina had the second-lowest union density in the country for a reason: the majority of the voters wanted it that way. This was an excellent opportunity to wipe out one union that had been making a bit too much noise for its own good while building a sound stepping-stone to the governor's office.

4

Taking up Positions

These things like the event on the docks I think are stories that have a very short shelf life.

—Mayor Joe Riley[1]

KEN RILEY STILL HAD BLOOD ON HIS SHIRT and in his cap the next day when he finished with the court appearances of eight of his guys who had been arrested. It wasn't over, though. Condon had sent two of his staff attorneys to Charleston to draw more blood, this time in the courtroom. The union's attorney, Peter Wilborn, warned Riley that they hadn't seen the last of the attorney general. Between the press coverage, including extensive video footage, and Condon's well-known political aspirations, this was shaping up to be a nasty and expensive court battle.

Riley's other men were out of the hospital, and it was time to regroup and assess the damage. But it was 2:30 p.m., he hadn't slept all night, and he still had to drive the hundred miles to Savannah to tend to his union's health plan. The Management/ILA (MILA) health plan trustees had already met for a day, and he was expected there.

Riley pulled into the hotel parking lot in Savannah around suppertime. As he walked through the lobby, familiar ILA faces from the North turned toward him, some glancing, some staring. No one walked up and asked if he was okay, or how the brothers in Charleston were doing. Instead, some gave him a look that said: "They should've *killed* you."[2] He'd come to expect that from his union up north.

After he checked in he walked toward the elevators. He rounded the corner, out of sight of the lobby, to face the three top men from one of the world's largest organizations of shipping corporations: USMX Chair David Tolan, Tolan's right-hand man Bernie Delory and USMX executive director Brian Duggan. The four stepped into the elevator together.

"That was quite something you did in Charleston last night," Tolan said. "It's those types of renegade companies that make it bad for everybody. To be driving down rates is uncalled for and it's time for the ILA to get some fight back in them."[3] When Riley got off on his floor, the three others rode the elevator back to the lobby.

It was the kind of moral support Riley had expected from his own union brothers, not the most powerful global transportation moguls in the world. But then these men didn't have to worry quite as much about feeding their families if they got thrown in jail for fighting a system a million times bigger than they were.

While Riley received a cool welcome from his New York-based ILA leaders, something that was unimaginable to the Charleston-born longshoreman was brewing on the West Coast. It started that morning before he left town, while he was still getting reports of injuries, dealing with arrests, and scanning the local press.

JACK HEYMAN WAS AN ACTIVIST who took seriously the slogan his union, the International Longshore and Warehouse Union (ILWU), had emblazoned on a banner to carry in parades: "An injury to one is an injury to all." Then an executive board member of the San Francisco Local, he showed his president Lawrence Thibeaux the *New York Times* story about what had happened the night before in Charleston.

Thibeaux called Riley and listened to his story. When he was done, Thibeaux said he'd get a $5,000 donation from his local, because it was obvious to him that the brothers in Charleston would need some help.

At a meeting, the members of Local 10 approved the donation and agreed that the local should pay for Thibeaux and Heyman to go out to the East Coast to see the situation for themselves. Riley gave the two Californians the tour of the port, the union hall, and the road leading into the Columbus Street Terminal where all the action had taken place. When Riley was done telling the story again, Thibeaux called his international vice president in California, Jim Spinosa.

"We're in Charleston supporting these brothers here," Thibeaux told Spinosa.[4] "This is a righteous struggle and we're inviting Ken Riley to attend our next caucus [the ILWU's name for its longshore workers' convention]."

"You can't do that!" Spinosa told the local president. ILA president Bowers had issued a statement that the Charleston workers had broken the law, and Spinosa didn't want to get the ILWU involved in another union's internal problems.

"Well, we're doing it," Thibeaux answered. The ILWU had grown out of a tradition of local independence and autonomy. This was just one more instance.

In the meantime, Riley had sent an appeal for support to every union, church, and community group his local had donated money or help to in the last three years. After years of groups coming to the union, it was ILA 1422's turn to ask for help. Small checks started trickling in, but it was going to take more than these groups could do. Riley knew about the lack of local resources for black organizations in Charleston. That's why he was willing to put his local behind them.

Back in California, Thibeaux firmed up plans for Riley to speak to the Longshore Caucus, the largest and most powerful section of the ILWU, an expansive union that includes warehouse workers, ferry and tugboat workers, service workers in Hawaii, longshoremen in Alaska, and others.

THIBEAUX CALLED RILEY AGAIN: "If you can get here by Tuesday, the caucus will match what Local 10 voted you—$5,000." Riley couldn't believe his ears. Perry Collins and WSI was suing his local for more than a million dollars, claiming 1422 was responsible for his monetary losses from the January 3 disruptions. Nordana was suing for compensation for its damaged cargo and was trying to root out the culprit who was responsible for the mischief. And the attorney general was trying to build a reputation for righteous indignation and law and order by going after the lawless "rioters" of January 19. But now union people Riley had never met and barely ever heard of were sending thousands of dollars to defend his members while his own union treated them like outlaws and his own community showed him empty pockets.

Riley asked his assistant, Fran Shuler, to book him tickets to California. At the ILWU Longshore Caucus the hundred and fifty assembled longshoremen and guests gave Riley a standing ovation. Riley watched in amazement as the West Coast workers made motion after motion to increase the amount of their donation, reaching $35,000 before one member asked what the ILA, Riley's own international, had done so far.

That's when David Arian, a former ILWU international president, took the microphone.

"We know the ILA," he said, referring to the often rocky relationship between the West Coast union more famous for its direct action and progressive politics and the East Coast one more infamous for its mobsters. "This is about workers," he said. "Here's something happening in our backyard. We cannot worry about what that international union is going to do." Then he sat down.

A member moved that the ILWU Longshore Caucus approve a donation of $50,000 to the Charleston struggle. The group approved.

When the meeting was over, Ramon Ponce de Leon, president of the ILWU representing Los Angeles and Long Beach, the largest port in the United States, approached the stunned Riley.

"When are you headed back?" Ponce de Leon asked.

"I was planning on going back tomorrow," Riley said.

"Can you possibly change your flight?" Ponce de Leon asked. "We've got a meeting tomorrow night and we should have five thousand people there. I'm sure we'll match what the Longshore Caucus just gave you."

Riley called Shuler, back in Charleston and asked her to change his flight; he was going to L.A.

ATTORNEY GENERAL CHARLIE CONDON was marshaling his own forces. Under normal circumstances the local solicitor, Republican Dave Schwacke, would pursue the case if he thought it had merit. But the press coverage was clear. Headlines screamed "Riot on the Waterfront" with ample photos on inside pages.[5] Television reports repeated the same headlines and newscasters reported the overturned vehicle, assaulted cameramen, and airborne railroad ties. The pictures said it all, and what they didn't say, the reporters filled in. The situation was "scary" and "dangerous to all parties involved." Union protesters attacked police with "a hailstorm of rocks, bricks, logs and other debris." Police dispersed the crowd using dogs, beanbag-like projectiles and tear gas.[6] Besides, the port was of statewide concern, and who better to prosecute than the state's top law enforcer? Was this union going to push South Carolina's business community around? Were black laborers to be allowed to run riot on the docks at the peril of the state's commerce?

Condon's office took over the case. He issued a press release the next day announcing a "comprehensive plan for dealing with union dockworker violence and attacks upon police officers." The plan was "Jail, jail and more jail."

"He said that there should be no bail or maximum bail, no plea bargaining, and no leniency for union dockworkers who attacked or are planning to attack police officers enforcing the law at the harbor in Charleston," the attorney general's office announced.

The statement said he would seek to upgrade charges against the "rioters," seek "maximum bonds for every offense committed," pursue civil enforcements, and that "contempt citations and fines were also an effective remedy against this type of union violence." It also asserted that six hundred longshoremen were at the terminal, though eyewitness accounts estimated from one hundred and fifty to two hundred and twenty-five.[7]

Local Charleston law enforcement wasn't quite as worked up about it as the attorney general was. Police had charged eight men with trespassing, a misdemeanor carrying a maximum of thirty days in jail. For their part, some longshoremen understood that some of them had behaved badly. One dockworker walked into the police department and apologized for the behavior of the men that night.[8] ILA president Ken Riley said no such event would ever happen again, and the mayor never referred to it as a "riot."

Nevertheless, the attorney general's staff was in court almost immediately, filing felony riot charges and demanding that the judge set high bail. The assistant attorneys general, who had driven in from Columbia, argued that high bail was necessary to maintain public order. Judge Jack Guedalia placed the eight longshoremen under house arrest with bonds from $35,000 to $100,000.

Ten days later, at a February 2 preliminary hearing, armed only with the testimony of Chief Reuben Greenberg as evidence, the prosecution lost the first round. Magistrate James Gosnell dismissed the charges against the eight men.[9] The prosecution had failed to offer evidence specifically related to any of the men charged. (One other man, Ken Jefferson, was arrested that day. His likeness was unmistakable in the *Post and Courier* front-page photo of the event. His bail was set at $150,000.)

Condon did not give up. The preliminary hearing was just a technicality, a leftover from English law that allowed defendants to hear the charges against them. Besides, that was city court. His new felony charges would take this case into another arena for justice—state court. In the provocative language South Carolinians had grown used to from their attorney general, Condon blasted the local legal establishment.

"The magistrate has usurped the role of the Grand Jury, the Jury, and the Trial Judge," Condon told the press. "The law makes it clear that riot is the proper charge for these defendants and we stand by those charges. Just as soon as the next Grand Jury is seated, we will seek indictments against each and every one of these defendants for riot."[10]

With newspaper photographs and videotape for evidence, Condon's office won county grand jury indictments against Ricky Simmons, Elijah Ford, Ken Jefferson, and Jason Edgerton. (In April, an additional defendant, Peter Washington, would be indicted.) For the next twenty-two months the one white and four black men were held under house arrest, not permitted to leave their homes from 7 p.m. to 6 a.m. except to work and attend church and union meetings. Most faced sentences of up to five and some up to ten years in prison. Even worse was the threat to their livelihoods. If convicted, none would ever work on the docks again. That would be a strong and chilling message to any other longshoremen who might consider protesting in the future.

Over the next twenty-two months, as unions, businesses, religious leaders, and politicians lined up in support, these five men, from the youngster Jason Edgerton to the most senior Elijah Ford, would follow the advice of their attorneys and maintain low profiles. Only a few times would they be publicly identified as involved in this case. Only rarely would the press have access to them. Their individual stories blurred and paled compared to what they represented. They, like Charlie Condon, would become a symbol of the fight that was to come, a fight bigger than any five ordinary workingmen had ever been or could ever be. They would be the dubbed the Charleston 5, and their story would inspire people around the globe to take a stand some had never before imagined.

CHARLIE CONDON WAS READY for this prosecution. He was the attorney general who endorsed what he called the "electric sofa" and said it was time to "speed up the death penalty."[11] He was the attorney general who had said, "Religion has a constitutional place in the public schools," when he wrote the opinion supporting the display of the Ten Commandments in schools.[12] His supporters knew they could count on him to maintain law and order. There was no doubt that an attack on the last remaining union with any power in South Carolina would do nothing but garner votes and other support from members of the state's chamber of commerce, one of the most powerful in the country, while Condon continued to build his support among upstate conservative Christians.

It would have been easy for Condon to believe that in these days of politically correct everything he had a quiet following of (white) voters who took offense at "rioting [black] union workers." They disdained uneducated (black) men who made demands and mob unions from the North that thought they could tell (white) South Carolina how to run its affairs, but no one would be boorish enough ever to put it in racial terms.[13] They didn't have to. Such deeply ingrained assumptions need not be voiced. His conservative base, of which Christian conservatives were a big part, would surely approve of his ongoing efforts to combat disorder in the streets.[14] Condon had been considering a run for the U.S. Congress for months, but this prosecution, among others, would lead Charlie Condon to change his mind and aim for the governor's office.[15]

As news of the "riot on the waterfront" settled on Columbia, Republican lawmakers eager to keep South Carolina attractive to international trade and sensing a local antipathy toward the "union riot" took the opportunity to make some headlines of their own.

By February 3, South Carolina's biggest newspaper, *The State*, announced "S.C. House Approves Anti-Union Measure." The vote was an overwhelming 83 to 32.

The bill, sponsored by state representative Harry Cato, a Republican from Greenville, home of Bob Jones University, strengthened the state's ability to investigate and punish union activity, or as *The State*'s Dave L'Heureux put it, "efforts to force workers to join unions."

Not surprisingly, the South Carolina Manufacturers Alliance applauded the move: "This legislation goes to the very heart of freedom for our workers," a group spokesman said.[16]

To fuel the fire, the South Carolina Chamber of Commerce released a report at the end of January highlighting the grave threat that unions posed to the state. "Labor unions attempted to organize employees at sixteen South Carolina companies in 1999, the highest number in the past decade, according to the South Carolina Chamber of Commerce," reported Sam Gresock of *The State.*

As a right-to-work state, South Carolina does not require those covered by a contract to join or support the union that negotiates the contract for them. In all, a simple majority of three hundred and twenty-one workers, none of whom would have to pay union dues to receive benefits from any new contract negotiated on their behalf, voted for union representation that year.[17] Yet the *Charleston Post and Courier*, taking the bait, picked up the story February 7 with the headline "Labor Activity in 1999 Sets Record for Decade."[18]

Ten days later a South Carolina House subcommittee renewed its effort to ban labor representatives and union members of any kind from serving on the State Ports Authority board.[19] It had been almost a year since the governor had nominated Riley to the board only to withdraw it under pressure, but at the statehouse they called the bill to ban such nominations the "Ken Riley bill."

"House Republicans are in the midst of an election-year offensive on unions," *The State* story noted. This bill was sponsored by yet another representative from Greenville.

The so-called union riot struck fear in the hearts of Upstate conservatives and corporations. A longshoremen's strike more than a hundred years earlier had inspired a series of violent strikes throughout Upstate rice and lumber mills from which South Carolina employers had taken decades to recover.[20] They weren't about to let *that* happen again.

From his vantage point in Charleston, police chief Reuben Greenberg wasn't surprised by the response.

"Much of the pressure I think, political pressure, came from the Greenville area, because they're afraid it would infect the BMW type stuff and [other industries]," he said. "We've come to an accommodation here in Charleston. We recognize the unions have power, but they didn't have that anywhere else in the state. [Upstate] saw this big cancer had gotten out of control in Charleston and they were going to get it back into control."[21]

But legislating the problem away wouldn't work this time. Both bills died in the Senate, where state senator Robert Ford, a longtime ally of unions and a black legislator representing Charleston, blocked them in committee.

THE BATTLE THAT WOULD BECOME the campaign to free the Charleston 5 was taking place in Mayor Joe Riley's front yard. While legislators had to look out for the state's reputation, Joe Riley was steward of Charleston's economic and cultural well-being. A white Democrat, Riley was elected mayor of Charleston in 1975. He was born and raised within the ambiguous and incestuous race relations of Charleston and understood the balance of power between blacks and whites, between the port and the city, between Republicans and Democrats, between the Low Country and Upstate. Early in his tenure as mayor, Riley recruited as his police chief Reuben Greenberg, a black Jewish law enforcement expert from Texas who had experience in civil rights on the West Coast.

Riley was reelected to the mayor's post without interruption for the next thirty years, serving as one of the most popular mayors in the history of the city. On the heels of the racial unrest of the 1960s and the marches of thousands by supporters of the striking hospital workers, Riley served term after term without a single significant racially charged incident—until January 2000. By then he had a healthy tuft of white hair hanging over his thin face, his suit hung loosely off a wiry frame, and his hearing was starting to go, but he maintained the usual hectic schedule of a midsized-city mayor. Now the state attorney general was going after the wealthiest black organization and the most powerful labor organization in South Carolina, threatening to disrupt the peace that kept a steady stream of cargo flowing through the port and a steady stream of tourists flowing through the streets of downtown Charleston. Condon, like the Upstate people he was coming to resemble, had no idea of the intricate balance of local interests and global forces that kept the waterfront functioning smoothly.

From the night of January 19 forward Mayor Riley's take on the altercation at the waterfront was low-key. "I felt like the actions of the attorney general in prosecuting these men for conspiracy to incite a riot and the potential punishment for that substantial jail time, wasn't necessary," the mayor explained later. "That was an overreaction." He spoke in an even, measured tone, not easily ruffled by questions about race or politics.

"We haven't had any real record of waterfront labor anger," he said. "If you put this aside, we've had really good relationships. We haven't had strikes, we haven't had real difficult times working out contracts and all that. I think the kind of collective feeling is one of admiration that these dockworkers are skilled, many are quite strong, but I think there's a kind of prideful recognition of that achievement."

Joe and Ken Riley also had one otherwise unlikely ally in Columbia who had similar Low Country interests: Senate President Pro Tempore Glenn McConnell, a Republican and Confederacy champion from Charleston County. McConnell had come from working-class roots, and also understood the power of the longshoremen at the port.

"Here is a respected leader in this community, with a positive outlook and a track record of trying to make the port run more efficiently," he said of Ken Riley. "And he was attacked in an anti-labor campaign by the big business in this state. I have not the first regret about supporting him."[22]

WHILE LEGISLATORS IN COLUMBIA rattled their chains to remind the chamber of commerce and business interests that they had that port union under control, and Joe Riley did his best to dampen the fallout from that night, Bowers, the ILA president in New York City, sent mixed signals into the local. He was the first to send a personal check to support the men, but also sent a letter to all locals instructing them to send only personal donations, not checks issued from union treasuries, per the union attorney's advice. He could not afford to ignore a local facing a $1.5 million civil suit and incalculable legal costs to defend five members against criminal charges, but he was in no rush to help a troublemaker like Ken Riley.

In addition to heading the ILA, Bowers was head of the dockworkers division of the massive International Transport Workers Federation (ITF), a coalition of national transportation workers' unions around the world. He had enough clout to decide exactly what level of response the ITF could offer. So within a few days, Bowers talked with Stephen Cotton, ITF's representative in London. On January 28, Cotton called Nordana's Claes Rechnitzer to tell him the ILA had asked the ITF to "instigate labour actions against. . . . Nordana ports of call in Europe."[23] Bowers never told Riley he made that call and there were no signs at other Nordana U.S. ports of call that Bowers was organizing any kind of response.

The next day Rechnitzer responded to Cotton with two pages full of counterarguments stated in more conciliatory terms than he'd ever used with the South Carolina State Ports Authority, SSA, or the union to lay out his case for the ITF to understand and empathize with Nordana working with a nonunion stevedoring firm, WSI, in Charleston.[24] He reminded Cotton that all of Nordana's officers were members of the Polish union Solidarity and argued that WSI was governed by the labor laws of South Carolina. He argued that WSI longshoremen made between $30,000 and $50,000 per year (later evidence showed that WSI paid them $12 per hour, less than $25,000 per year)[25] and claimed that right-to-work laws are democratic because in a "fully democratic process, the state of South Carolina had decided that all workers . . . in the state has [sic] the freedom to decide whether to belong to a union or not."

Rechnitzer could ill afford Nordana's cargo being disrupted across Europe, but busy dealing with those risks he never saw what was coming from the bosom of his own Danish company. A local newspaper carried photos and the story of the Charleston troubles and named Nordana as the source. Nordana's reputation among its countrymen was at stake; Danes don't take kindly to social injustice and virtually every Danish worker belongs to a union. Indeed, unions are an integral part of the policymaking machinery of Denmark. But South Carolina was an ocean away from Denmark, not to mention its concepts of social justice and equality.

Nordana's owner, a son of the founder and a man twenty years younger than Rechnitzer, stormed into his office and threw the newspaper down on his desk. "You really put us in a mess here," he said angrily. "Do you remember we are just concerned with our business, Nordana, and you have to get us out of this mess? I cannot accept that we are put on the front page of the papers and customers are getting worried. Do consider the consequences and get us out of the mess. Please reconsider the whole thing and don't be pulled away with whatever is going on, political things in Charleston. Find some way so we can get back to our normal operations, because I won't accept this situation."

Rechnitzer's attitude changed dramatically after that. He had considered the situation in Charleston to be under control, but things were unraveling. The ITF he could handle, if with kid gloves, but his own employer's reproach jarred him. The entire business and its owner's reputation were at stake, and he needed a new approach.[26]

BACK IN CALIFORNIA, members of the ILWU, who control the pace and movement of every cargo container from Seattle to Los Angeles, were quickly awakening to the breadth of the fight the longshoremen in Charleston faced. ILWU activists had just played a big part in the previous month's World Trade Organization (WTO) demonstrations in Seattle, the largest and most effective mobilization of American workers, environmentalists, anarchists, globalization opponents, and other activists that any could recall.

The AFL-CIO's usually impenetrable bureaucracy had actually helped mobilize some 50,000 union members for the Seattle action. The demonstrations disrupted the meetings of the most powerful nonelected body in the world, the men who decide where, when, and at what rates commerce moves. The rules that the WTO drafted would supersede the laws of nations. ILWU members and hundreds of thousands of Americans who converged on Seattle that week were well aware of the dangers that lay there. With the AFL-CIO involved, it looked as if labor might just be getting the hang of the social movement activism that motivated it before it began its backslide in the 1940s. ILWU had its roots in that earlier tradition of social movement activism of the IWW and allied organizations. And their members were proud of that heritage.

That last week of January, the ILWU was buzzing with news about Charleston. Jack Heyman was furiously sending emails and making calls to radical activists he knew all over the world, many of whom he had met during the Liverpool dockers' lockout in 1995. Not since Liverpool had workers put up such a fight on the waterfront, and with this renewed awareness of global economic forces, the world's labor movement would surely respond this time better than it did for those dockers. While the activists and leaders of the ILWU didn't look to the rest of the world to decide whether to support a cause, they knew the meaning of solidarity and did what they could to foster its spread. Heyman was doing what he loved to do: connecting people with like interests in the hopes of sparking something.

The ILWU and ILA 1422 had an old and checkered past that only some of the old timers would have remembered. At least twice in the last hundred years—the last time in the mid-1960s—the radicals from the West Coast had come to Charleston to try to lure the black dockworkers into their union.[27] ILA's Bowers was old enough to remember and to be worried. The East Coast always stayed with the East Coast, in spite of black-white and North-South antagonisms. Now the next generation of West Coast longshoremen was aiding the next generation in Charleston. Since the 1960s, the threat to longshoremen everywhere had become more real as the results of containerization, globalization, the North American Free Trade Agreement, and the blatant disregard for national sovereignty the WTO had shown began to filter through working people's consciousness.

"We read about your valiant efforts to defend your union and your jobs from incursions by the nonunion Winyah Stevedoring company [WSI]," wrote Local 10's Thibeaux in a January 27 follow-up letter to his phone call to Riley that first day. "Your stand, in the face of police provocation, was inspiring to us longshoremen on the West Coast who will be facing the same problem."[28]

Thibeaux, a black man born in Louisiana and transplanted to Oakland, California, didn't have to be convinced of the challenges well-paid black union men in Charleston had to face, but he also knew it was a sign of much bigger things to come, a global assault on all of them, one of the last remaining unionized workforces in the great global logistics system that kept the global economy moving at the speed of light.

When Riley read Thibeaux's letter to Local 1422 members they cheered and applauded. It was good to have friends, especially ones with deep pockets and open hands. The letter mentioned a lesson from the Liverpool dockers that Riley didn't quite understand. He remembered Bowers once telling him something about the ILA honoring Liverpool dockworkers' picket lines, but he had never seen one in Charleston, so it hadn't been an issue for him. It was enough to know that other dockworkers around the world had faced trouble, but that wasn't so surprising. Whatever happened in Liverpool couldn't have been as bad as what he faced in Charleston, or surely he would have heard about it.

For four months Riley had tried to settle with Nordana and nothing had worked. Charlie Condon had managed to get grand jury indictments against five longshoremen, WSI had upped its suit against the union by a half-million dollars, Bowers wasn't coming to Riley's aid, the union was looking bad in the press, and Nordana was still out there operating nonunion. With five men under house arrest, some of his members were worried the local was in more trouble than it could afford to be. He looked everywhere for a strategy. His men moved cargo in the second biggest and most efficient port on the East Coast—there *had* to be a way to leverage that.

5

On the Waterfront

To remain a player in an industry whose boundaries span every ocean on Earth, you've got to be capable of delivering a variety of cargo with unprecedented precision—and you've got to do it on a huge scale. This is reflected in today's super-competitive and ever-evolving shipping industry, where a Darwinian current running among carriers is bringing together the biggest and the best.
—Jamie McAlister, *Port News*, Port of Charleston [1]

TRUTH RUNS AGAINST THE GRAIN of South Carolina's business. Some people would simply like it to disappear. The history of the State Ports Authority, for example, is documented in a book it commissioned in 1990, yet the story has been called into question by none other than its original author.

Richard Coté, a freelance writer the SPA paid to document its history, called the final version "a historical fraud and utterly without merit as a documentary history."[2] The changes the SPA made to the original manuscript were so egregious that the author refused to allow the SPA to print his name on the cover and instead donated his original manuscript, along with annotations listing the changes the SPA made, to the Charleston County Public Library. The omissions range from small copyediting changes to censoring descriptions of criticism of the SPA and its programs.

But a particularly objectionable and indefensible "edit" was the SPA's removal of all references to slaves or blacks in the history of the port. Forty percent of the American slave trade was conducted through the Port of Charleston and 98 percent of the longshoremen working there now are black.[3]

Charleston's economy thrives or dies on its history. Without history there is no tourism industry. The Civil War's first shot rang out from Charleston's Fort Sumter, the slave revolt led by a freed man named Denmark Vesey was thwarted there, and schoolchildren and tourists can visit the past of its grand mansions and sprawling plantations. Without its history, Charleston would not be the city it is. So the history that makes it between covers is critical.

This isn't news to blacks in the South. Al Brown's Gullah Tours, which points out Denmark Vesey's home as a national historic landmark, for example, offers a radically different version of slavery and the South than one of the many tours guided by whites, where a tourist can hear a description of Vesey as "a man who didn't like white people" and the unnamed slave who exposed the plot to free 22,000 blacks as "a slave who loved his master."[4]

The power brokers for the port understand the need for a version of history that meets their political needs. For more than a century, the Port of Charleston was a cash cow for a handful of powerful Charleston families. From the beginning, slaves were used to unload the ships, and there is reason to believe that they themselves unloaded slaves who came in as cargo from the West Indies. The port fell into ruin for some time around the turn of the century, but by the 1960s it was going strong again. Then came the containerization of cargo, possibly the single most significant development in the history of contemporary global trade.

"Old blue-blood families controlled the waterfront, they controlled the agency, the stevedoring, the line handling," Robert New, a waterfront businessman and transplant from the North, explained. "They made tons and tons of money, especially in times of war. During the Vietnam War, they used to sit down at the Colony House downtown and fix rates and became fabulously wealthy. Times changed after containerization. In the 1960s, national lines came in and they started to lose their grip on it. People like me said they're going to change things.

"As containerization came in, the old families started to lose everything. [Shipping] lines became more efficient; they had M.B.A.s and bean counters," New said. "They didn't care about the cotillions and the blue bloods down here; they just wanted to make a profit."

Lee Tigner, now vice president and general manager of SSA in Charleston, experienced the changeover firsthand. Tigner graduated in 1961 from the Citadel, which, created in response to the failed Vesey slave revolt, remains a military academy and the pride of many South Carolinians. It is something of a finishing school for a cabal of elite young white men who grow into a tight-knit group of alums. The closest thing to a union member on the State Ports Authority board, harbor pilot Whit Smith, is a Citadel graduate.

"The Citadel is an institution in South Carolina," SSA's Larry Young, another graduate, explained. "I asked someone, Why you wanna go there? 'Because you guys have the best network going; Citadel grads tend to look out for each other.'"

Thus when Tigner graduated from the Citadel, he had a commission in the Army, which posted him in Fort Jackson, near Columbia, his "old briar patch" as he called it in his archetypically colorful Southern accent. He left the Army as soon as he could, reconnected with friends from the Citadel and was soon working for the Street brothers, who owned Carolina Shipping.

"Back then there were a lot of things done strictly by hand, carting, toting with the old longshoreman's hook," he explained. "They had just gotten forklifts five years before. They were just beginning to modernize, and the company was just wildly successful. Everybody was making money."

As old age and family relations began to unravel Carolina Shipping, Tigner could see the technological changes coming on fast.

"In the sixties Charleston was a sleepy little place," he said. "New York knew it was a port, that they brought cargo here or picked it up, but that was about it. Nobody was counting anybody's money. But then comes along this soon to be ubiquitous can or box, in 1974–75. During the next five years there was a huge move toward containerization."

By 1980, Charleston was building the Wando Terminal, outfitted with the port's first giant container cranes. The waterfront was changing in more ways than that, though.

"About this time also all of these shipping lines began to get a handle on our cost," Tigner said. "There were about twelve stevedoring companies in Charleston. When I first started there were three." Those were the "blue bloods" New referred to.

Throughout the 1980s, Tigner saw firsthand the major transitions in world trade: shipping companies consolidated and formed consortiums. One ship might have containers from five shipping companies.

"Different people own the ships," he explained. "Israel will have three, United Arab Emirates will have two, and someone else will have three. They might not get along any other way," he laughed, "but they'll come together for this, in one consortium."

The next period brought consolidation. The shipping lines that survived the fuel crunch of the 1970s were looking to cut costs. Their most visible expense was stevedores, and as shippers put the squeeze on them, the bigger stevedoring companies started swallowing the smaller ones. Tigner and his colleagues at Carolina were fighting off Ryan Walsh and Cooper T. Smith, both based in Mobile, Alabama.

Stevedoring Services of America, a company based in the Pacific Northwest, also tried to move in. Tigner helped fight them off, too, calling on his relationships with the port and the local authorities and telling them that letting SSA operate in the Southeast was a bad idea. It worked.

"In retrospect *that* was a real bad idea," Tigner, who expects to retire from SSA Cooper soon, said, smiling.

Sometime in 1988 or 1989, Tigner was in New York City calling on Carolina's shipping customers. It wasn't going well. That's when he put a call in to Jock Stender, who was running Carolina Shipping with his brothers.

"I'm not encouraged by what's going down these days in our industry," Tigner told him. "These big guys are gonna eat our lunch. We gotta face up to the fact that we are still just a regional company; we're not huge like ITO, or SSA, Ryan Walsh with all these resources that we just don't have. They're covering Dixie like dew. We don't have it in us. Let me tell you and your family what the smart thing for us to do: Sell this company."

He set up a meeting with SSA co-owner Ricky Smith and the Stenders. Six months later the deal was sealed.

TODAY A DIRECTORY of Charleston port services includes barge services, container leasing, warehousing and storage, purchasing and sales, harbor pilots, launch service, insurance, marine cleaning, marketing, medical services, ship equipment and repair, waste handling and waste oil handling, stevedoring contractors, ship and pier diving services, railroads, moving

and storage, chassis leasing, air cargo and air freight services, courier services, international marketing, and more.

Every year, these services move goods such as 16,500 tons of candy,
15,000 tons of gloves, 19,000 tons of toys, 65,000 tons of nuts, plus thousands of tons of paper and paper products, chemicals, textiles, tractors, boats,
cars, and consumer goods through the port.[5] Cotton is still a major export,
but millions of dollars' worth of iron pipefittings, appliances, clay, and
unwrought aluminum pass through as well.[6]

"Charleston is different than New York, different than ones that historically
had mob ties," said New, who grew up in Philadelphia. "This is a sleepy
Southern town, and that permeates the relationships on the waterfront.
Because it's tight, because it's small and because it's like family, the production levels are very, very high."

Charleston in fact brands itself as "The Pros of Productivity." Charleston
is the most efficient port on the East and Gulf coasts, making it a "weekend
port." Since shippers have to pay overtime after regular weekday hours, they'd
rather pay fewer overtime hours at an efficient port like Charleston, so as
frequently as possible they schedule their ships to dock there on weekends.

Driving this overtime engine is the contract the International Longshoremen's Association negotiates between the longshoremen of the East and Gulf
coasts and USMX, the industry's East Coast coalition of shipping corporations. Because of their union and its history, longshoremen get what most consider a fair slice of the pie (and what some consider more than fair). But their
union wasn't powerful enough to fend off job-killing technology.

So as containerization came, longshoreman jobs went out. The ILA
1422 hall in Charleston is lined with historical paintings of muscular black
longshoremen, large metal hooks in their thick hands, hoisting cargo in
sacks, or looking up at large loads in massive rope nets lowering crates from
the ship. When containers replaced nets and burlap bags, the change over
was devastating. For example, in 1954 it took 35,000 longshoremen to
move 13.5 million tons through the Port of New York. By 1989, thanks to
containers, it took only 8,000 longshoremen to move 20 million tons.[7]
Loading 11,000 tons of cargo went from more than 10,000 man-hours to a
mere five hundred and forty-six.[8] To compensate for the lost work opportunities, the union negotiated "royalty checks," which amount to $16,500 per
longshoreman every year, a per container charge.

"When the check comes out it flushes the economy," said New, who added that he pays his workers $130,000 to $150,000 per year. "The car dealers know when it comes out, everyone does." He said the shipping industry pays well for most everyone involved. Harbor pilots, who navigate ships into port, make between $250,000 and $400,000 per year, stevedores who manage the longshoremen make $60,000 to $80,000, and full-time longshoremen's wages can run from $60,000 to more than $100,000 because they can work as much overtime as their seniority and union rules allow. Longshoremen work in all kinds of weather and all hours of the day or night. The difference between getting the job done right and getting it done wrong can cost a shipping line hundreds of thousands of dollars in delays or damage for a single ship. For that, most are willing to pay well for the reliability of the ILA.

"These guys are not oppressed," said Larry Young, of SSA Cooper, whose family spans five generations on Charleston's waterfront. "They're off Spam a long time ago and eatin' thick ham. These are big jobs."

PERRY COLLINS, ORIGINALLY FROM ALABAMA, was a relative newcomer to South Carolina in 1999. He was working for the Federal Emergency Management Agency (FEMA) in 1979, helping Hurricane Frederic victims rebuild Mobile when his future father-in-law told him to get "a real job."[9] So Collins went to his father, just retired from sixteen years in the Alabama state legislature and still chair of the Alabama State Docks board, who told him, "Son, I think you ought to go to the waterfront."

So Collins joined the stevedoring firm Ryan Walsh, owned by a family friend. He eventually landed in Georgetown, the State Ports Authority's smallest port, located an hour's drive north of Charleston. Two years later the port director came to him and encouraged him to start up a nonunion stevedoring firm.

In 1985 with the blessings and a loan of equipment from his employer, Collins launched Winyah Stevedoring Inc. which he eventually shortened to WSI. He offered his nonunion stevedoring, trucking, and warehousing services to shipping companies from around the world. He hired his own nonunion longshoremen and line handlers, truck drivers, and warehousemen at a fraction of the rate union workers made, and created a niche for himself in the one area of the waterfront the union couldn't control: break bulk and bulk cargo—loose cargo that can't be packed into a container. His old employer, Ryan Walsh, later became part of SSA's rapidly expanding global enterprise.

"We do melons, we've done orange juice, we've got a lumber distribution center in Florida," explained Collins. "We've done heavy lifts, like a generator; we do projects like a new cement project here in South Carolina. We unloaded the largest burlap shipment that ever hit the U.S. waters, coming from India, over ten thousand metric tons of burlap—they had never done that before," he said proudly. The burlap is used for roadbed material, to stabilize shoulders, he explained.

It was WSI's reach into container cargo that set off the events on the Columbus Street Terminal in January 2000. "We don't do containers," Collins said wryly five years later. "We cause riots when we do containers." He explained that Nordana, which shipped mostly break bulk cargo but had some containers, was looking to lower its expenses. Collins saw an opportunity and took it.

THIS WAS THE TERRAIN that was the changing waterfront in Charleston and every port in America in 2000. The good ol' boys had reorganized. They were bigger and badder than ever and answered to no government but their own board of directors. Little fry like Collins were carving out their niches and hoping to stay alive and thrive off the crumbs left by the SSAs of the industry. Longshoremen had leverage, but only with companies willing to agree to the rules. Collins represented someone operating outside of those rules.

Ken Riley had hoped that Nordana would see the wisdom of labor peace with professional, efficient, union longshoremen. He had hoped the disruptions on the port might talk the language of business, the one he read about so often in port press releases and magazines: teamwork means the free flow of money into the state, and a lack of teamwork means that free flow is jeopardized. But he hadn't been able to convince local or state policymakers of the need for this teamwork. He hadn't been able to convince one small shipping line of the error of its ways, and with newspaper and TV coverage of the "riot on the waterfront," he had a larger audience than ever to convince.

Now, in addition to his problems with Nordana and WSI, Riley had to persuade the state of South Carolina, and Attorney General Charlie Condon in particular, to end this prosecution. The financial help from the West Coast was a great gift, but $100,000 wouldn't even cover the legal costs that were sure to mount. And in the end, the legal battle was a gamble.

He needed to get the port's attention, and it *owned* so much of South Carolina politics. He needed to get business's attention, if it meant pressuring the attorney general's friends and followers. But he had already felt the strength once of the chamber of commerce's opposition. He had to make the governor, a man who had proven he had no integrity, stand up for what was right. He had to wake up the civil rights movement, the labor movement, anybody who'd listen, for these five men who had been indicted and the rest of the men he represented. This was too big for one man's imagination, expertise, or willpower. It overwhelmed this small group of longshoremen, who were still stunned by the court proceedings. It overwhelmed their community of friends and leaders, who stood shaking their heads in awe and anger. And it was too much, or not enough, too far away and too troublesome, for his union's weary and wary leadership in New York, a leadership in no rush to come to his aid.

6

Nordana Bows to Global Pressure

Global labor organizing among dockworkers will depend on a keen understanding of diverse national and regional political economies to identify concrete actions that can be used in different countries.
—SSA Marine Strategic Corporate Research Report, 2006[1]

KEN RILEY FACED IMMEDIATE BATTLES on at least two fronts: Nordana and Charlie Condon. He was receiving more help from the West Coast, in that Jack Heyman seemed to know people all over the world. Because of Heyman, Riley was giving interviews to leftist newspapers he had never heard of. Riley didn't care about their politics, he needed the press, and he needed the help. Besides, these socialists weren't exactly what he'd expected. When they said they were going to do something, they did it. Those were the kind of people he needed.

But Riley was convinced that without the ILA, the local could not make Nordana cave, and he hadn't heard one good word from John Bowers in New York. And without the help of the mainstream labor and civil rights movements, Local 1422 wouldn't be able to short-circuit Charlie Condon. Letting these five court cases go the full fifteen rounds would hurt the union for decades to come, not only in its treasury but in its community.

Unbeknownst to Riley, Nordana executive Claes Rechnitzer was receiving troubling reports from Christy Hunt in Charleston. Nordana was beginning to suffer the fallout of the national press coverage of violence at the port. Coleman Marine Supply refused to deliver batteries to Nordana's ship *Skodsborg*.[2] Anxious about deliveries of its boats through Charleston, Sea Ray was recommending that its cargo be routed through Baltimore until the situation was settled and expected Nordana to absorb the additional cost of the rerouting.[3] Hunt was concerned Nordana might lose Caterpillar, its biggest customer, if something wasn't done soon to secure cargo better.

Rechnitzer was no longer gloating over the poor media image the longshoremen were suffering. The situation had become more complicated. He now had to deal effectively with the odd assortment of interests involved—the port, Nordana's customers, the authorities in South Carolina, the union, and now the International Transport Workers' Federation, which represented transportation unions around the world and was threatening actions around Europe.

The Nordana ship worked by nonunion WSI workers had left all of the problems in Charleston in its wake. Ten days had gone by since the altercation at the Columbus Street Terminal, and now another Nordana ship was heading for Charleston. Still nothing had been settled.

At the end of January, another full contingent of six hundred law enforcement officers, once again in riot gear and accompanied by an assortment of helicopters, personnel carriers, and dogs, stood braced for a rumored 3,000 ILA members for that day's arrival of the *Skanderborg*. No protesters showed up.[4] Ken Riley had given his word that there would be no more altercations, and there were none.

Rechnitzer was in South Carolina that day. He and Perry Collins from WSI were meeting with Governor Hodges in Columbia. The governor reiterated his support for the two companies.[5] The next day, Rechnitzer scheduled another meeting with Ken Riley. He hoped that between the union president's recent reelection and what Rechnitzer interpreted from the news coverage as a "public condemnation of the riots," Riley would be feeling more pressure to settle than the company did. Rechnitzer would offer the same deal he had offered January 19 for WSI to subcontract the work to a union stevedore and he'd see if the ILA would accept it this time.

Meanwhile Rechnitzer called upon his colleagues to assess the potential threat of ITF-sponsored work stoppages at various ports around Europe. Nordana agents in Italy and Spain assured Rechnitzer that the ITF was no threat. Marseille was the only port the company considered a problem because of its reputation for radical labor activity.[6]

That day, Riley and Rechnitzer were able to talk without the static of intervening groups like the stevedoring companies SSA and WSI, but they could not reach an agreement.[7] Nordana had signed a five-year contract with WSI and wasn't willing to pay the price to get out of it.

This issue had grown larger than one local president under the East Coast master agreement had the power to negotiate. So Riley called on Benny Holland, the Southeast District president for the ILA. For the next two months, the South Carolina Department of Labor, Licensing and Regulation mediated talks between Nordana, represented by Rechnitzer, and the ILA, represented by Holland. It would not go smoothly, but the new communications would enlighten the Nordana executive about the dealings of the world's fifth-largest global logistics company, SSA.

It was during these discussions that Nordana learned that SSA, not the union, had been the obstacle in earlier negotiations. In fact, Nordana learned that ILA 1422 had been making offers to cut costs by exactly the 40 percent that Nordana had demanded for months. It was true that Riley had done all he could to avoid a confrontation at the port. It was SSA, the stevedore, that never passed that offer along to the shipping line. Stevedore contracts are cost plus; their profits are based on a percentage of fixed costs. The higher their costs, the higher their profits. SSA had no interest in reducing the cost of freight handling.[8]

A week later, on February 4, the ILA and Nordana signed their first agreement. It called for Nordana to switch its stevedoring services from nonunion WSI to a Nordana-owned operation, Dannenborg, which would use union longshoremen. But this agreement was contingent upon the State Ports Authority reducing its fees by the amount Nordana would lose hiring ILA longshoremen—an estimated $600,000 over three years. The SPA, having no incentive to accommodate a shipping line that had tried to leave, or the union that had given it a black eye, refused. Rechnitzer was learning about the complexities of business on the Charleston waterfront. Now it wasn't the stevedore or the union that was in the way, but once again the State Ports Authority.

The second agreement, proposed in early March, provided better economic terms for Nordana than the signatories to the ILA master agreement enjoyed. To add insult to injury, Nordana had refused to join the employer group, USMX. So when the world's largest shipping corporations caught wind of it, they demanded the same uniformity that the ILA demanded on the

East Coast ports. Any terms the union came to with Nordana must apply to the master agreement for all ports and all shippers. That would gut the ILA contract. From New York, John Bowers reneged on the verbal agreement his representative Holland had made with Rechnitzer.

On March 23, an increasingly frustrated Rechnitzer received a letter from the Danish general consul based in New York.[9] The New York City Federation of Labor had contacted the Danish consulate requesting a resolution on the issue of the Charleston longshoremen. Bowers never told Riley about his request to the New York City Federation. But it added one more straw to the camel's back of Nordana's woes.

Finally, another week later, Holland and Rechnitzer found a way to cover Nordana under the ILA's "small boat agreement," a clause of the master contract usually applied to ro-ro (roll-on/roll-off) carriers. Half of Nordana's cargo was ro-ro and the small size of its ships fit the contract language, so Nordana began getting their ships properly reclassified as "small boats." The two men combined good ideas from earlier proposals and had already agreed to allow Nordana's wholly owned stevedoring company Dannenborg to hire smaller ILA crews and therefore bring the costs to a level Nordana could afford.

But before the ILA could sign off, Bowers received a letter from the South Carolina Stevedores Association inquiring about the agreement. SSA and other stevedores belonged to the association and its members were concerned that the agreement allowed for "double breasting." A contractor can employ union workers or nonunion workers, not both, and "double breasting" means a company operates under a union contract with some customers but remains nonunion with others. This provides an unfair advantage to the double breasters who can always come after new business with their nonunion, and lower paid, services while maintaining peace with the union on the other side of its business.

They were back to square one. It seemed that no agreement could satisfy everyone.

Whereas the shorthand these men used included terms like "union" and "nonunion," every player was in fact protecting industry and area standards. The workers employed by stevedoring companies who used the ILA as a hiring hall were not all union members. By South Carolina law, the union could not require it. Hypothetically, any man or woman could walk in off the street and get hired. So union versus nonunion was a moot point. But the wages and benefits that stevedores and shippers had agreed to pay as the price of doing business under the union contract served as the floor upon which everyone else's wages and benefits rested, the standard by which all others determined their own worth. It was the basis upon which every one of them measured the value of the labor they provided for keeping billions of dollars of cargo moving smoothly through the world's ports.

SSA employee Wayne Pinkleton, a thirty-year stevedore at the port, explained not long after the January incident at the Columbus Street Terminal the importance of the ILA contract for the entire region: "The ILA, stevedoring companies, the State Ports Authority, freight forwarders, agents, truckers and shipping lines have worked cooperatively to make Charleston the great productive port that it is today. The wage standards of the ILA have been the greatest bargaining chip for all waterfront employees to obtain decent wages."[10] Pinkleton said many people who work on the port are second- and third-generation waterfront workers, and that black and white workers "laugh together, cry together, help one another, and unfortunately witness injuries and occasional loss of life.

"Yes, the waterfront is not a pretty place to work, but it is a community and culture, and it functions well as structured. The recent introduction of nonunion labor into this previously peaceful environment threatens not only union members, but everyone who garners a living from the Charleston waterfront."

That is what hung in the balance as the lawyer from Denmark and the union leader from Houston negotiated their way to a settlement over a handful of jobs in Charleston.

AS TALKS DRAGGED into the spring, Jack Heyman was sending a steady stream of emails to former docker Jimmy Nolan in Liverpool and to Coordinadoras union staffer Jose Bernejo Llorca in Barcelona. If anyone could throw some leverage behind negotiations in Charleston, Heyman believed these men could.

To Heyman, a self-proclaimed Marxist, this struggle in Charleston was just one more move by global capital more emboldened than ever by the new global economy and the support of conservative regimes around the world from Reagan to Thatcher, from Bush to Blair.

The ITF wasn't built for worldwide worker mobilization. The Cold War was over, and the ITF, like many global union federations, was taking a long time to recalibrate itself to focus more on employers and less on what it considered The Red Menace.

In 1995, on the heels of a Thatcher government directive that divided waterfront unions, the five hundred Liverpool dockworkers, known as some of the most militant workers in the country, refused to cross the picket line of fellow waterfront workers. The refusal, which would have been legal just a few years earlier, was now illegal. Every docker was fired.

Without an ally in Great Britain (their parent union feared further retalia- tion from the Thatcher government) the dockworkers went international. Docker Terry Teague employed his recently acquired Internet skills to con- nect with waterfront workers from Sweden to California. Fired dockers stood on Liverpool street corners holding out buckets, raising money for airfare.

Soon the Liverpudlians received approval from a number of union locals to set up pickets whenever a ship from Merseyside, the company that had fired them, arrived at port. Two men with picket signs were enough to shut down a terminal, so the British dockers traveled around the world doing just that.

Dockers' wives organized Women of the Waterfront and traveled through- out Great Britain raising funds and support for their husbands' efforts. Protests involving dockers and non-dockers who had come to their aid included hanging massive banners across buildings and occupying gantry cranes so a port couldn't operate.[11] These were new allies and their radical tactics caused the Liverpool local, already a pretty leftist group, to be red-bait- ed by the mainstream labor movement—highly placed British union leaders accused local leaders of letting Communists run their fight for them.

The Liverpool dockers' pressure wasn't enough. By 1997 they were still out of work, and their hope of ever again working on the waterfront was fad- ing. They wanted to turn their tragedy into a lesson learned for other dock- workers. Nolan in Liverpool, Garcia in Barcelona, Heyman in California, and Bjorn Borg in Sweden turned their organizing skills to another endeavor. At a conference in Montreal in 1997, dockworkers representing locals from Sweden, the U.S. West Coast, Japan, France, Italy, Portugal, and Spain agreed to create a new, rapid response network for dockers, by dockers. They also voted to send a delegation to address the ITF's Dockers Section about the Liverpool situation, now two years old, and give the ITF one last chance to prove it could make a difference.

At the ITF Dockers meeting in Miami, the Liverpool delegation was given just a few minutes on the agenda. The parent union of the Liverpool dockers was an affiliate of the ITF and as far as it was concerned, these men were renegades, a naive group who had stuck their necks out without thinking and then been co-opted by radicals. (The parallel with the ILA and its Local 1422 was not lost on supporters of the Charleston longshoremen.) The national-level union had done all it could for the Liverpudlians, but now the fight was over. Liverpool was a dead issue and those dockworkers were out of luck. But the men from Liverpool weren't in the room when at that same meeting Dockers Section members, representing ports on almost every continent, voted to sign an International Solidarity contract that the ITF could call upon when necessary.

Feeling stonewalled by the ITF, Nolan, Garcia, Heyman, and the others kept organizing. Representatives from their unions met in Barcelona in 1998, then Sweden in 1999. They were working out the details of organizational structure so a worldwide dockworkers organization could grow into the future. Liverpool showed them they all needed an organization of dockworkers locals that could respond globally to any local dockworkers' problems. If their current national and international labor organizations were moribund and incapable of responding, they would organize a new and vital organization that could and would respond. They directed attorneys well versed in international law to draw up articles of incorporation, and in 1999 they launched the International Dockworkers Council (IDC). They met one last time in Liverpool to finalize the details, and set their founding convention for June 2000 in Tenerife in the Canary Islands off the west coast of Africa.

By this time, Greg Dropkin, an expatriate American living in England, had created www.labournet.net, a clearinghouse of information for the global labor movement, such as it was. In the spring of 2000, Dropkin and Heyman were exchanging emails, and Dropkin was translating emails between the Californian and Spanish dockworkers. Familiar with shipping routes since his days assisting the Liverpool dockers, Dropkin had looked up Nordana's shipping routes on the company's own website and discovered that the same ship that landed in Charleston, *Skodsborg*, would also go to Barcelona and Valencia in Spain, home of key IDC founders.

So on February 13, 2000, four months before the IDC's founding convention, Garcia and Borg received an email from Heyman in California, pointing the way, in classic ILWU style, to direct action.

"If you want the ILWU to become an affiliate of the IDC then you have to show concretely the difference between the ITF and the IDC," Heyman told them. "Your call for solidarity is a genuine one built on a concrete action.

Here's a good time to do it. You have these ILA workers on the East Coast, and the ships are going into Valencia and Barcelona. If you take action to help these brothers being isolated just like the Liverpool dockers were, you can show the difference and it will win the ILWU over to joining the IDC."[12]

The Europeans not only agreed with Heyman that this was just the kind of effort they had created the IDC to support, but knew that having the powerful and militant ILWU join the IDC would give the fledgling organization a much-needed financial and political boost.

Llorca and Garcia, the more seasoned union leader and a thirty-five-year waterfront veteran, planned the next move.

"I understood that we could not have another Liverpool," Garcia explained later. "If we looked the other way and didn't want to help the Charleston dockworkers, then that meant we were not going to have another meeting to form an organization." Three years of planning would come to nothing. Garcia was a broad-shouldered longshoreman graying at the temples, crossing over from longshoreman in his prime to wise elder on the docks. "And if we help, we are going to help with all that we have."[13]

Barcelona and Valencia were major ports for Nordana, but the dockers had learned from Liverpool, where workers had stormed the barricades, at least figuratively speaking, and been immediately shot down. In studying what had gone wrong, allies of the Liverpool dockers had learned to be more strategic. They would escalate actions so that workers built toward more power and unity and the company would never know exactly how bad it could get.[14] The fear of what *could* happen is often more effective than the action itself.

First, the Spanish union would lodge an official protest with Nordana. Then if that didn't work, they would discuss their next move. After taking the issue to the rest of the members for approval, the two men sat down and drafted the letter they would deliver the next time a Nordana ship came to port. Because of his long relationship with the dockworkers, they gave Nordana's agent in Barcelona, Paco Rivero, a copy of their letter. He had faxed it to Nordana headquarters with a rough translation. The ship's captain and Nordana officials read the same letter:

Dear Captain,
We hereby inform you that due to the specific stowage and unstowage operations on the vessels and the high risk of accidents in these operations, it is

required that both stowage and unstowage operations must be effected by duly skilled professionals.

We have detected that the stowage effected recently in your company's vessels do not reach the minimum quality required to ensure an efficient operation, in terms of productivity and considering that in such operations you are not using professional dockers, for which we request that in future operations you do it with professional dockers, which will grant an unstowage in accordance with labour prevention risks requirements.

We hope our request will have an efficient reaction from you.[15]

THE DOCKERS AGREED that Garcia and an English-speaking dockworker would go together onto the *Skodsborg* when it arrived in Barcelona around April 10. When the Nordana ship finally tied up in Barcelona in mid-April, the two men stopped their fellow dockworkers and the dock fell quiet. Dockworkers looked on as their coworkers boarded the ship and requested to see the captain. As Rivero watched, they asked the captain to tell them what happened in the United States with the cargo, because it didn't look loaded and lashed correctly.

"The cargo is in very bad condition. It is very dangerous for us," Garcia told the captain.

"There's a problem," the captain admitted to the Spanish dockworker.

"Are you telling me that the stowage has been done by nonprofessional dockworkers? People who usually don't work on the docks?" Garcia asked.

"Yes," the captain said.

"The next time that you come back to Spain with a ship loaded by someone who's not professional we are not going to work the ship," Garcia said, and then left.[16] Their action had already delayed the ship and showed that the Spanish dockers were disciplined.

Everyone there understood the dockworkers' code. Unlike most countries, union members in Spain can legally strike in solidarity. But workers in any country can refuse to work a ship if they think the work situation is unsafe, and that was what awaited the captain at his other ports of call if this situation in Charleston was not resolved.

"Believe them," said Rivero, who had known the dockworkers for years. "They are telling the truth."

Then the Nordana port agent wrote to his colleagues in Denmark: "They stopped the vessel's ops for 20 minutes just to show us their power, and that this warning is real, and advised that they are ready to stop any of Nordana's vessels at any port in Europe anytime."[17]

The next day in Valencia, the same captain received Llorca and his letter. By then Rechnitzer was on a plane to the States for yet another negotiating session with the ILA. The problem was spreading. It was getting out of control. This time they would *have* to settle.

KEN RILEY DIDN'T KNOW JULIAN GARCIA or anyone else in Spain. He had never heard of the International Dockworkers Council. He had never even been to Europe. One day Heyman asked Riley if he could contact friends in the IDC and enlist their help. Riley said, "Sure, why not?"

So Riley was surprised when Nordana finally came to an agreement at their April negotiations. Nordana's ships would once again be worked under the ILA contract, by Local 1422 members, under terms of the small boat agreement SSA could have offered the company seven months earlier and that Local 1422 did offer five months earlier. Nordana would also drop its lawsuit against the union, a great relief to the local president. The mood at that month's union meeting was optimistic for the first time in months, but the WSI lawsuit and the house arrest of five of their own was a cloud that dimmed their collective relief.

Back in Barcelona the Spanish dockworkers' union published an article in its newsletter about Garcia's delivery of the letter to Nordana and the union's commitment not to work Nordana ships until Charleston was settled. By the time the article came out, Nordana had signed the agreement under the ILA contract. Rivero called Garcia to tell him, "All the problems we have with Charleston are over." IDC members across the globe celebrated. The young group had faced its first challenge and won. Dockworkers' locals responding to each other with direct action had proven more effective than established national and international labor federations and associations left over from the Cold War.

For the leaders of ILA 1422, the immediate threat to area standards for wages and benefits had been eliminated for now. Stevedores and the hundreds of other companies and services on the port could rest on the ILA's success as well. The standards for port services had remained healthy, and Perry Collins had been sent packing to the tiny port of Georgetown. Ken Riley's visits to every key player in South Carolina had not succeeded in doing what, as far as the longshoreman knew, the delivery of one letter by a Spanish long-shoreman to a ship's captain had done. Riley was just beginning to appreciate what he and others could accomplish together.

Collins refused to sign off on an agreement that put him out of work. Since originally filing suit against the union he had amended it to include twenty-seven individual union members for the loss of work he incurred by the protests leading up to January 19, 2000. Now he raised the ante to $2.5 million for the loss of the contract with Nordana. What he had lost on the waterfront he would seek in court.

In the meantime, the five men under house arrest needed attorneys of their own to defend them against Condon's criminal charges. With the union's help, Peter Washington, Ricky Simmons, and Elijah Ford retained Lionel Lofton, former federal prosecutor. Andy Savage, Condon's former assistant prosecutor and a former Charleston County Council member, would defend Jason Edgerton and Ken Jefferson.

With Nordana out of the way, the union needed new friends and an infusion of cash for its mounting legal fees. In May, Riley attended the Coalition of Black Trade Unionists' (CBTU) national convention on Memorial Day weekend 2000. He flew out a day early to address the executive board, but first he met with the civil rights director of the AFL-CIO who was attending the convention. Riley carefully spelled out his case.

"If you need anything, give me a call," the director said, then shook his hand and left.

President of the CBTU, Bill Lucy of the American Federation of State, County and Municipal Employees, the country's largest public sector union, was a legend in the labor movement. But Riley didn't know most of the other people sitting around the table. He just hoped that out of all the activists in the labor movement, the people in this room would understand the kind of help his guys needed.

He laid out his case again. When he was finished, he could feel a collective sigh in the room. It sure wasn't the standing ovation he'd received from the ILWU in California. He looked at Lucy expectantly. Lucy thanked him for bringing the situation to the CBTU board and told him the board would pass a resolution on the matter at their meeting after the convention.

"Then what would I have?" Riley said later, disgusted. "A resolution. What good is a resolution? Nothing."[18]

So far, Riley was striking out with his fellow black union activists.

With the encouragement of his ILA longshoreman friend Royce Adams from Philadelphia, Riley stayed at the convention to see where else he might find help. Adams had been receiving and distributing bundles of the ILWU publication *The Dispatcher*. It was by way of California that Adams had kept up with the latest news of union support for the Charleston longshoremen. At the opening plenary, Adams walked up to Riley and said, "C'mon over here. There's somebody I want you to meet."[19]

Bill Fletcher, assistant to AFL-CIO president John Sweeney, was standing outside the meeting room talking on his cell phone. Adams, who had worked with Fletcher in the Black Radical Congress, interrupted him and said there was someone he needed to meet.

The two men stood in a quiet corner while Riley told Fletcher what had happened in Charleston.

"You gotta be shittin' me," was Fletcher's first response to the audacity of the state of South Carolina.[20] Riley handed him newspaper clips. The local president then explained how he had been trying to find someone in the labor movement who could help him, had come to the CBTU for that reason, and was having trouble getting the attention of the leadership.

"What's your international doing?" Fletcher asked.

"Nothing," Riley said.

"Do you have the support of your state AFL-CIO?"

Riley said yes. No local union is permitted to request support from the AFL-CIO, the American federation of international unions. Only an international union leader, in this case, John Bowers of the ILA, could request support. Riley, and Fletcher after he heard the story, didn't expect that to happen. But the federation is made up of local and state federations, any of which can also request support.

"Then have your state fed president write a letter to Sweeney asking for me to help her," Fletcher told him. "In two weeks, I'll have a strategy worked out and we should talk. Call me."

Riley left the CBTU convention hoping but not expecting Bill Fletcher to come through for him. So many union leaders had said "call me" and so many had let him down. But he asked his friend and president of the South Carolina AFL-CIO, Donna Dewitt, to send a letter to Sweeney asking for support. Dewitt sent a letter off immediately.

7
Black Longshoremen:
When Race and Class Collide

If you start arresting blacks in this state when they're protesting something that has to do with their rights of any kind, that has nasty implications. . . . We do not have a blank slate in our history in South Carolina.

—Hoyt Wheeler[1]

RILEY'S OWN UNION WAS USELESS. Internationally, he couldn't budge the ITF without Bowers's help. In America, the AFL-CIO was asleep; in South Carolina, it was so small it was barely functioning. Maybe Fletcher would help; he was an experienced, knowledgeable black man high up in the AFL-CIO. The West Coast longshoremen were backing him up, too, but except for Thibeaux, it was hard to believe they could relate to the kind of overtly racist system Riley was dealing with in Charleston.

Black Charlestonians talking about the longshoremen's protest inevitably turned to stories of the local hospital workers' strike of 1969. White Charlestonians would point to the rock throwing and broken car windows, intimidated reporters, the overturned news van that filled the papers and newscasts for weeks after the event.

Most black people believed any attorney general would have prosecuted some longshoremen, if maybe not those particular five. Similar things had happened before and would happen again. It was part of the way things were.

Most white people believed that only the eccentric Charlie Condon, driven by his political ambitions, would have made so much of such a minor case. It was an aberration in the otherwise smooth family-like operation of the port.

Why did it matter, anyway? It was a simple legal case, something for the courts to settle. It mattered because ultimately everyone understood that those "uneducated" black longshoremen could shut down and restart a multimillion-dollar economic pipeline on a moment's notice while those highly educated white men in charge were still trying to figure out who had flipped the switch.

This was the racial and economic divide across which Ken Riley and Charlie Condon watched and studied each other as they prepared to enter the battlefield with whatever legal, political, and economic leverage they could muster. To Condon, it was one case of many he could assign to young staff attorneys. To Riley, it meant the future of these five men—and of his union.

Each man came prepared with the wisdom of his respective history. For Condon, it was the importance of a status quo that had given South Carolina its strong Southern economy and its Confederate pride. For Riley, it was the unique role generations of longshoremen had played in Charleston since the days of slavery.

ECONOMICS HAS ALWAYS driven race relations in Charleston. It was because they were deeply entrenched in the South's economic system that a number of light-skinned free blacks supported the Confederate war effort.[2] When Charleston was occupied by Union troops, including several units of blacks from Massachusetts and South Carolina, liberated blacks celebrated, but the brown elite didn't; the emancipation of all blacks threatened the economic middle ground they had staked out between the races.

The light-complexioned blacks were incensed that after the Civil War whites did not distinguish between them and other blacks so they used their economic resources to gain the approval of whites and to show them that they were different.[3] Light-skinned blacks continued to form separate organizations scorning other blacks and blaming them for the new predicament they were in.[4]

Once the war was over, Charleston whites and light-skinned blacks came to a tacit agreement that the emancipation of blacks did not require the kind of radical protests that had fired up the rest of the South. Many light-skinned

blacks then became entrepreneurs who built their businesses with capital provided by their white ancestors and had an overlapping interest in maintaining
a peaceful community.[5]

Later, the NAACP, the Avery Institute, and elite brown clubs formalized
the collaboration between the white establishment and light-skinned blacks,
who became the intelligentsia and the successful businessmen of black
Charleston. From its inception the elite Avery, funded by the New England
American Missionary Association, reinforced barriers between classes and
favored light-skinned, well-off African Americans.[6]

Dark-skinned Charleston blacks, among them longshoremen, quickly
learned that life in Charleston was not black and white; it was black, *brown*,
and white.[7] Black workers were clearly on their own to navigate a new post-
slavery society and began to stake their own claim to economic prosperity. In
1869, Charleston longshoremen, performing some of the most brutal work in
the city, incorporated the Longshoremen's Protective Union Association.[8] It
was referred to at the time as "the most powerful organization of the colored
laboring class in South Carolina."[9] By 1875, the union had more than eight
hundred members and, within its first ten years, became known for its long
record of strikes.[10] Recently freed slaves and their sons were willing to jeopardize the first paid work they had ever experienced for the hope of something
better. They were making the demand that Frederick Douglass had so elo-
quently stated they must.

During the decades flanking the turn of the century, the port fell on hard
times. In 1936, as the Port of Charleston enjoyed a recovery, longshoreman
George German reorganized the dockworkers and they elected him union
president. He hired as their attorney William Morrison, whose grandfather
had owned German's grandfather until freeing him in 1861.[11]

Morrison was a powerful but progressive white man who served as mayor of
Charleston from 1947 to 1959. He was the first to appoint blacks to the police
force, extend sewer lines into black neighborhoods, and rebuild slums. He was
also, not surprisingly, a key proponent of port expansion in the mid-1950s.[12]
Employers and Morrison would negotiate at a hotel in downtown Charleston.
In those days of staunch segregation, German, unwelcome in the hotel, would
stand outside on the sidewalk until someone came down to show him the proposals, which he would hand to his schoolteacher daughter. She would look
them over and discuss them with her father and the union delegates.[13]

Charleston entered the 1960s with black students marching against the same segregation their ancestors had protested after the Civil War. A "riot" broke out when between five hundred and a thousand people marched up King Street to the *News and Courier*'s printing plant to protest biased news coverage. A magistrate jailed sixty-eight protesters. Their bonds totaled almost $700,000—enough to strain the finances of the entire civil rights movement.

The mayor, Palmer Gaillard Jr., whose grandfather had been mayor a hundred years before, called on the governor to send in state troopers while pickets continued in front of merchants who refused to integrate. Behind the scenes, Charleston's brown elite negotiated continually with the white establishment and appealed to both sides for a peaceful move toward integration.[14]

In early 1969, as the city recovered from a sixty-seven-day longshoremen's strike and a one-week protest by other ports authority workers demanding union representation, twelve of the local medical college's housekeepers, most of whom were black women, tried to gain recognition for their union, New York's Drug, Hospital, and Health Care Employees Union District 1199. This union had harnessed the power of the civil rights movement and blacks' workplace disenfranchisement to a new social movement style of organizing inspired by Martin Luther King Jr. and Cesar Chavez. (King had been assassinated just months earlier in Memphis after marching with striking black garbage workers.)

Four hundred hospital workers walked off the job when management fired the twelve who had made their union recognition demands to management. Black ministers kept the pressure on throughout the strike with full-page ads in the local newspaper, and the expansive Morris Brown Church became the rallying point for protests. Four days into the strike, the guest speaker at a previously scheduled NAACP awards dinner in Charleston called on "affluent Negroes to 'do a little profit-sharing with their brothers and sisters sweating on the picket line.' "[15]

The strike expanded to two more hospitals. Civil rights leaders Ralph Abernathy and Coretta Scott King made repeat visits to Charleston as more workers were arrested. When Abernathy, Hosea Williams, Andrew Young, and others led two hundred and fifty people in an evening march and prayer vigil in Charleston, they were arrested, charged, and convicted for marching without a permit and, interestingly, for rioting.[16] (Their case would become critical to the legal arguments in the Charleston longshoremen case almost forty years later.)

County officials voted to raise the minimum wage to lure strikers back to work. As thousands marched almost weekly and violence broke out around the city, the governor called out the National Guard. Five weeks into the strike he declared a state of emergency. After months of marches and hundreds of arrests, the longshoremen put an end to it all. The ILA threatened to shut down the port in support of the hospital workers.[17] The strike was settled immediately.

Harry Dent, special assistant to President Richard Nixon, emphasized the power of the ILA's threat. "The secretary of labor is a very fine person and a professional mediator," he said. "The threat of a longshoremen's strike and sympathy strikes across the nation concerned him greatly. The secretary used his personal influence on labor leaders to avert the dock strike on a day-by-day basis."[18]

It wasn't the Voting Rights Act of 1965 but the hospital workers strike of 1969, won with the vital assistance of the ILA, that changed the attitude of Charleston blacks about themselves and their power.[19] Black voter registration rose, and in 1970 a new black leadership began to emerge among elected officials, replacing an old brown elite cadre that had helped maintain the status quo through the early 1960s.[20]

But even by 2000, race was still the defining factor in almost all relations in South Carolina, as it was in the rest of the country.

"White folk don't want to talk about race, because they might be seen as racist, and black folk are just frankly tired of it," explained state representative Gilda Cobb-Hunter. "I think there's a resentment among white people here in Charleston of the longshoremen. When they see a black man making over $100,000 they got a problem with that. They see uneducated black men driving around in expensive cars and they resent it."

Black legislator David Mack agreed. "There's this sense of denial that people have and it gets back to where we stand as far as race in the state of South Carolina," he said. "There are so many folks who are in complete denial in regard to that. There are so many folks in the white community who when the subject is broached get very uncomfortable and they give you that jargon, 'Everything's okay,' 'I have black friends,' 'That was just an aberration.' I cannot get excited about singing 'Dixie' and *Gone with the Wind* because during that time a good time was not had by all."

It was no different, and perhaps even more starkly evident, on the docks.

"I believe race is an issue," said white port businessman Robert New. "It's not entirely about race, but it's an issue, and on the waterfront, you have long-shoremen who are mainly black, checkers who are white, stevedores who are white. And nobody wants to change it—and if you try to change it, who's going to fight it most? Kenny Riley. He doesn't want to integrate his union."

"The clerks and checkers [union local] down here is loaded with Irish Catholics, but it's been split by Greeks now, who tend to be clannish," SSA's Larry Young explained. "These good ol' Irish, you gotta beat their ass to take women and blacks. The whites went into the checkers and management. Kenny [Riley] over there ain't any better that way," he said, nodding down the road to the union hall. "Mechanical—blacks basically got control of that, too. It was a mixed union, but they've just about weeded the white boys outta there, too."

As THE COUNTRY PREPARED to enter the twenty-first century, South Carolina still refused to remove the Confederate flag, which had been placed atop its capitol building not during the Civil War but in 1961 in response to the civil rights movement. In January 2000, after months of debate and national attention, the NAACP launched a long-anticipated boycott of South Carolina that scared the hell out of South Carolina's tourism trade, its number-one industry.

South Carolina's investment in the successful, uninterrupted, and practically unregulated flow of commerce has paid off in poor education, high unemployment, low wages, and low union membership.[21] By the millennium, South Carolina ranked forty-third in income growth.[22] Less then 5 percent of the workforce was unionized. Black workers usually suffer the brunt of the bad news in this kind of economy. Not longshoremen. Whereas the average worker in South Carolina made $582 a week, $139 a week below the national average,[23] the average full-time longshoreman was making $1,350 a week.[24]

Low wages make the state attractive to local, national, and international business. So do keeping the workforce union-free and strengthening the state's "at-will employment" language, which clarifies that employers have the final say in who works when and under what conditions, giving employees few rights. South Carolina can justly sell itself to business as a third-world country within the United States.

Constantly honing business's leading edge is the South Carolina Chamber of Commerce. The chamber, with glassy skyscraper offices looking down on the state capitol, boasts 4,500 members including BMW and the State Ports Authority.[25]

The chamber has been powerful for many years. In the late 1990s, South Carolina lured a record number of businesses to its borders, yet the state's total corporate income tax revenue actually fell by 6 percent. Local property tax revenue on business equipment dropped 13 percent from 1993 to 1997. The state slashed taxes for one class of businesses by $2.7 billion, a benefit they will enjoy into the year 2010.[26]

"South Carolina has always been a very conservative state, very pro-business," explained S.C. Chamber of Commerce executive director Howard Hunter. "When I was at the Department of Revenue before I came here, South Carolina was the only state that carried its tax administrator on its trade missions because we had such a positive tax climate for business."[27]

BMW, for example, got the deal of the century when it first moved to South Carolina, because taxpayers and the State Ports Authority wrote the check for $35 million for the land on which the auto plant would be built, and now leases it back to BMW for $1 per year. It just kept getting better for BMW, who by 1999 wasn't even paying property taxes.[28]

But when pockets get pinched, business blinks, and the NAACP boycott, much like a disruption at the ports, was a distinctly economic threat with the added insult of being orchestrated by blacks. BMW and other Upstate business interests are affected more by the threat of a port shutdown, but Charleston and the Low Country count heavily on tourism, thus the two events of January 2000 caused an unusual consensus of concern between the two regions of the state. Black workers kept almost invisible millions flowing through the port, and black tourists spent a very visible $280 million in the state in 1997 alone.[29] Both economies were in jeopardy. Because of black people.

The Confederate flag debate was almost unfathomable to people who lived outside the South, but for South Carolinians, it tapped more than just strong feelings of "heritage," as flag supporters call it. To blacks and many whites, it was a symbol of racism, but more deeply it was "a measure of the isolation, self-absorption and morbid sense of inferiority that have haunted generations of white Southerners."[30]

"The Confederate flag goes to the heart of all Southerners," Myrtle Beach motel owner, George Trakas said. "It reminds us that we are a conquered nation and we have in common with each other certain cultural values. . . . We fear no man. We fear Jesus Christ only. Christianity and Southern thought and ideology go hand-in-hand with each other. . . . If it says it in the Bible, then it's true."[31] Trakas identified what Charlie Condon embodied in his politics: the marriage of neo-Confederacy and conservative Christianity epitomized the white South Carolinian.

Charlie Condon's response to the events that night on the waterfront is as deeply rooted as Ken Riley's. But in South Carolina, those roots grow in different pots. Some of them go back before the Civil War; some from a hundred years later during the struggle for civil rights and some were just sprouting when Condon announced his opinion that the Confederate flag should remain atop the capitol building and Riley helped fund buses to transport flag protesters.

The flag debate vaulted South Carolina into the national and international limelight. For months, national news correspondents descended upon the capitol to interview black and white legislators. The state became openly polarized as the top blew off the genteel white and tired black debate over race relations and history. The NAACP was business's Public Enemy No. 1 for months leading up to and including its 46,000-person march on Columbia. Now, with the trouble on the docks, ILA Local 1422 was quickly moving up to take its place.

8

Condon and Riley Launch Their Campaigns

Calhoun was the South's most profound political theorist since the time of Jefferson. But his political theory was only a logical statement of the status quo in the South Carolina of his day. . . . James Knox Polk confided to his diary that Calhoun mounted the slavery controversy as a political hobby to keep himself before the public in his designs on the Presidency.

—Clement Eaton[1]

IN JANUARY OF 2000, the horse race that was the Republican primary was at a full gallop. Texas governor George W. Bush, the conservative establishment's favorite, was running ahead of John McCain, a moderate senator from Arizona. But in South Carolina, Bush was not a sure favorite. Some Republican voters were still smarting from Bush Senior's betrayal on tax increases. Two South Carolina Republican activists, Mark Sanford and Lindsey Graham, fell in behind McCain, splitting the Republican Party.[2]

Christian voters, no tax increase voters, and veterans were coming out of the woodwork for McCain. Establishment Republicans who were supporting Bush were on their heels. McCain was everywhere, generating new excitement in the primary. Suddenly a Republican machine used to turning out 250,000 voters was faced with more than a half million of them heading to the polls.[3]

The stakes were high and tensions deep within the Republican Party and state Attorney General Charlie Condon, South Carolina chair of the Bush campaign, had a lot riding on Bush's success against the liberal Republicans pushing for McCain.

For a man who was a Democrat until 1990, Condon had a surprisingly deep association with the conservative wing of the Republican Party. His work chairing Bob Dole's South Carolina presidential campaign four years earlier gave the candidate the boost credited with vaulting him to the Republican nomination for president.[4]

During the 1996 campaign Condon had become close with the Doles. When the story broke that Condon was supporting Elizabeth for president in 1999, national "Draft Dole" campaign chair and native South Carolinian Earl Cox said, "The many people who have been working behind the scenes in our area now have a well-respected and powerful leader."

This "powerful leader" eventually landed with the 2000 front-runner, Bush. In his role as one of the top Republican statewide officeholders in South Carolina (the lieutenant governor being the other), Condon had the responsibility as symbol if not front-line coordinator to provide the legitimacy of the Bush campaign across the state.

As McCain showed up at every parade, tent revival, and church picnic in South Carolina, the Bush campaign scrambled to put together a larger ground campaign than it had ever anticipated needing. Then McCain won the New Hampshire Primary, and panic set in. Less than two weeks after Condon's successful grand jury indictment of the five longshoremen for felony rioting, radio ads linking the "union riot" to John McCain's election reform proposal began running on South Carolina radio.

> The Charleston union riot reminds us why South Carolina is a right-to-work state. Unfortunately, big labor comes out a big winner in John McCain's campaign finance plan. Senator Strom Thurmond says it would be disastrous for conservatives. Almost every conservative senator opposes it.

It continued, with a string of carefully selected buzz words:

> The McCain plan curtails free speech rights of individuals and citizens groups, limiting what they can do in elections. But it does not prohibit union

bosses from taking mandatory dues from working people and spending them to elect liberal Democrats. That's not right. . . .

The McCain plan would give union bosses and the liberal media more control over elections by restricting First Amendment rights of individuals and citizens' groups. Those are not South Carolina values. Paid for by Bush for President.

The voice on the radio was Charlie Condon's.[5] Given that less than 4 percent of the state's entire workforce was unionized at the time, the commercial may have seemed out of place, but the scary images of "union bosses" and the "liberal media" stealing rights away from "working people" was classic neoconservative propaganda at its best.

These ads coincided with Bush's controversial early February visit to Bob Jones University in Greenville, South Carolina, to build momentum for the February 19 primary. The campaign later called that stop "the single most ill-considered decision of the campaign" in light of a national backlash against the anti-Catholic, anti-Semitic, anti-interracial dating institution.[6] The campaign suffered the political fallout for months, with Bush issuing numerous apologies, including one to the pope. But Bush had done what all other conservative Republican candidates had done before: he sent a strong message to the religious Right that its issues would be an integral part of his campaign, and his presidency if he won.

The New York Times identified Warren Tompkins as "a seasoned strategist who ran Mr. Bush's operation in South Carolina" and the real decision maker behind the visit. "To ignore that block of voters would be like running on a Democratic ticket and ignoring African-Americans or labor unions," Tompkins said.[7]

Pat Robertson, founder of the Christian Coalition, questioned the wisdom of the visit: "I'd have advised him not to go. Bob Jones has been known as a rather extreme place. Those people are really far out."[8]

Clearly, times had changed since Robertson, a former presidential candidate, had campaigned at Bob Jones University.

In the end, Tompkins's strategy was the winning one for the Bush campaign. George W. Bush won the South Carolina Republican Primary 53 percent to McCain's 42 percent.[9] (Alan Keyes received 5 percent.) Among the Bob Jones faithful, he whipped McCain by an impressive 77 to 18 percent.[10]

Exit polls showed conservatives voting for Bush by a two-to-one margin and
the religious Right voting three to one for him.[11] Condon's brand of polarization spread beyond his home state as he helped Bush capture the right-wing
Christian conservatives that the future president would later cater to by sys-
tematically eroding the barriers between science, religion, and the state
through both policy and law.

As THE NATIONAL MEDIA picked up its gear and left South Carolina for the
next primary, Ken Riley was on the phone pulling together the meeting that
would launch a kind of campaign Condon and his kin had never seen before.
Between daily union business, building the new union hall, and local politics,
Riley had already managed to plant the seeds of a campaign. He and other
leaders had traveled to national meetings where they hoped to build new connections and successfully toured the West Coast where their new longshoremen friends and allies helped get their story on radio and television for the
first time.[12] But what Riley was doing, all he knew how to do, was piecemeal
and based more on luck and good wishes than any kind of grand plan.

     Having researched the issue and garnered as much support as he could get
from his colleagues, Bill Fletcher flew from his office at the AFL-CIO in
Washington to Charleston in late June to meet with Riley, DeWitt, Cobb-
Hunter and Jimmy Hyde, director of the AFL-CIO for South Carolina and
Georgia. Later they would consult Local 1422 attorneys Armand Derfner and
Peter Wilborn, but first they had to discuss whether to include them at all.[13]

     At that meeting they laid out the strategy and potential tactics of the cam-
paign. A local judge had already limited pickets at the port to nineteen, and
Condon's office had already weighed in trying to get that number slashed to
four, so to be effective this fight had to quickly move away from the Columbus
Street Terminal. They named their group the Charleston 5 Defense Committee,
and its first work was to organize defense committees around the country to
raise funds and awareness about the case of the five indicted men and what
had brought it about.[14]

     The group needed to identify their biggest obstacles and most likely allies.
One unfortunate obstacle, they all agreed, was the International
Longshoremen's Association, based in New York, which had remained oddly
quiet until then. The local and the AFL-CIO could go only so far without the
declared support by the union's international, but that support was unlikely

to come willingly. The Riley brothers and Eddie McBride were already plenty visible in their work building the Longshore Workers Coalition to reform the ILA, and the word was out.

To complicate matters, the man Riley had unseated in the 1997 union election for local president and beat again just days after the incident in January was now causing problems in Charleston. Ben Flowers still held his position in the ILA as district vice president and international vice president. In December, during one of the pickets of a Nordana ship, Flowers went to the picket lines and told members that the protests were wrong.

After the January incident, Flowers told members that the men arrested that night had broken the law. Riley wrote and asked John Bowers to tell Flowers to stop using his position to influence the members.[15] When Flowers continued to voice his opposition to the local's efforts, Riley filed charges with the international executive committee asking that Flowers be reprimanded.[16]

It was a classic battle between the older-generation union leader, raised in the ways of accommodating the South Carolina establishment, and the new generation, willing to stand up and fight, even take a blow to the head, with confidence. Each approach had its own price to pay, but now Riley was president, and Flowers was aging; his days as an officer above Riley were numbered.

More complications arose when Benny Holland sent a letter informing Riley that he could not use union dues toward the legal defense of the 5. Then Riley lost his case against Flowers at the international level, another indication from New York that it was displeased about Riley's handling of events in the South. It was clear Bowers would not come to their aid unless pressed, and he would have to be pressed by people he respected such as John Sweeney, AFL-CIO president, and David Cockroft, head of the International Transport Workers' Federation. In the meantime, there was plenty of work to do for the Campaign to Free the Charleston 5.

The second obstacle was Condon, who as the white conservative Christian and Republican attorney general had the full weight of the South Carolina establishment behind him. But Condon was also known for his provocative public statements, quirky legal arguments, and political opportunism. This campaign would have to vilify Condon effectively without libeling him personally, a tricky and thin line but one these activists were more than glad to draw. They would turn Condon from obstacle into target and make the campaign not about five unruly longshoremen but about police provocation and a man who took advantage of an unfortunate convergence of circumstances for his own political gain.

The third obstacle was resources, in the form of both people and cash. Within the AFL-CIO, Fletcher was waging his own battles. The Harvard-educated activist had been promoted to assistant to the president in June of 1999, a position that put him in a relationship of both contention and coop-eration with the chief of staff, Bob Welsh. Both men had come with Sweeney from the Service Employees International Union when Sweeney was elected president of the 13-million-member AFL-CIO. The senior staff was well acquainted with the tensions between Fletcher and Welsh. By the time this campaign came along, Fletcher's dissatisfaction with his work situation was well known. When he brought the project to the senior management team of the AFL-CIO, some of whom he'd worked with since their days at SEIU, he was met with a less than an enthusiastic response, but all agreed he could pur-sue it for the time being.[17]

The local, with the help of the West Coast longshoremen, had already amassed an impressive war chest, but there could never be enough money. It was impossible to know how long this fight would last. The legal fees for five defendants and the local were mounting fast. Flying three or four speakers around the country and the world, putting them up in hotels, eating on the road—all of this would add up quickly. (Dewitt's expenses would be paid by the South Carolina AFL-CIO.) The local had organized a few crab-cracking and fish-fry nights that had raised almost $10,000, but it was like holding a bake sale to pay for a new school. Ken Riley his brother Leonard would have to hit the road to tell the story of the Charleston 5 and raise money at any gath-ering of workers they could find.

Politically, the governor was worthless compared to the kind of pressure Condon, who had just delivered South Carolina to the most conservative presidential candidate of the pack, could exert. Charleston mayor Joe Riley was sympathetic but had done nothing to help when Riley approached him earlier. Police chief Reuben Greenberg had maintained friendly relations with the local and Riley gave him the benefit of the doubt, but the outspoken chief was hardly a player in Condon's circles. They couldn't hope for a repetition of the scene a decade earlier when Greenberg, during a public feud covered extensively by the local media, waved around a ten-pound roll of bologna in front of the press to drive home his opinion of Condon.[18]

Besides, Joe Riley and Reuben Greenberg were "Low Country," as locals refer to it, and Charlie was talking to "Upstate" when he talked about prosecuting union people. Ever since the textile union was busted in the violent suppression of the uprising of '34, Upstaters perceived unions as bad, and believed that what unions still survived were over on the coast, in the Low Country.[19]

Unfortunately for Local 1422, the unions on the coast were mostly made up of building trades—carpenters, plumbers, ironworkers, and electricians. These "craft" unions were like guilds. They grew from a tradition of training programs to protect white craftsmen from incursions of skilled slaves whose owners contracted them out to work in the cities. Not much had changed over the years, and those unions were still almost all-white.[20] They were not a group that could be considered an automatic ally just because they were called unions.

To complicate matters, the construction of the new union hall had gone out to bid. Due to a combination of miscommunication and ignorance of the process it was awarded to a nationally renowned nonunion construction contractor, fueling local building trades union members' animosity toward the longshoremen's union to such an extent that someone filed a complaint with the Department of Labor that launched an investigation of the ILA project. Rumors even circulated that Ken Riley was recruiting black construction workers from out of state to build the hall.[21]

Organizers searched elsewhere among their acquaintances for allies. Leftist political groups from the International Socialists Organization to the Communist Party USA had already published sympathetic stories about the 5. Their own friend Brett Bursey was publishing stories on the website The Point out of Columbia and would continue to rally the troops under the banner of the South Carolina Progressive Network. Most reporters from the Left had taken down word for word everything Riley, Dewitt, and others had told them. They never questioned the facts as union people related them. They seldom if ever got direct quotes from Condon, but they gleaned information from other news sources. The message of peaceful pickets attacked by cops was one they understood immediately. They didn't need to be persuaded of a story of black workers in the South standing up for their rights. Photos of the men throwing rocks and railroad ties at riot police only convinced these journalists that the longshoremen had been provoked.

What a relief it was for both Riley brothers, Dewitt, and Local 1422 members to read one of those articles compared to the *Charleston Post and Courier*, which never published a story without using the word "riot" and stating that longshoremen made $100,000 or more per year, something only a few senior ones, working long hours, managed to accomplish. Riley added to his list of tasks getting a meeting with Tony Bartleme from the *Post and Courier*. He needed to sit the reporter down and walk him through an ILA contract to give him a more realistic view of longshoremen's wages.

New connections through the International Dockworkers Council, which Riley hadn't known existed until a few months earlier, had caused the Spanish dockworkers to pressure Nordana to settle its dispute with 1422. In March the head of an ILA local in Canada had sent $5,000 and had referenced the Liverpool dockers in his cover letter and asked Riley to consider joining the IDC.[22] It was apparent that a passionate group of longshoremen had pulled together for those Liverpool dockers and Riley was scheduled to speak at the group's founding convention in Tenerife in a few months. He was confident he would build even more international relationships there. Fletcher, for his part, had not only whatever AFL-CIO power he could bring to bear on the campaign, but also had his long association with the Black Radical Congress to call upon.

Dewitt and Riley's heads were spinning from their sudden immersion in this new political scene, a world they had only heard about from a very long distance. Dewitt, a white woman with a Southern peaches-and-cream inflection to her voice had only the most basic experience with such things. Her grandfather had been a politically active Democrat. Her uncle was sheriff in 1968 when police killed three young black people who were protesting segregation at a bowling alley on the South Carolina State University campus, an event that became known as the Orangeburg Massacre.

Dewitt had grown up best friends with the girl whose father was the most powerful man in the state at the time, Senator Marshall Williams. Years later the senior legislator would take Dewitt under his wing in her early days as a Communications Workers of America Union lobbyist in Columbia to teach her the importance of allies and coalitions in winning legislation as well as strikes.

When she was first elected president of the state AFL-CIO in 1996, construction trades union members, traditionally the more conservative wing of the labor movement, wrote to John Sweeney, Dewitt's national counterpart, to complain that she was consorting with gay pride groups and Communists (more accurately one gay pride group and one self-proclaimed socialist, Bursey). Sweeney wrote back in a letter he copied to Dewitt that the AFL-CIO was a broad umbrella that worked with many diverse groups.

So whatever shade of politics these new friends claimed didn't matter to Dewitt. Her political experience taught her the practicality of coalition building. Her union experience taught her the rest.

Riley had spent a lifetime developing his people skills and his ability to assess complicated situations in the complex racial politics of Charleston. But Riley's twenty years of reform work within his all-black union taught him that sometimes it isn't just about race but about something much bigger and more complicated. His experience growing up as a Southern, Christian son of a longshoreman in Charleston had taught him humility, kindness, and something about the complexity of people of any color. His good-natured but sincere manner made him a popular union leader and someone both blacks and whites could quickly appreciate and respect. His deep religious roots and faith in God also taught him not to judge but to accept. Now he was happy to accept the help and support from these people he had never met. They were human beings, and they were willing to help. That's all he needed to know.

Gilda Cobb-Hunter, by then a seasoned legislator, could see the challenges ahead. Over the next eighteen months she, along with Senator Robert Ford, Representative Joe Neal, and others, would offer the campaign informal advice, regularly take the pulse of the state's General Assembly, and ward off any sudden legislative assaults. This extroverted black woman from Florida, with decades as a social worker in the South and eight years as an outspoken South Carolina state legislator, had learned some hard lessons. She didn't shy away from controversy, and some would say she willingly engaged it.

Jimmy Hyde, a native Georgian, brought to the table a long history as a union autoworker in Doralville, Georgia and his position as the go-to guy for the AFL-CIO in the Southern region. While Fletcher had almost daily but sporadic and interrupted face time with Sweeney, Hyde would soon have more coveted alone time with the AFL-CIO president as the Southerner drove his esteemed guest to and from a convention more than an hour from the airport where he would land. If America's top labor leader wasn't completely on board by the time he landed in Georgia, he would be by the time Hyde got done with him.

With this list and a strategy of building legal and political pressure on the South Carolina power structure, Fletcher, Dewitt, and Riley with their cast of lawyers, activists, and legislators set out to get five longshoremen out from under the state charges that could imprison them for years, and surely ruin their work lives forever.

If they lost, it would signal the end of any meaningful, effective protest against global employers anywhere in the United States. It would also represent the final throes of the last significant civil rights and union presence in the state. That sizzling Charleston day in June two native South Carolina labor activists, one a black longshoreman and the other a white retired telephone company operator, a strategic thinker from Washington, a feisty legislator, and a good ol' boy from Georgia put their heads together for the strategy session of their lives, then broke bread together to cement their pledge to do what had to be done until this fight was over.

Within weeks of that first meeting, the group would grow into a Tuesday afternoon cross-country telephone conference call with as many as twenty participants some weeks, reporting in on defense committee work, legal progress, and international solidarity. Fletcher would be the taskmaster, running the calls like a drill sergeant. Everyone had a job and each person would make a progress report each week. When someone came on the call, he'd ask, "Who is that?" and when someone left the call, "Who left?" He made it clear there wasn't time or energy for people who didn't get their assignments completed. Everyone was responsible to each other and to the campaign.

The steering committee decided there was no way to win this without the local's legal counsel, voting rights legend Armand Derfner and his young protégé Peter Wilborn. Both progressive lawyers were dedicated to civil rights in the South, and they understood the careful balance between social movement tactics and legal maneuvers, the advantages and constraints of both. Because of that, they would eventually become the mediators between the campaign and the legal team, including Savage, Lofton, and each other.

For now, though, they helped the committee determine its message to the public. First, campaign spokespeople would emphasize that this had been a peaceful picket, that workers were provoked by the sheer presence of the amassed army of police, and that not only workers' rights but civil rights were at stake. The six hundred and sixty police in riot gear who shot at longshoremen with beanbag bullets and concussion grenades were unnecessary armaments against gravel from a railroad bed. Riley would tell the story of Nordana versus the ILA leading up to the big night, but with the WSI lawsuit pending, it was important not to jeopardize the local's legal position. He could do it in a few simple lines: Nordana went nonunion after twenty-seven years, union members had been picketing that decision for months, and then police thugs came in one night, beat on them, and arrested them.

Fletcher knew someone at *60 Minutes* and hoped he would eventually get the AFL-CIO communications experts on board. Would the lawyers for the five defendants permit their clients to talk to the media? If not, how could the media part of the campaign be effective? Was there any way to get any of the 5 on a speaking tour? These questions would become the source of intense debates between attorneys and organizers and would challenge, strengthen, and at times tear at the committee during the coming months. Fletcher and Derfner, both familiar with so many other legal cases that had become causes célèbres, were familiar with this dynamic, but that made it no easier.

Members of the committee fanned out across the country, or used the phone and email, to enlist their respective friends and organizations. They were soon disappointed. Most people outside of this budding campaign didn't think this mattered to anyone. Where was the news in five union guys getting arrested for getting carried away at a demonstration? Hell, it could've been worse. At least no one got killed. And who was involved again? They were mostly black guys, right? Must be a civil rights thing. No, they were union guys, must be a labor thing. So while the Charleston 5 encompassed so many overlapping social justice issues—class, race, organized labor—it risked becoming an orphan to all of them.[23]

Cobb-Hunter, straddling all of these interests, could be heard repeating what had become a mantra during her time in the General Assembly.

"What role did race play in this? How do you separate it?" she asked. "I don't—and the reason I don't separate it is because they're the same thing. White legislators separate it because they see race but don't see class. I suggest the most important color in America is green."

Cobb-Hunter was a prophet. The color of money would overshadow this campaign all the way to the end.

RILEY'S NORMAL UNION ACTIVITIES up to this point had helped to slowly build his circle of contacts. He and other members had attended the A. Philip

Randolph Institute meetings and were connecting with black political activists across the country. In March he and a group had attended Howard University's Charter Day convocation in Washington where he had been able to socialize with great and respected black academics and leaders like keynote speaker Dr. John Hope Franklin, Ossie Davis, and others receiving recognition from the university that day.

But with the meeting in June, Riley and his allies now had a vision and a plan ahead of them, and organized support behind them. He and Local 1422 Vice President Robert Ford went to the IDC founding convention in the Canary Islands with a determination to meet and enlist these dockworkers from around the world. Delegates representing union dockworkers' locals of eighty-five ports in thirteen countries attended the three-day meeting. Riley finally had the chance to meet in person and thank Julian Garcia, the veteran Barcelona dockworker who had presented his letter of protest to the Nordana captain, and they made fast friends. He also met Swede Bjorn Borg and others who had been supporting the Charleston dockworkers from afar.[24]

By the time Riley returned to the States, Condon had made the news once again, this time announcing his disappointment with the U.S. Supreme Court's decision to uphold Miranda. His office had written the amicus brief to overturn Miranda, the ruling that requires police to inform an arrested person of his or her right to an attorney. Condon's response to the high court's decision? "Miranda does not protect constitutional rights of the innocent as much as it gives lawyers a loophole to help the guilty go free. Miranda has always been a decision which puts the handcuffs on the police rather than on the criminals."[25]

For Labor Day that year, Riley had the opportunity to make his case to the local community about what good wages do for a region. The union's massive Labor Day picnic was the perfect venue. The media still referred to the events of January 19 as a "riot" but they were willing to give the union some ink to explain its position.

"Riley and other labor leaders say the riot was unfortunate, but they believe their stance with Nordana was vital to the union's future on the waterfront," *Post and Courier* reporter Jonathan Maze wrote. "They say the union is needed because it provides workers with higher wages and better benefits in a difficult and dangerous industry. They also point to their productivity, saying the union has created an efficient and highly trained work force."[26]

By mid-December the ILWU on the West Coast approved an official policy of support for the Charleston longshoremen, tying it to other events around the world and to the recent presidential election.

"The global attack by steamship lines, terminal operators and stevedoring companies on the unions, wages and conditions of longshore workers has moved from Mexico and Brazil, from Liverpool and Australia, and has landed on American shores," the resolution read. "Charleston is the opening salvo in the war against American longshore workers and the American labor movement, an indication of things to come under a possible George W. Bush administration. It must be stopped here." [27]

Condon took the only opportunity he was given to address the union issue before the year's end. Just days after the ILWU announcement, his office issued an opinion to the Georgetown City Council stating that the South Carolina Constitution prohibits the "donation" of public funds to labor unions. The council had contributed $3,000 toward a Labor Day parade sponsored by the United Steelworkers of America. [28]

By December 2000, defense committees had formed in a half-dozen cities across the country, and Riley, Dewitt, and Leonard Riley had told their story dozens of times. The money they raised covered their travel costs and a little more, but at least they were keeping the issue alive and getting the word out about the Charleston 5. It was slow progress for the amount of work and time they were putting into it, and it would be hard to keep up that pace for much longer.

Fletcher noticed a significant increase in enthusiasm among the AFL-CIO staff after Sweeney's return from Georgia. Hyde's passionate outrage at the events in Charleston had persuaded Sweeney of the merits of the campaign, but there was more to do before he and the organization could come out publicly for the campaign.

Still there was no movement from the prosecutor. Legal machinery grinds slowly, and even slower when lawyers expect a simple resolution to a simple situation. Attorneys on both sides had reviewed the press and police videotapes and seen the event from beginning to end, not just what had ended up on the nightly news.

Defense attorney Andy Savage contacted one of his expert witnesses in law enforcement who would be prepared to speak to the overuse of force that night, but he didn't expect to have to use him. The lawyers, the police, and the entire Charleston legal establishment understood these were nothing more than simple misdemeanors on the part of the longshoremen and that the police had their own answering to do if it went to trial. Any reasonable judge would probably defer and dismiss the charges if the defendants had no other violations in a six-month period and everything would go back to normal.[29]

But the Charleston legal establishment had a wrench called Charlie Condon in its works, and nothing was proceeding as usual. So as prosecutors reviewed videos and photos and collected reports and statements from police in three agencies, defense lawyers filed motions and more motions to compel discovery, then sifted through thousands of documents, viewed hours of videotape, and hoped against hope that Charlie Condon and his staff would just go away.

9

The Tide Starts to Turn

Solidarity, unlike charity, is a two-way street. It means accepting mutual responsibility. The essence of solidarity is mutual aid. And the most effective and meaningful assistance to workers can be delivered through organization.
                                   —A Trade Union Guide to Globalization[1]

BY JANUARY 2001, a year since the trouble on the docks, defense committees were forming from San Francisco to New York, Chicago to Atlanta. Committee members mobilized potential supporters around speaking engagements, often combining them with radio and television interviews. Local union newsletters and independent newspapers published excerpts from the talks, but "Charleston 5" was not a household word, even among labor activists.

The local had already incurred $87,000 in legal bills defending the $2.5 million civil suit from WSI.[2] With two of the area's best-known criminal lawyers assigned to the 5, the legal fees were bound to escalate, yet most of the speaking engagements covered little more than the expense it took to get speakers there and back.

Fletcher kept the campaign on course with his weekly conference calls, but the organizers of defense committees, Riley, Dewitt, and others reported that they were meeting opposition from union leaders who were telling

Then came the pivotal words, the words Riley, Dewitt, and so many others had awaited for a year:

"The national AFL-CIO is assisting in this effort and I ask your help."

As if that weren't enough, Sweeney then made a request that most certainly did not go over well with Bowers, who believed donations to the campaign were being misused at best and illegally channeled to the Longshore Workers Coalition at worst. Sweeney told unions to send their donations to Charleston.

The funds would not go to the international—the official affiliate of the AFL-CIO—but to a local union. The call was rare if not unprecedented for the AFL-CIO, but Riley, Fletcher, and Dewitt wanted to make sure that whatever money went to the ILA's New York office made it the rest of the way to the campaign in Charleston. Fletcher, still in charge and watching out for the AFL's interests, also wanted to be sure the ILA kicked in its fair share. There would be no way to know that unless all funds came to South Carolina, without being filtered through the ILA in New York.

Sweeney also requested that unions form defense committees across the country. For more information, he directed labor leaders to Dewitt's South Carolina AFL-CIO rather than Bowers's International Longshoremen's Association in New York.

"We wanted to do a rally but we knew we could not plan anything without it," said Dewitt of the memo. "This gave us the ability to begin mobilizing for the things we wanted to do."

Once the dam broke, letters, emails, and calls came flooding in. It couldn't have come at a better time. The trials were set to begin in June; it would take six months to plan the rally and all the publicity they could get.

CHARLIE CONDON'S STAFF was having its own troubles getting their case off the ground. The assistant attorneys general were not getting the broad unequivocal support from the local police they could usually count on. In fact, they were getting quite the opposite.[3]

"I recently met with the Charleston City Police Department to discuss preparations for trial in this case," assistant attorney general Brad Cranshaw wrote to Condon. "Lt. Colonel Edward Hetherington [Hethington] was present and speaking for Chief Greenberg at the meeting . . . Colonel Hetherington asked that the matter be handled short of a trial." Cranshaw explained to

Condon that the police believed nothing good could come of a trial and that the attorney general's office should accept guilty pleas "on any number of various magistrate level offenses." The police wanted to bring the case back to city court, where the men would face misdemeanor charges and thirty days or less of jail time.

"This position has been consistently maintained by the city," Cranshaw continued. "No general sessions warrants were sworn at arrest, and the department supported this form of resolution when we originally pushed for a trial date last June before Judge Cottingham."

Condon asked for recommendations. Cranshaw suggested guilty pleas to misdemeanor-level riot charges or to higher-level resisting arrest and aggravated assault charges. The greatest weakness in the case was that the police had never treated them as anything more than a trespass, a magistrate level offense, nothing that warranted a state level trial.

"The original trespass warrants sworn by the city are the Achilles' heel of this case," Cranshaw said. "The defense will exploit it and a jury will not like it. However, public sentiment was certainly in our favor when the riot occurred."

A year had already passed and the trial was at least another six months ahead of them. Condon had other things on his mind. Just days after he received the news from Cranshaw about the Charleston case, the attorney general announced his candidacy for the Republican nomination for governor.[4]

Condon's announcement confirmed what many believed, that his desire to attain higher office was motivating him in the Charleston case. Long before the announcement was official, everything he did was suspect. Or as one Democratic Party operative put it, "Condon has been running for governor since the day after [Democrat] Jim Hodges was elected governor."[5]

Charleston 5 defense committees were forming in Washington, Louisiana, Texas, Milwaukee, and Miami. By February 21, 2001, Riley, Local 1422 vice president Robert Ford, and two of the Five, Peter Washington and Elijah Ford, were in San Francisco for a whirlwind four-day tour of the West Coast. While the ILWU remained the backbone of the defense committees on that coast, Sweeney's memo created new opportunities.

"The Charleston longshoremen wasted no time in reaching labor's ear," Jack Heyman reported via the Web. "No sooner had they disembarked from their airplane than they headed for a mass picket line of some 400 United Air Lines mechanics. Local TV crews filmed the labor protest that was addressed by Executive Secretary-Treasurer of the California AFL-CIO, Art Pulaski, and other labor officials. Riley was introduced, spoke from the platform and received resounding applause."

On that trip alone, the campaign received coverage by Fox News and Soul Beat TV (with a black audience of 400,000), appeared on KPFA's "Flashpoints" radio show, and attended the National Labor Conference for jailed journalist Mumia Abu-Jamal. The Charleston delegation spoke to two hundred people at La Peña cultural center and to another two hundred at Local 10 ILWU's membership meeting, and at a fundraising breakfast at the Crowne Plaza Hotel hosted by the ILWU, the California AFL-CIO, and the San Francisco Labor Council. They also walked with strikers from the Hotel and Restaurant Workers Union (HERE) on their picket line at Castagnola's Restaurant on Fisherman's Wharf.[6] The tour was co-sponsored by the Black Radical Congress.

ON MARCH 2, just a week after the California tour, an officer with the Charleston Police Department was searching the Internet. Among his other tasks was monitoring the Black Radical Congress. In one of their discussion groups someone had posted an article from the Communist Party USA's newspaper, *People's Weekly World*. It reported on the West Coast trip and announced a worrisome development:

"Riley reported that he had recently attended a meeting of the International Dockworkers Alliance [*sic*] in Spain where the dockworkers of 14 countries agreed to take actions with U.S. dockers unions on both coasts on the day that the trial of the defendants begins."[7]

The fight had moved not only beyond South Carolina's borders and beyond the American leftists, it had somehow become international, and all eyes were fixed on Charleston.

AS BOWERS REMAINED OFFICIALLY SILENT in his New York office, California activists continued to set the pace for fundraising and political support for the Charleston 5. In February, the more conservative West Coast Maritime Trades Department and the Plumbers and Pipefitters union, buoyed by the AFL-CIO memo from Sweeney, passed resolutions supporting the Charleston 5. ILWU locals were beginning to plan "stop-work meetings" for the first day of the trial. Closing the ports could cost the logistics industry millions of dollars per hour. In Long Beach, California, longshore workers voted to assess themselves $20 per member per month for the legal defense fund. (In a larger membership meeting, the approved amount was reduced to $5 per member.) The local representing the largest port in the country, Los Angeles, voted to assess itself $10 per member, a move that would net more than $40,000 per month for the Charleston defense fund. ILWU members were signing up for the long haul.

In Local 1422's backyard, Southern black longshoremen were stepping up to the fight. The Savannah longshoremen worked with Jimmy Hyde and the Georgia state Federation of Labor to coordinate statewide campaigns. Riley's trips to Georgia had him speaking to workers during shift change at auto plants and to hundreds of workers at the state convention. Hyde even arranged a meeting with the building trades unions so Riley could make amends over the union hall construction issue that still lingered. In Jacksonville, Florida, ILA President Charles Spencer pledged his support and convinced the Florida Federation of Labor to take on a statewide campaign. Farther north, longshoremen in Philadelphia reached out to the Wilmington local to coordinate organizing and fundraising efforts.[8]

Workers in New York City were organizing. The International Socialist Organization invited Leonard Riley to speak to the three hundred who attended their East Coast Conference in New York in February. On the heels of that talk, a committee of thirty from the Service Employees International Union, the Laborers Union, the Democratic Socialists of America, International Socialists Organization, New Directions, the Black Radical Congress, and others were meeting to create the New York City Charleston 5 Defense Committee.

It was the invitations to the Communist Party USA convention and the other socialist events that got the attention of the AFL-CIO. In the midst of his other travels, Riley was summoned on short notice to Bowers' office in New York. When he walked in, Joe Uehline, of the AFL-CIO's field mobilization department, was sitting with Bowers waiting.[9]

"The reason the mainstream labor movement isn't turning out in the numbers we expected is because of the people organizing some of these events," Uehline told Riley. "You're getting support from some pretty shady people."

"Well, let's be for real," Riley said. "The mainstream labor movement has been very slow in joining this struggle." He turned to Bowers. "The ILA has been very slow in joining this struggle. If we had waited for *you,* my guys would all be in prison now." Then he said something he later regretted, because he believed it cost his friend Fletcher his job. "If it hadn't been for Fletcher saying, 'We'll have to go around the ILA to win this,' we wouldn't *have* a campaign." Riley refused to distance himself from the leftists who had helped him in the union's time of need.

Riley's travels and speaking engagements continued. In March a large 1422 delegation attended an event at Spellman College in Atlanta. That same month, Ken's brother Leonard Riley spoke at Columbia University, the Northeast Regional A. Philip Randolph Institute Conference in Wilmington, Delaware, and did the rounds in Chicago including the University of Illinois, Chicago, and various churches. Ken Riley was the invited guest to the Longshore Division Caucus of the ILWU and a speaker at a community-labor breakfast at Tulane University.[10]

"This campaign has taken on a whole new life since Sweeney and [ILWU President] Spinosa have come on board," Riley said in an interview in California. "The letters and contributions to the defense fund are rolling in."[11]

And so they were.

In March, Benny Holland Jr., the highest-ranking ILA official in the Southeast, wrote a letter to every ILA president in his district. He explained that since a year earlier ILA's counsel had issued an opinion that union treasury funds could not be used to support the legal costs of the Charleston 5, Local 1422 had set up its own defense fund. Holland sought a second opinion from another attorney the ILA trusted, Stuart Davidson.

"It is Mr. Davidson's opinion that such [ILA treasury] funds may be used for this purpose 'so long as the contributions to the legal defense funds . . . are duly authorized pursuant to the donor union's constitution and by-laws, and so long as those contributions are duly recorded and reported to the donor union's membership,'" Holland wrote.[12]

This bulldozed one of the greatest obstacles Bowers had erected against the Charleston local. Now local leaders could simply bring it to their members at a meeting, vote on it and write a check, a process with which the East Coast union, unlike its always mobilizing West Coast brothers, was much more familiar.

"I am asking each of you to give such support to this fund as you deem appropriate," Holland said. "In addition, we are asking you to canvas your membership for individual contributions to this worthy cause." He also instructed unions to send their checks to Charleston.

The ILA's obstacles were collapsing. First Sweeney's letter, now this from its own Southeast District. Two weeks after Holland's letter, Bowers spoke out publicly on the Charleston 5 for the first time. In a letter to every ILA president, he called the Charleston members "brave" and then spelled out all he had done for them:

"When Nordana Lines first made the wrong decision to replace ILA members' jobs with scab labor in the Port of Charleston, I held a series of meetings with officials from the International Transport Workers Federation in London, including David Cockroft, General Secretary, Kees Marges, Dockers' Section Secretary and Stephen Cotton, Special Seafarers Department. The ITF is a worldwide labor organization representing more than six million transport workers in seventy-eight countries.

"I traveled to London personally to ask ITF leadership to generate and promote international labor solidarity for the striking ILA members in Charleston and urged Nordana Lines to negotiate a settlement with the ILA,"[13] Bowers continued, claiming that his efforts brought Benny Holland and Nordana to the meetings that resulted in a settlement between the shipping line and Local 1422.

Bowers then explained that even after the contract settlement the dispute wasn't over; five members were still being prosecuted. "Shortly after the riots and arrests of the Charleston 5, ILA Local 1422 established a Dockers Defense Fund in January 2000 to which I immediately made a personal contribution," he said. But then the local requested a donation from the International, which Bowers said his lawyer refused to allow.

Fifteen months after the altercation on the docks Bowers announced in his letter that the ILA Executive Council had just voted to form the International Dockers Educational Association (IDEA), "which will be used to publicize the plight of the Charleston 5 and organize nationwide and worldwide support for them."

Presumably at the same meeting, the Executive Council, joined by the Atlantic Coast District and the South Atlantic and Gulf Coast District (Benny Holland's district), voted unanimously, by Bowers's account, to condemn the Workers Coalition, the group of ILA members Ken Riley had been working with to reform the international union.

Bowers tried to make his condemnation of the troublesome reform coalition credible by reference to the higher outside authority of national and international federations of labor unions. "John Sweeney, the president of the AFL-CIO, on whose Executive Council I am honored to serve, contacted me over concerns he and the Federation had about the Workers Coalition and its appeals for help," Bowers wrote. "He and the leadership of other AFL-CIO affiliated unions were uncertain whether their contributions were earmarked for the Charleston 5 or the Longshore Workers Coalition. The ITF also expressed confusion and reservations about the Workers Coalition and their appeals for contributions. In fact, the ITF recently instructed the International Longshore and Harbor [sic] Workers Union (ILWU) to direct its request for support of the Charleston 5 through the office of the President of the ILA"—contrary to what Sweeney had requested in his earlier letter to American union leaders.

Finally, Bowers announced the creation of the ILA Defense Fund, to be managed by his office for the benefit of the Charleston 5. He repeated that people could only send personal contributions to his office for the defense fund, but not funds from union treasuries.

The Charleston dockworkers haunted Bowers at every turn. He and Gleason couldn't escape Charleston in a meeting with ITF general secretary David Cockroft and Paddy Crumlin, president of the Maritime Union of Australia. Crumlin was an active member of the ITF and would eventually succeed Bowers as chair of the ITF Dockers' Council. But in 2000, he was just an outspoken Aussie union president who served on the ITF executive board.

"It looks like it's going to happen anyway, so you better get behind it," Cockroft advised Bowers.[14]

"We've got to support the Charleston 5," added Crumlin. "We didn't do enough for Liverpool."

Crumlin had already threatened "industrial action" or some kind of strike, but sitting there with the men he appreciated the dilemma Bowers faced. Crumlin was proud of Bowers for the solidarity the ILA had shown Liverpool workers. He said the ILA stopped ships when the Liverpool dockers set up their picket lines and faced a $3 million lawsuit because of it, but this Charleston situation was much more complicated because of the reform group's agitation and Riley's association with the coalition, the Australian leader explained later.

"Johnny Bowers saw it [the Charleston defense fund] as support for reform within the ILA," Crumlin explained "He didn't want to be so close to the reform group of Kenny and his brother." Crumlin said he thought the workers' coalition was about workers' rights, but Bowers saw any move to reform the ILA as a threat to his power and control. The ILA president was still feeling the aftershocks of the Canadian ILA threatening to leave the international union after a dispute, and now with these problems to the south it looked as if the ILA was falling apart. He described Bowers's dilemma this way:

> If you go down there encouraging them, you're encouraging new leadership, but if you let them run their course, they run out of steam and you can show what kind of leadership they are and say, 'You want *them* running the ILA?'

Crumlin also spoke with Cockroft alone. "Talk to John [Bowers]," the Aussie told the international leader. "He needs to take some leadership on this thing or it'll look like an ILWU and 1422 collaboration." But he had more to tell the ITF head, who argued that the ITF could do nothing without Bowers's approval. "That is the same argument as the Liverpool dockers. All it does is demonstrate the inadequacy of the ITF," Crumlin told him.

Everyone in the room that day discussing Charleston had been around long enough to know how long it takes distressed workers to forget both the loyal acts and the vicious betrayals of others in a time of need. With mounting national and international support, Riley and the Charleston dockworkers were gaining momentum, not running out of steam, and Bowers finally had to back down.

Crumlin wasn't the only one talking to other dockers around the world. The IDC, through Julian Garcia in Spain, Bjorn Borg in Sweden, and Jack Heyman in California, had extended its reach, and unions that belonged to the ITF were beginning to ask where the ITF stood on this Charleston dockers issue. Crumlin's and the IDC's public stance over the Charleston 5 showed the world that in contrast the ITF was standing still. Some unions were feeling pulled in two directions between the two federations—one impressively large and legitimate if conservative, to which they'd been loyal for decades, but which had never been militant and the other young and small but innovative and speaking to the needs of workers in conflict without the interference of dinosaur organizations from a bygone era.

Just two days after the Dockers' Section Committee meeting in London in April the section issued a strongly worded statement supporting the Charleston 5 and announcing the ITF's $71,000 contribution to the ILA Defense Fund. It asked affiliates to contribute to that fund, based in New York. The author of the announcement, Kees Marges, secretary of the dockers' section, noted the ITF's intervention almost a year and a half earlier that brought Nordana to the table and settled the dispute. Now, fifteen months later, the ITF was announcing its "global campaign."

What the ITF lacked in timeliness it made up for in fire. Marges had been corresponding with Stallone, ILWU communications director, for some time. Stallone, under Spinosa's direction, had been using the ILWU's position in the ITF as leverage to force the federation into action.[15] When Marges was finally given the chance, he called on affiliates to be prepared to *act*, yet he had to remind them that they had agreed to do so. This was not an organization, after all, used to such things:

"The Dockers' Section Committee . . . came to the conclusion that ITF affiliated port workers unions should be asked for further support and international solidarity, in line with the discussions which took place back in 1997 at the Miami Dockers Section Conference, where dockers affiliates all signed an International Solidarity Contract and unanimously adopted a resolution against union-busting."

The labor movement is too often long on threat and short on action, and the ITF's inertia had caused the birth of the IDC. The elder organization still had decades to go, but in this one letter, Marges helped the group make one of its greatest leaps:

"It may well be that in the very near future you will receive an urgent request to participate in a global action in support of the 'Charleston 5' and against union-busting. If possible and if it is appropriate this call will correlate with the final date for the court case against 'Charleston 5.' On the basis of the pledges made in Miami the Dockers' Section Committee expect that all port workers will do their utmost to respond to the request, if and when they receive it. . . . Please prepare yourselves for International Solidarity and be ready to act."[16]

Marges sent the letter to affiliates but it would not be long before it was on the web for everyone, including South Carolinians, to see.

A WEEK LATER, in early April 2001, Peter Wilborn and Ken Riley flew to Denmark. The $2.5 million lawsuit filed by Perry Collins and his company WSI was slowly percolating and it was time to take a key deposition. WSI was suing for damages, first for the ship that wasn't worked properly because of ILA protests and then claiming that Nordana had reneged on its contract with the company because of the union. Wilborn and Riley were in Denmark to prepare for the trial, to get the sworn testimony of Nordana executive Claes Rechnitzer on the record.

This case, like the original negotiations with Nordana to stay union in Charleston and even more than the prosecution of the Five, would determine the wage standards in the Port of Charleston for years to come. If WSI won this suit and individual longshoremen lost their homes and their savings accounts for picketing and protesting, what longshoreman would ever take that risk again? Other shipping companies would be free to go nonunion without risk. If the ILA won this suit and sent WSI packing, it would be a long time before another shipping company tried the Nordana stunt in Charleston again. The fight might move to another port, but at least for the moment, Charleston would stay strong.

The 34-year-old Wilborn was more comfortable than most American attorneys would be among Danes.[17] Less than a decade earlier, disillusioned by a summer internship at a high-powered Washington law firm, Wilborn talked to an international studies professor who introduced him to the work of the International Commission of Jurists. Before long he was living in Geneva, Switzerland, and traveling regularly across continents doing their work building legal institutions around the world to ensure the rule of law. In just a few years, he had administered international human rights training programs with and for attorneys and judges in thirty countries.

But Wilborn grew increasingly ill at ease with his own lack of experience in the law. He returned to the United States and continued his search for meaningful work. He found Armand Derfner, a legendary voting rights attorney, tucked away in Charleston. Wilborn's family was from Virginia; he had attended a racially mixed high school just outside of Washington. He was comfortable in the South, and in awe of Derfner's legal record.

Derfner, in his 60s, widowed and expecting to retire soon, didn't have enough work in 1996 to hire Wilborn full time, but that would soon change. In January 1997, Ken Riley and his slate were elected to lead the black longshoremen of Charleston and came to Derfner looking for an attorney. From that moment on, Riley and Wilborn's fates were joined.

Now they were together in Denmark, where Wilborn, an avid cyclist, could expose the car-collecting longshoreman to the sight of other full-grown adults riding bicycles to work. But more seriously, Wilborn's familiarity with the Danish culture and his love for all things and people Scandinavian would serve him well in dealing with the Nordana executive over the next two days.

"I have great admiration for your society," Wilborn said to Rechnitzer near the beginning of the deposition. "You know better than anyone in this room, better than Kenny Riley who is sitting here, the importance of respecting minimum standards for paying people for all walks of life, correct?"[18]

Rechnitzer agreed.

"Have you ever considered that this Nordana issue in Charleston is a civil rights issue in the tradition of American civil rights issues in the South?"

"Yes. Yes." Rechnitzer answered. "On a very, very late stage of events came the issue of civil rights in some form, but as I said it was on a very late stage after several of these incidents, and from articles in the local papers I can remember that I saw that phrase a few times."

And finally, Wilborn got personal. "What I meant to ask you as a man, you as an individual, when you look into your heart, do you consider the Charleston protest to be an issue of their basic social rights that you enjoy so beautifully in Denmark?"

"I will answer your question," said Rechnitzer, "but I will first have to explain to you that before we made the agreement with WSI . . . we talked to some of their employees. . . . We had a good feeling of how they treated their people. And so . . . no, it didn't strike us that this could have some higher principle implications when we started all of that."

With the Dane established as a reasonable man, Wilborn went for the kill. He needed to nail down the dollar figure that would make most of WSI's $2.5 million figure go away. It was a number that conveniently appeared in Article 13.2 of the contract between WSI and Nordana, an article Rechnitzer had formulated himself as an escape clause. Nordana would have to pay WSI a mere $60,000 if they broke the contract. Rechnitzer's testimony established the true value of Nordana's relationship to WSI.[19]

By the time Riley and Wilborn returned to Charleston on April 11, Wilborn had his case in his pocket. Nordana's escape clause with its $60,000 payoff figure put the suit in an entirely new light—and in an entirely smaller economic ballpark.

RILEY SPENT THE REST OF APRIL speaking to the Queens College Labor Resource Center in New York, the Black Workers for Justice banquet in North Carolina, the Labor Notes conference, a UAW meeting, and Michigan State University. The pace picked up even more after that. In May he was in Montreal, Greensboro, N.C., New York, and Massachusetts speaking about the Charleston 5.[20]

IN A SUBDIVISION of Columbia, South Carolina, in a ranch-style house that served as the office of the South Carolina AFL-CIO, Donna Dewitt was working with her allies to build for a massive rally. The organizing of a rally for thousands landed mostly on the activists in South Carolina and a handful of dedicated AFL-CIO staff there to pitch in where they could. Dewitt called on old friends from her days as a union officer at the telephone company, Linda Houck and Cindy Rickards. Albertha Glover, from Dewitt's hometown of Orangeburg, came to her aid, too. The AFL-CIO provided Jimmy Hyde from its Southern Region and John Cox from Alabama to offer their time and expertise.

The attorneys said that the trials were likely to begin in June, so organizers settled on June 9, in Columbia, within sight of Charlie Condon's and Governor Jim Hodges's offices.

Brett Bursey organized the logistics of the march from training marshals to reserving tents and a caterer. There were the police to alert and a soundstage to build, portable toilets to rent, and booths with water bottles to staff. A banner hung over the street would welcome the marchers.

UAW retiree Rudy Feagin helped mobilize locally, Selwyn Carter, the political director for the Southeast AFL-CIO pitched in with grounds logistics, Jim Evans contacted politicos but also pitched in wherever necessary, Rev. James Orange helped the AFL mobilize clergy for the march. Matt Painter, a student from the University of South Carolina, distributed leaflets, ran errands, and worked the local media. Lee Sustar, a volunteer from Chicago, slept and showered at the office, filling in where needed. Soon the AFL-CIO dedicated professional communications staff to assist with national media relations. The house/office/rally headquarters was kept stocked day and night with junk food, fresh food, and drinks for volunteers and staff.

Of course, the key component was turnout. No point throwing a party if nobody comes. As if suddenly thrown into high gear, the AFL-CIO supplied ten summer interns with room and board for four weeks to help with mailings, visibility, phone calls, and logistics. Staff from the AFL-CIO started writing checks for buses: eight buses from Atlanta, fifteen from the rest of Georgia, five from North Carolina, and three from South Carolina. All told, the AFL-CIO would spend more than $30,000 on bus transportation for marchers.

Individual unions like the ILWU and others sponsored buses and airline flights from as far away as New York, Chicago, San Francisco, and Washington State.[21] Lawrence Thibeaux's local sent the union's famed drill team. Another hundred or so ILWU members would come from the West Coast. Defense committees around the country organized caravans and buses from Illinois, Missouri, Florida, and Tennessee.[22]

Organizers set up a booth for press credentials and another for information for people with disabilities. A signer was hired to translate the speeches for the hearing impaired. Organizers had a first-aid station and an information booth. T-shirts, fliers, bumper stickers, banners, and signs were printed and stocked.

The AFL-CIO spent thousands on mailings to get the word out, and staff in Washington reached out to national press contacts from Boston to San Francisco to run stories and columns about the rally. Volunteers leafleted neighborhoods in Columbia and Charleston.

The speakers list would define the rally as a high priority for the AFL-CIO and eventually cause a confrontation between local organizers and AFL staff the day before the march. The list of speakers grew and grew: AFL-CIO's second officer Linda Chavez Thompson; Charleston native Nelson Rivers III, executive director of the NAACP; the United Mineworkers President Cecil Roberts; Ashaki Binta of the Black Workers for Justice; Bjorn Borg, the IDC member and longshoreman from Sweden; Kwang-Jun Yu from the Daewoo Motor Workers Union in South Korea; Joseph Lowery, president emeritus of the Southern Christian Leadership Conference. The final agenda included enough speakers to melt even the heartiest rally-goer in the Carolina summer sun—more than twenty.

On May 1, Fletcher was moved from his job as assistant to the president of the AFL-CIO to the George Meany Center, the national labor education center run by the AFL-CIO, but continued to advise the campaign from there.

By the end of May, Charlie Condon's staff was busy preparing for the June 25 trial. The two attorneys most familiar with the case traveled to Charleston again to meet with police. In preparation, Cranshaw, who had advised leaving the case in Charleston, wrote to Condon to ask for guidance:

"I have been informed that Chief Greenberg wants to meet with me as soon as I step foot in the Holy City [Charleston is so called because of its numerous churches]. Is there anything in particular that you would like me to pass along to him during this meeting?"[23]

On May 31, while Cranshaw and his coworker, attorney David Avant, were in Charleston preparing the police for a trial the police had said repeatedly they did not want, Brett Bursey led about two-dozen members of the South Carolina Progressive Network to visit the attorney general at his office in Columbia. When he wouldn't meet with them, the group issued a press release generously sprinkled with unkind statements about Condon, including a charge from Charleston 5 defense lawyer Andy Savage that the indictments reflected, "Attorney General Condon's confusion between his political ambition and the proper performance of his job. Charlie is more concerned with running for governor that he is with impartial justice." [24] It was a mantra the campaign would repeat for months to come.

The press release served to promote the upcoming rally, but it reaped more than expected when the attorney general responded, "The attack launched today against me and the Attorney General's office by the South Carolina Progressive Network is ridiculous and absurd. This is nothing but a propaganda ploy by labor union sympathizers."

Condon then called out the network on its name, "Progressive," saying it should support an individual's right not to be in a union. "The disruptive effects of the SC Progressive Network and its comrades are designed solely to divert attention from the very serious criminal charges of riot and conspiracy to riot against these five defendants."

After restating the charges against the Five, Condon reiterated his position on the prosecution: "We intend to prosecute these cases fully and vigorously. Again, let me emphasize that as long as I am Attorney General, the laws of South Carolina will be enforced and the right of South Carolina citizens to refuse to join a labor union will be upheld." Then, practically as an afterthought, the press release ended with: "Of course, all defendants are presumed innocent until proven guilty beyond a reasonable doubt."[25]

The day after the state's attorneys met in Charleston with the Charleston Police Department, attorney Avant repeated to Condon the department's position, this time more emphatically, point by point:

1. We have already won the matter: The AG got an injunction. There have been no other violent protests. The media and public battles were decided in favor of the police.

2. The prosecution would result in, no matter the outcome, a loss for the City. There would be nothing gained and the continued peaceful operation of the City would be in jeopardy.[26]

Then Avant reported that he had dutifully passed along the attorney general's position on the matter:

"I advised the Lt. Col. that we understood his concerns, but that it was the obligation of this office to pursue this matter. The Chief Prosecutor could not let these actions pass. I made reference to the actions amounting to terrorism. I did advise that we were prepared to make a reasonable offer—Misd. Riot w/recommendation of Jail time, but that the matter must be pursued as a riot."[27]

That same day, Cranshaw received a letter from Andy Savage, representing two of the Five, notifying the attorney general's office that Savage would be requesting a continuance.

The judge granted the continuance. The next time this case was docketed, Judge Victor Rawl, a man who understood the Low Country, would be presiding.

THE NIGHT BEFORE THE RALLY, at a party at the Columbia hall of Donna Dewitt's union, Communications Workers of America, Dewitt, Riley, and Cobb-Hunter visited with volunteers and marchers who had come in early for the next day's rally. It had been a year since they first met with Bill Fletcher, who couldn't attend. It had been a solid year of hard work, a year of two steps forward, one back. Now some of the biggest names in American labor, progressive clergy, and civil rights were coming to Columbia because of what this group had accomplished. Even the IDC would be represented. The Charleston 5 had become a cause, a campaign.

How times had changed . . . and how *they* had changed the times.

Across America, times were changing as well. After what many considered an election stolen from black voters in Florida, a black union was on trial in South Carolina. The country was increasingly polarized on political, religious, and cultural grounds, with states now identified as "red" or "blue." The United States had a new president closely advised by neoconservative Karl Rove and a new attorney general, conservative John Ashcroft, former U.S. senator from Missouri known for his opposition to desegregation and the 100 percent backing he received from the Christian Coalition. Charlie Condon was a part of the administration's first days, named one of forty key justice policy advisers to Bush's transition team along with more familiar names such as Edwin Meese, Harriet Miers, and Michael Chertoff.[28] A massive shift in the relationship between the United States and the world was under way, but no one knew exactly where it would end up.

But as the union activists waited for the next day's rally, and greeted their jet-lagged Korean and Swedish guests, there was a feeling of hope. No matter what happened, they were building something good here and people all over the world would know about it.

10

Free the Charleston 5!

Longshoremen around the world fully understood that their well-being depended on collective action, because otherwise the large supply of men desperate to do manual labor would force wages to near-starvation levels.
                                                    —Marc Levinson[1]

THE DAY OF THE COLUMBIA FREE the Charleston 5 rally started earlier than expected with an argument about who would speak at the rally and who would not. The organizers—staff from the AFL-CIO, Donna Dewitt, Ken Riley, and attorney Peter Wilborn could not agree.

Wilborn reported to the rally organizers earlier that week that the five defendants would not be attending. The attorneys had all agreed it was better they didn't. Organizers were furious, saying the campaign was counting on people seeing the Five and hearing them speak, but the lawyers were adamant. They would do nothing to muddy the jury pool.

The same went for talking to the *60 Minutes* crew that had been interviewing people in the area. There would be no Five on camera. Organizers scrambled to produce large cardboard photo portraits of the Five. They would place them on folding chairs on the stage, with volunteers standing behind them to hold them steady for the duration of the rally.

With that disappointment still burning in her gut, Dewitt had no patience for AFL-CIO staff dictating the speakers list. The group finally agreed that the national figures would get the main stage at the state house at the end of the march, and the local people would get the Teamsters' truckbed at the Memorial Park rally to speak as marchers gathered from around the country. She would have to live with the compromise, but to show her solidarity with the local activists Dewitt, now nationally known as president of the South Carolina AFL-CIO, spoke at the pre-march rally.

More than 5,000 people descended on Columbia that day in what was billed as the largest gathering of union people in South Carolina in recent memory.[2] They came from Miami, San Juan, Mansfield, Ohio, Hopewell, Virginia, and Lake Charles, Louisiana. They came from Brunswick, Canada, and Tacoma, Washington, from San Francisco to Los Angeles, from Chicago to New York. One came from Copenhagen and another from Seoul. And they came from every corner of South Carolina.

The march down Washington with Thibeaux and the ILWU drill team leading the way was an impressive sight but hardly anyone saw it. Most businesses were closed and the churches stood quiet on Saturday. Police lined the rooftops guarding against trouble, but Jim Evans, a state representative, minister, and AFL-CIO staff member from Mississippi had gone to school with the mayor of Columbia and paid him a visit before the march. There would be no overreaction from the police that day. Local officers did confiscate the drill team's chrome-plated cargo hooks (and returned them after the march), but the California longshore workers still stepped sharply in their black and white striped shirts, black jeans, and white caps.

Behind them, carrying the main banner that read simply "Free the Charleston 5" were some of the biggest names in civil rights and in the labor movement: the fiery mineworker president Cecil Roberts, the legendary dean of civil rights Reverend Joseph Lowery, State Representative Gilda Cobb-Hunter, AFL-CIO executive vice president Linda Chavez-Thompson, State Senator Robert Ford, ILA president John Bowers walking side by side with ILA 1422 president Ken Riley, Screen Actors Guild actress Anne Marie Johnson, best known for her role in the TV series *In the Heat of the Night* and fresh off an actors' strike, Nelson Rivers III, president of the NAACP, Donna Dewitt, and Bill Lucy, a leader of the country's largest public sector union (and president of the Coalition of Black Trade Unionists when Riley had approached the group more than a year before). The group chanted and sang while "Union Summer" interns from the AFL-CIO kept up the cheerleading with bullhorns at locations up and down the parade route.

The Confederate flag had been removed from the top of the state capitol building and both chambers of the General Assembly, but that day a contingent of police stood guard around a smaller version that now flew over a Confederate Soldier memorial on the statehouse grounds. As AFL-CIO organizer Jimmy Hyde put it, "They cut some kind of deal and got it down off the capitol and on the ground, where you can *really* see it." Some of the speakers referred to it during the rally, but they could bask in the achievement of the recently-dedicated monument to African American history, the first in the country that provided visitors an important and little-recognized facet of South Carolina's history. One after the next, speakers told stories of inspiration and hope, fired up the crowd, and called for Charlie Condon to end the prosecution. And one after the next threatened repercussions if the Five walked into a courtroom. When ILA president John Bowers and when ILWU President Jim Spinosa walked to the microphone, the crowd chanted "Shut the ports down!" But attorneys had warned the speakers of the legal implications of publicly stating that ports would shut down over the issue. The labor-unfriendly Bush administration could come down hard on the unions under federal law, most notably the Racketeer Influenced Corrupt Organizations (RICO) Act if it could prove there was an organized effort to impinge on commerce to influence the outcome of the legal case.

The ILWU's Spinosa, who had earlier vowed to shut ports down from Alaska to Hawaii the day the case went to trial, said his union was ready to do whatever the Charleston local asked of it.[3]

Bjorn Borg, who had traveled from Sweden to represent the International Dockworkers Council for Julian Garcia who could not get to South Carolina, said if the Charleston 5 went to jail, it wouldn't go without actions at ports around the world. Pat Riley, head of one Canadian ILA local, told the crowd that Liverpool "taught us that courage is not enough."

"Plenty of working people in other countries, from Denmark to Australia to Chile, are giving the Charleston longshore workers all the help they can," Chavez-Thompson told the crowd. "We pledge here and now that we're going to stand alongside them and give them all of the support they need, until the morning comes when the union-bashers of South Carolina go down to defeat, and Charleston becomes a city where justice is finally done."[4]

Adding to the dignitaries on the stage were greetings from around the world, from the Maritime Union of Indonesia, Italian shop stewards from Genoa, Cuban workers, Mumia Abu-Jamal—the black journalist on Death Row in Pennsylvania—and the general secretary of Coventry National Union of Teachers in England.

But to everyone's surprise, the crowd went wild over the one speaker it could hardly understand. Kwang-Jun Yu, director of policy for the Daewoo Motor Workers Union in Seoul told the story of Korean workers struggling against GM, comparing them to black workers in the United States.

"We know about the vicious racism of the rulers of South Carolina and the corporations here—they want to keep people divided so they can continue to pay lower wages and give fewer rights. Racism against black people is horrible and wrong. The descendants of slaves should be honored not be the victims of more injustice. We too have been the victims of racism. GM treats all workers badly—but they reserve the worst treatment and the worst wages for those in Asia, Africa, and Latin America."

The heat was baking everyone, and the rally had gone on for hours, but the energy surged as Yu continued to speak. He said the average pay for Korean workers was $4.33 per hour, and said GM exploits them while threatening American workers with layoffs. But then he tied it to the global market:

"Ever since the IMF and the U.S. bankers came in they have been demanding privatization, layoffs, and a move to lower wages," he explained, adding that almost every law protecting the workplace is being dismantled and that there was a move to make it illegal for the community to support strikes.

"When we come out to protest, we have been faced with brutality just like that inflicted on the Charleston 5," Yu said. "Thousands of police have massed against us. Hundreds of us have been beaten and sent to the hospital. Some have had their ability to see taken from them by the police clubs and beatings. They use bulldozers to smash through to get at us. We know about police brutality.

"The brutality that you face here and the brutality that we face in southern Korea comes from the same place. It is the hammer that they use to keep us in our place, to drive us back from having our basic human rights. It is a hammer wielded by GM and by the IMF and by all of the Big Business interests that we are facing. The Daewoo workers have raised one of our hands to stop the blows of this GM hammer. We extend our other hand in solidarity to you and we hope you will reach out for us." [5]

As the rally rose to its climactic end, some of the greatest American orators of the day lit up the stage. Those who had never heard Cecil Roberts, the president of the United Mineworkers Union, were shocked but pleased when he let loose his fiery oration about how "Moses didn't send no fax or email; Moses went to Pharoah." As one organizer said, "I doubt they'd heard a white guy speak like that before." But Roberts made them cheer the loudest with: "My grandfather always told me, 'If you ever come across a bear in the woods, son, don't go kicking it.' Well, Charlie, you gone and kicked the bear!"

Then the eighty-year-old Reverend Joseph Lowery, speaking as president of the Georgia Coalition for the People's Agenda, and holding up well after three hours in the heat, set the crowd on fire with his call for justice. Both men had been steeped in the Southern tradition of spirited preaching, and the reverend, a man *Ebony* magazine named one of the nation's Top 15 preachers, had been doing it longer.[6] (Hyde later said glowingly of the rally's keynote speaker, "Jesse [Jackson] can't hold a candle to him. You should see him and Jesse up on the stage. He always wants Jesse to go first.") The older Charlestonians gathered there would harken back to the days of Ralph Abernathy, Coretta Scott King, and the 1969 hospital workers strike as both Roberts and Lowery vowed to fill the jails for the Charleston 5.

COMING OFF THE RALLY, Fletcher spelled out the priorities for the campaign.[7] They had raised $330,000 so far, with more than $100,000 of that coming from the ILWU.[8] The lawyers had successfully moved the trials to the fall, and the campaign had new resources from the AFL-CIO to help turn up the heat. Speaking engagements would focus on the West Coast, Gulf Coast, and the Midwest and would be better coordinated with union and community groups to broaden the audience and raise funds more effectively. The national steering committee, now fifteen people from California to D.C., would discuss and coordinate an international day of solidarity, including the option of shutting down ports around the world. Anticipating that the trials would go forward, Fletcher suggested getting celebrities to sit in the courtroom. The group would continue to struggle to find a pressure point with the state, including organizing a product boycott, lobbying members of the State Ports Authority or demonstrating at a popular local beach. Other possibilities included a countersuit against the state, a national advisory committee composed of celebrities, and anything that more research on WSI might bring to the surface. Then there was the question of the media.

"What steps should we take to get our story further out there and keep it out there?" Fletcher asked the group.

The *New York Times* had picked up a syndicated Associated Press article on the rally. Tom Joyner had discussed the campaign on his national morning radio show. A senior editor from *The Nation* was writing a story. The *Charlotte Observer* had just run a long story. The buzz had begun, but it was about to run headlong into the attorneys, who had already warned that their clients were not available to speak to the media. NPR and *60 Minutes* were asking to speak to the Five.

MEANWHILE SOUTH CAROLINA'S other campaign was heating up. Charlie Condon was working to earn the trust and support of the Upstate conservatives in his race for governor.[9] One opportunity came when the *Charlotte Observer* contacted him for an interview about the Charleston longshoremen just days after the union demonstration in Columbia.

"The evidence speaks for itself," he told the reporter. "They're the ones who are using mob violence and threats of violence. What is going on here is a purposeful plan, union-backed, to use violence to cause us to not enforce state right-to-work laws."

Condon took the opportunity to once again illustrate his ability to represent the entire state and his capacity to forsake local allies in the Low Country, just as he did when he skipped over the local solicitor and prosecuted the dockworkers himself. It appears he didn't utter a single sentence about dockworkers without including the words *mob* and *violence*:

"You had a number of principles at stake," he said. "These mob violence intimidation tactics that have been successful in other states ought not to be allowed to succeed in South Carolina."

Ninth circuit solicitor David Schwacke, from Charleston, was quoted in the same article saying he "might have been content to have left the charges where they were. The police made that decision, and if anyone was assaulted, it was them."[10] The lines between Low Country and Upstate were becoming clearer with every escalation of the battle.

But Condon needed more than a Charleston-based union prosecution upon which to build his candidacy. Candidates from the Low Country coastal areas had always had trouble garnering support from the more rural, conservative and Baptist areas. Condon's competition for the gubernatorial nomination was a neighbor from Sullivan's Island, Secretary of State Jim Miles, who had moved there from Upstate Greenville after being elected to statewide office. The two candidates also shared the advantage of having won a statewide office from which to launch their campaigns.

Condon had the disadvantage of being Catholic in a statewide election in which he would need the support of staunch Baptists. Bob Jones, one of the more visible people among a variety of Baptists, considered Catholicism "a cult." Condon had to find common ground with the fundamentalists, and that ground was a faith in God. So, at the end of June he announced the creation of a new Commission on Marriage and the Family. The announcement was largely lost in the usual flurry of faxes coming from the attorney general's office and received little attention in the press. So he wrote an opinion piece that landed in the *Charleston Post and Courier*, missing his ideal target Upstate audience by hundreds of miles.

"Nothing is more important to South Carolina than our having policies which support rather than undermine the institutions of marriage and the family," he said as he announced three appointments to the commission.[11] Anne Badgley of Charleston, a major anti-abortion, abstinence-based education proponent proposed the commission, according to Condon. Cyndi Campsen Mosteller, a former Department of Health and Environment Control Board vice chair would serve as this commission's vice chair. The DHEC was responsible for handing out condoms instead of teaching abstinence, Condon explained, indicating that reversing this reprehensible practice might be one of the commission's first projects. Reverend Jerry Clark, pastor of the Freedom Baptist Church in Greenville would serve as the chair.

Walking the careful line between Upstate and Low Country, Condon didn't mention Cyndi Mosteller's active membership in the Christian Coalition, a group which admittedly was on the decline by then but still had pull with hardcore Baptist voters. He also didn't mention that she was from Charleston, perhaps in the interests of not alienating those hardcore Baptists. And lastly, he didn't say a word about Freedom Baptist Church being one of a minority of Baptist churches in Greenville endorsed by Bob Jones University.[12]

With an Upstate Baptist leading the way, the attorney general commission's charge was to "explore ways to use faith-based initiatives. The church or synagogue can often address social problems far better than government."

In July, Republican Charlie Condon sued the Democratic governor of his own state over the governor's proposal to increase higher education funding.[13] The lawsuit was one of a long list of contentious exchanges between the two, and one easily pegged by a reporter who noted high in his story that "it's only likely to get worse as Condon seeks the Republican nomination to challenge Hodges' reelection bid next year."

In August, Condon "launched an inquiry" into allegations of race discrimination against a white employee by the governor.[14] The state had already settled the suit, filed by former human services deputy director, Roger Posten, who claimed he was fired because he was white. In his suit, he charged that the Legislative Black Caucus, of which the white Hodges was a member, had pressured Posten's boss to fire him because a black deputy director had been fired.

Condon, facing a racially charged sea of yellow "Free the Charleston 5" signs in his own backyard, announced, "We simply will not tolerate a person being fired because of the color of his skin, be it black, white, or any other color."

Condon's campaign was well under way, and prosecution of the Five would come in the fall, an ideal time for political media coverage.

AFTER THE FREE THE CHARLESTON 5 RALLY, AFL-CIO strategists Jimmy Hyde and John Cox moved their operation to Charleston. They talked with Ken Riley and other local community members, met with key leaders, and quickly assessed where they could count on support and who was blowing smoke.

Hyde was an old autoworker born and bred in Georgia. He quickly understood the lay of the land in Charleston. He realized that Riley and Dewitt's national and worldwide travel to spread the word about the Charleston 5 had left out one important element: Charleston. Nobody in town had heard of the Charleston 5. Even some of the local legislators didn't know there were any issues left over from the troubles on the waterfront more than sixteen months before.

Hyde helped John Cox create the campaign that would have everyone asking "Who are the Charleston 5?" After learning where Condon lived, organizers, including another batch of AFL-CIO union summer interns, plastered his route to work with "Free the Charleston 5" yard signs. They purchased a billboard on I-26 that read "Free the Charleston 5." For added measure, when they heard about a NASCAR race up the road in Darlington they had a plane fly over it with the same slogan trailing behind it. By the end of the day some quick-thinking Condon supporter had the plane pulling a banner that read "Charlie Condon's a Good Man."

Summer interns erected yard signs around town and from one end to the other of Sullivan's Island, Condon's neighborhood. They leafleted downtown intersections including some not so far from Condon's brother Tommy Condon's popular restaurant. Someone suggested going to the conservative Catholic Stella Maris Church on Sullivan's Island that Condon and his family attended, because "John [Cox] was Catholic and would've known how to do it," Hyde said, but the campaign had word that Condon's wife was ill, so out of respect organizers scratched that idea.[15]

The blue-on-yellow signs became so popular that they went through the first five thousand almost immediately and had to order more. Years later, faded "Free the Charleston 5" bumper stickers would still peer through the dirt and grime on car bumpers, street signs, and even garbage dumpsters on the College of Charleston campus. Some were seen as far away as Manhattan. Months later in Atlanta, Hyde saw a man standing at a busy intersection with a handwritten sign asking for food. The note was written on the back of a "Free the Charleston 5" sign.

The sudden sea of yellow signs, bumper stickers, and fliers caused Mayor Joe Riley's office to call the longshoremen's hall to call a meeting with Ken Riley. These signs weren't good for business, yet the veteran Democratic mayor understood the effectiveness of a good ground campaign. In the face of an unreasonable attorney general's refusal to let go of the case, the mayor wasn't unsympathetic to the union's tactics. After that initial phone call, Wilborn and Riley met regularly with the mayor to update him on the status of the legal case.

City council members were getting involved, too, either to support the union or to undermine it, with calls to the union and to the attorney general's office with tips one way or the other.

WHILE VISIBILITY WAS PICKING UP on the local level, the steering committee continued to meet roadblocks at the national level. The national media were starting to take note, and wanted to talk to the five defendants, but couldn't get through the attorney firewalls. AFL-CIO media specialists were beating their heads against a wall about it. By the end of July, Lyndsay Barenz, staffer from a public relations firm contracted by the AFL-CIO, was insisting on access to the five.

"We will be more successful attracting media and delivering our message at rallies, speeches, press conferences, hearings, and other events if the members of the Charleston 5 attend these events and speak at these events,"[16] she told Riley and Fletcher. "Media access to the five men can be tightly controlled, but their presence is key to media interest."

She continued to press her point. "The most appealing aspect of the Charleston 5 is the human interest story of the hardship these men and their families are enduring under the assault of the attorney general. The media finds this interesting and it is the message we want the public to hear."

She was barking up the wrong tree. Riley and Fletcher weren't controlling media access to the Five; the attorneys defending the individuals in their criminal cases were. And the attorneys had one job: protect their clients. The Charleston 5 would not speak to the media.

While media work was difficult, it still met with some success. On July 23, columnist William Raspberry, writing in the *Washington Post*, dedicated his column to the Charleston 5. The legal nuances of the case were not lost on the journalist.

"I'll have to defer, of course, to those who have seen the video," Raspberry wrote. "But it does seem likely that if the five men under indictment had been seen assaulting police, they'd have been charged with criminal assault."[17]

Five days later, Teamsters president James Hoffa Jr., whose international union is based in Washington, D.C., called for an end to the prosecution of the Charleston 5. The Teamsters and the ILA had had their share of turf battles over jobs on the waterfront. Unqualified support from union truckers at ports around the country could magnify by the thousands any action taken by American dockworkers.

KEN RILEY, FOR HIS PART, was traveling more than ever. He had addressed the National Baptist Convention in Charlotte in July, was in Barcelona for the second IDC convention a month before that, and made it to Boston and New Orleans in between. In July he took another swing through California, this time with more coordination and assistance from ILWU'S

Stallone and Evelina Alarcon, the head of the Los Angeles Charleston 5 Defense Committee.

The day before Riley arrived in California, an estimated 10,000 people marched across the Vincent Thomas Bridge separating the ports of Los Angeles and Long Beach to celebrate the hundredth birthday of ILWU founder Harry Bridges. The campaign had sent two hundred yellow signs, and the ILWU had agreed to put them at the front of the march, near their "An Injury to One is an Injury to All" banner. The *Los Angeles Times* ran a page 3 story the next day with a Charleston 5 sign in the photo. While in California, Riley met with politicians and taped a radio show on Northern California's KPFA. He then attended an International Dockworkers' Solidarity Conference, called by the ILWU, where organizers raised $1,400 selling T-shirts. Largely due to Riley's presence, the Charleston 5 became a dominant theme of the gathering.[18]

In August Riley headed to San Francisco again, to Chicago for the Rainbow/PUSH convention and a rally at Teamsters auditorium, to Cleveland twice, and to Manhattan and Newark, N.J. In Chicago, Lee Sustar had been organizing a defense committee for almost a year. One event drew 250 people and raised $5,000 at Teamster City, with Jerry Zero from Teamsters Local 705 handing over a check for $2,500.

A week later Riley was in New York, speaking to another two hundred and fifty people at an event hosted by Roger Toussaint, president of Transport Workers Union Local 100. (Five years later Toussaint would defy a court injunction and take the entire city's public transit system out on strike.) In a sign of the new times and momentum of the campaign, Riley was invited by the ITF to speak at the Norwegian Transport Workers Union conference in September. He would be followed by David Cockroft, general secretary of the ITF. The grudging support from the ILA had turned more enthusiastic. In any case, it was continuing to pay off.[19]

BY AUGUST, JUDGE VICTOR RAWL was assigned to the Ninth Judicial District. Andy Savage, who had requested the continuance in June, now complained to the judge that the attorney general hadn't contacted him since then. The veteran defense attorney, knowing Rawl was from the Low Country and familiar with its dynamics and politics, quickly requested that the judge set a date for a status conference for the cases.[20]

"The way our community, from the mayor through the police department through the defense attorneys, the way we viewed this is we can take care of this, this isn't something outsiders from Columbia have to tell us how to handle," Savage explained. "We all had our respective positions, but underneath this whole thing everyone was on the same page. But," he said in hindsight, "I think that created a false sense of security."

Enough time had passed and the case wasn't going away. Savage was losing his patience with the entire situation, and Judge Rawl had been assigned. Savage had already sent a letter to the other attorneys suggesting he file a motion to dismiss the indictments for "outrageous governmental conduct." He laid out his case and asked them for a meeting.

"I know we are all busy, and I don't want to get behind on this case," he said, then ended his letter pointedly: "I'm starting to see red and I am out of Ativans."[21] "It became clear we had to cut that son of a bitch off at the knees," Savage said of Condon later.

The trial was set for November 12, and the legal team moved into high gear.

11

Countdown to Trial

It was a calculated bald political move to gain political favor. [Condon] knew the newspaper in this town would overreact. The law wasn't with him. . . . Anyone looking at what happened to the Charleston 5 from the outside—It's as easy as a child eating baby food. It was politics. Sheer politics.
                    —Andy Brack, former Democratic gubernatorial candidate[1]

ON THE MORNING OF SEPTEMBER 11, 2001, attorneys Peter Wilborn, Andy Savage, and Armand Derfner and longshoreman Ken Riley sat at a small round table in Savage's office on the second floor of a fashionably renovated warehouse in downtown Charleston. The attorneys were going to show Riley the entire videotape they had retrieved through the discovery process. They began early; there were at least six hours of tape to view.

This was the first time Riley saw for himself what happened that night more than eighteen months earlier. As he watched the police, the captain telling them to prepare for "a battle" and the officers lining up to get their riot helmets and handcuffs, chatting as if they were going to a football game, he whistled low and shook his head.

Then Savage slipped in another video and Riley saw the searchlight from the helicopter.

"That's how they knew it was me!" Riley said, pointing. "That light was on ME!" All this time, he had wondered if the baton to the head that he had suffered was a random act, an officer out of control. Now he knew otherwise.

The next video was from behind the police line at the railroad tracks. It showed longshoremen throwing rocks at the temporary light, trying to take it out. Riley knew most of them. Some picked up broken and rotten railroad ties and were jabbing them at officers, or tossing them overhead into the line of police.

Riley saw his brother motioning for people to follow him down the railroad tracks. Over to the side, a white checker, the brother of a leader in that union, was taunting officers nonstop. The temporary light went down, but the police got it back up quickly. Longshoremen stood around the generator, resting their hands on it as though it were a table, talking to the police, telling them in typical longshoreman language that these were their jobs, the police didn't belong there. Then some of the delegates were waving people off, and others were pointing at some and yelling at others to stop throwing the rocks.

Riley thought this was about the time he got there to try to calm things down. On the video there was an eruption, maybe when he got hit, and the longshoremen started pelting the officers. None of the camera angles were clear enough to see who struck Riley that night, but his own cousin yelling, "You didn't have to do that!" was enough. Now he realized beyond a doubt that the police knew exactly what they were doing when he took that whack to the head that required twelve stitches.

The videos showed that not long after Riley was hit two police cars and a white Suburban—Greenberg's car—plowed through the back of the longshoremen's group. They threw tear gas canisters out of both windows to clear the crowd, but one man rolled over the hood, stood up on the roof and jumped off the back.

By then the police had arrested Leonard Riley as he walked among the train cars sitting inside the terminal. Then another arrest. The video is dark, muffled against the backs of the officers near the front line, jostled, and fuzzy so only the sound is clear. Then Riley cringed as he heard the cries of Charles Brave taking a beating behind the police line.

Then came the video the attorneys hadn't talked about until now, taken from the side of the road and in front of the police line—more from the longshoremen's point of view. Riley was in the hospital when these events occurred. When Riley's childhood friend and 1422's Recording Secretary Anthony Shine picked Riley up at the hospital, he had told Riley it got worse after he'd left, but that night Riley's only concern had been finding his missing brother.

This video was Rodney King kind of footage that could shock any jury into an acquittal and send more shock waves through the community. It was the kind of public relations ammunition no one uses unless absolutely necessary.

By 12:45 a.m. the longshoremen had retreated from the police line, which had held steady at the railroad tracks. The tear gas had caused most of them to disperse and go back to the hall. The remaining forty or so were backing up and most had turned away from the railroad tracks and the police, heading back up Immigration toward Morrison. Most of the media had retreated to Morrison as well.

When someone fell behind to yell back at the police or hesitated in his withdrawal, another longshoreman would go get him and pull him toward the union hall where their cars were parked. One of the delegates saw a few longshoremen maintaining a low profile in the dark by the railroad tracks and returned to pull on their coats, saying things like, "C'mon man, let's go. It's over for now."

Shine and Freeman stayed behind to talk with Greenberg at the railroad tracks as half a dozen troopers moved up and took positions in front of the line. Greenberg, still wearing a suit and tie under his police windbreaker, was telling the longshoremen to get their men out of there. So they walked away, sometimes walking backwards facing the police line, and at other times turning around to face away from them, their arms wide and low, their palms open to the front, herding the widely spaced stragglers forward even though they were waving at empty air because the men were gone. The street was clear and the gap between their backs and the police line widened. The demonstration was over. They had made their point and it was time to go home. The police could guard their railroad tracks all night. Who cared?

When they were about a hundred yards from the police line at the railroad tracks, near the corner of Immigration and Morrison, off State Ports Authority property and on the public thoroughfare, the longshoremen slowed down to mingle and talk about what happened. The leaders were still herding them forward toward the union hall, but now, with so much room between the stationary police line and the longshoremen, there was no reason to force them farther.

The longshoremen didn't notice what the video camera showed—how in the dark and distance the police line suddenly re-formed and tightened up.

Then the entire line, about four officers deep, stepped over the tracks and stopped. The officer at the bullhorn was still reading his arrest announcement to a vacant street. Some of the remaining longshoremen huddled just barely in sight under a street light on Morrison.

Six officers at the front of the police line lifted their rifles to their shoulders, aimed, and started shooting. Sparks flew. Smoke filled the air. Flares hit the ground. In the distance, longshoremen fell, got up, and fell again. Then the entire police line marched in quick step, with the officers up front still aiming their shotgun-like beanbag launchers and plastic bullet guns. More shots rang out.

By now the longshoremen had turned the corner onto Morrison and were almost in front of the union hall. The police made up the distance between themselves and the longshoremen. Now they were only a few feet from the slowest longshoremen, the ones turning around with their palms up as if asking, "What are you doing?"

Checker Joe McPherson stood closest to the police line, facing it from only five feet away as it approached. A trooper lifted his rifle and shot him in the leg at such close range that his feet whipped out from under him, sending him airborne and then slamming him onto his back. Others leaned over to help, but the police kept advancing and kept shooting, most aiming low. One man jumped as if on hot coals; the others retreated as the police line moved forward to swallow the fallen McPherson in a sea of riot shields and gunfire. Behind the line, three officers leaned on McPherson's back and injured leg to bind his wrists in plastic handcuffs as he yelled. Somewhere in the dark chaos another three longshoremen were arrested.

Officers shouted to residents of the housing development on the other side of Morrison to get back inside. Longshoremen shouted from the parking lot. A few longshoremen and checkers continued to try to talk to the police, who yelled at them to get off the road. The helicopter hovering overhead, its rotors beating the clouds of smoke and tear gas, the fiery flares burning in the middle of the road, and the dim light reflecting off gun barrels and riot shields made the city landscape look and sound like a scene from a war.

Riley sat in the comfort of Andy Savage's plush office, staring at the video, stunned, as it showed police lining up to circle the union hall. Colored pink in places by flares, white smoke floated above the union's parking lot, highlighting the silhouettes of longshoremen standing bewildered and talking in groups with police stiff in formation in the foreground.

As Riley watched the video screen, there was a knock on Savage's door. When no one answered the summons, a secretary opened the door to announce that a plane had just flown into the World Trade Center in New York. The lawyer, thinking it must be some crackpot in a Cessna, sent her away.

A few minutes later the video ended. Riley took a deep breath and reached his hands behind his head to stretch, trying to absorb what he had just seen. As the last tape finished, the video player turned off to allow the television set to return to broadcast mode. On the screen was a World Trade Center tower with flames coming out of its side. Then, as the four men watched, a second plane flew into the second tower. They sat there, transfixed, and with the rest of the nation for the next three hours tried to interpret what they saw and heard from that faraway city New York, home of the ILA.

THE VIDEO KEN RILEY WITNESSED put some other pieces of the puzzle perfectly into place. While the local maintained decent relations with the Charleston City Police Department, Riley still found the story that appeared in the local paper over Labor Day surprising. The local police seemed to be bending over backwards to make this case go away.

'Having these guys under house arrest for this long is ridiculous,' said Jeff Osburn, a Charleston Police detective working on the case. People arrested in shootings and even more serious crimes often have more lenient bail conditions, he said. 'These are normal, everyday, hardworking citizens, the backbone of the community. They had a right to be there that night and a right to make a statement. It's just unfortunate that it got out of hand, and it's a shame that the prosecution has gone as far as it has.'

Police Colonel Ned Hethington noted that several longshoremen who were arrested made personal apologies to the chief after the riot. 'They were just caught up in the moment. No good is going to come out of this. The police won't look good, the workers won't look good, the port won't look good. It was a bad night, and we need to put it behind us.'

. . . That may not happen. Condon said he won't back down. 'This is about the rule of law. This rough 'em up and scare 'em up effort to intimidate is a problem when it comes to union activities around the world. It won't work here, and it won't work with me.'[2]

THE NEXT DAY, Savage was back on the Charleston 5 case.

"I was involved in a hearing at the courthouse yesterday and ran into Chief Administrative Judge Vic Rawl," he wrote to Brad Cranshaw and Lionel Lofton on September 1.[2] "Judge Rawl advised me that he has recently been appointed by the Court Administrator to handle all of the cases arising from arrests made at or about the Columbus Street Terminal on January 19/20, 2000."[3]

Charlie Condon had received a number of phone messages from the mayor of Charleston. A phone call would have been a friendly chat suggesting a different tack, but Condon wasn't returning the calls, so Joe Riley resorted to writing him a letter. Having decided to take a stand, the mayor was willing to speak on the record.

"The reason that I was calling and the reason I am writing is to urge you to transfer the matter of the Charleston 5 to the Ninth Circuit Solicitor's Office," the mayor wrote.[4]

> That will allow this matter, I believe, to receive the justice and local solution that it deserves and that controversies like this require.
>
> What happened that night is inexcusable and can never happen again. It was a civil protest that got out of hand, way out of hand. I know that those involved will never be party to something like that again and I know that the Union learned a very important lesson as well. These are good people who, in a moment of civil protest, got carried away. All of the issues of that night have been resolved, and the Ports Authority and the local unions have, I believe, put the matters of that night behind them, and our port is again operating efficiently and peacefully.
>
> I feel strongly that this event should be put in that context, and that this matter should be resolved in the fashion that you would normally resolve situations like this, on a local level by a locally elected Solicitor. I feel that if it is sent back to the Solicitor, he, in consultation with the defendants, their lawyers, the Ports Authority, the Police Department and others, can find an appropriate way to see that justice is done and that our community's commitment to security, order and safety is preserved.[5]

The next day Assistant Attorney General Brad Cranshaw alerted his boss that Andy Savage was trying to set a motions hearing in front of Judge Rawl.

Condon responded that he would call the chief justice (who had appointed Rawl) and told Cranshaw not to do anything until Condon got back to him.[6]

That day the State Law Enforcement Division (SLED) received an email from Vanda Murphy of the Georgia Bureau of Investigations. It had been forwarded to her from a sergeant in the Emory University Police Department, in Atlanta, who had received it as part of an email blast. It announced a September 29 Workers Democracy meeting in Washington, to focus on the Charleston 5: "We are planning direct actions to shut down the ports on the first day of the trial."

Andy Savage's Ativan supply was long gone, and he was itching to escalate the legal battle. Armand Derfner had just the cure. He called in his old friend in Washington, Michael Tigar. Famous for defending the Chicago 8, Communist Party member Angela Davis, and Oklahoma City bombing conspirator Terry Nichols, Tigar knew a lot about aggressive defenses. Derfner, Wilborn, Tigar, and Savage, and Lofton when he could, met frequently and brainstormed to develop the strongest legal arguments they could make.

On September 28, the legal campaign shifted into high gear as the team filed a motion to quash Count I (conspiracy to riot) and Count II (riot) in the indictment against Ken Jefferson and Jason Edgerton. Four days later they filed a motion to dismiss all the indictments against all of the men. On the same day, in a bold move that would either vault their case forward or drastically backfire, they filed a motion to disqualify the attorney general from the case.[7]

On October 3, Judge Rawl presided over a status hearing on the case. City of Charleston attorney Bill Regan attended and repeated that the mayor wanted to resolve the case in municipal court. He told Cranshaw that the Charleston City Council might pass a resolution regarding the incident at its next meeting in six days.

That evening, Condon appeared on a popular Charleston television call-in show, *Live Five Talk Back*.[8]

"We've got Attorney General Charlie Condon with us tonight here in our studios, and we're going to talk about the men charged in that ILA riot and why he does not plan to drop those charges," said host Warren Peper. The first caller asked if Condon had ever checked to see if the police had provoked the men. Condon responded that he couldn't discuss the facts of the case, and that he believed they should be tried in court and not in the media, then answered the question.

"The charges speak for themselves. Again, they're presumed to be innocent, but they're charged with rioting. And that's a very serious matter because, as you can imagine, a riot can get out of control, lots of innocent people can be hurt. And I think the allegations certainly speak for themselves."

The host asked about the date for trial and Condon confirmed that it had been moved to November 12, a change that had occurred at the status hearing less than an hour before.

The next caller voiced approval of Condon, and the host moved on to the next, who said the charges seemed harsh, and Condon responded.

"I'm not antiunion, but I'm against forcing people to join unions in order to get a job. And so, this whole idea of ends justifying the means, as we know these terrorists that killed so many people, that's exactly their argument. I think it's important to note that ends do not justify the means." The September 11, 2001 attacks on the United States were still raw in the minds and hearts of Americans. The term "terrorist" was becoming commonplace, but to associate any American with the word was at the very least provocative.

"How could they get a fair trial when this thing goes to court if peoples' minds are already made up because of the media?" another caller asked.

Condon responded that in his experience "jurors are really fair." Then the host asked Condon about a resolution opposing the prosecution that city council member Wendell Gilliard had proposed.

"I'll simply say this," Condon responded. "There's been tremendous political pressure brought to bear against me, and I'm not going to bow to political pressure." Then, to drive home his point, Condon added:

"We're talking about people taking railroad ties, rocks—these are allegations in the indictments—of taking metal bars and hitting police officers simply doing their jobs."

One more supporter of the prosecution called and then the show was over. The damage, however, had been done.

The next morning, city council member Robert George called the assistant attorney general's office looking for Condon. He wanted to talk about the city council resolution and offer information "favorable to the State's position."[9]

Cranshaw worked fast to make sure no one at the city level could make an end run around the state's prosecution. For the third time in eighteen months he called and sent letters to the attorneys in the Office of the City Prosecutor to get assurances that they would not move forward on the prosecution of the municipal charges before the state had its day in court.[10]

On October 5, Cranshaw received a supplement to the motion to disqualify the attorney general, with quote after quote from Condon's television appearance two days before.

The hearing on this pile of motions was scheduled for October 12. Cranshaw and David Avant, who had been assisting him, had one week to respond to arguments prepared by some of the most respected legal minds in the country—Derfner and Tigar—while defending not only their legal position but the public actions of their boss, Charlie Condon.

The Charleston police were less than enthusiastic about the case, the local solicitor agreed that there should be a local solution, the entire community was plastered with yellow signs, the threat of a worldwide port shutdown loomed and the mayor wanted it to go away. The two young assistant attorneys had only the staff in the attorney general's office to help them with legal research and strategy and they had to juggle their other more substantial criminal cases as well.

The AG's staff research had dug up some good decisions on the riot argument. The key one was *Abernathy et al.* from 1970, a case right out of Charleston.

Cranshaw read it over. Southern Christian Leadership Conference members Ralph Abernathy, Hosea Williams, David Bright, Elijah Pearison, and Andrew Young had appealed their case against Charleston police chief John Conroy and practically the entire state of South Carolina.[11] The circumstances were eerily similar though not identical.

On June 20, 1969, near midnight, about 250 civil rights supporters assembled at Memorial Baptist Church in Charleston. They had completed their civil disobedience training and were planning to march four blocks to a park to conduct a prayer vigil against racial discrimination in employment at the local medical college and Charleston County Hospital, the two medical centers that were then on strike.

Marchers only made it two blocks before the police told Abernathy to stop under the pretense that the marchers didn't have a permit and parades were only permitted until 8 p.m.

Abernathy asked Chief Conroy if the group could split up and walk in small groups, or even individually, to the park. Conroy said no. "Abernathy and the others immediately knelt in the street, and Abernathy began leading the others in prayer. Conroy ordered them to stop. Abernathy refused and admonished him not to interrupt the praying," according to the uncontested facts stipulated in the case.

The civil rights leaders were charged with "riot" and jailed in lieu of $50,000 bond each. They argued that the permit limiting parades from 8 a.m. to 8 p.m. was unconstitutional because working people couldn't be expected to leave work around 5 p.m., get home, eat supper, tend to their children, assemble for the march *and* receive instruction in Southern Christian Leadership Conference's nonviolence tradition before 8 p.m. The group also argued that the definition of "riot" was overly broad and therefore unconstitutional, but the court ruled that though peaceful picketing and parading are methods of expression entitled to First Amendment protection, they are methods subject to greater regulation than other forms of expression.

Cranshaw knew this would be a good case to argue to the judge. More than thirty years old, this was the last recorded civil protest case in Charleston and spoke to the heart of the matter—the definition of "riot." If a bunch of people kneeling and praying in the street could be considered a riot, surely longshoremen throwing rocks and railroad ties was a riot.

Cranshaw and Avant got to work writing their responses to the motions and preparing for October 12, the hearing that would set the tone of the trial to come.

TWO DAYS BEFORE THE MOTIONS hearing, Charlie Condon transferred the cases to Walter Bailey, the solicitor from the First Circuit, the counties north of Charleston. A 1972 graduate of the University of South Carolina School of Law, Bailey had earned a reputation for his ability to put people on death row in South Carolina. Like Condon, he was no liberal.

In transferring the cases to him, Condon wrote to Bailey:

> The reason I am assigning these cases to you is to remove any charge, albeit false and totally unwarranted, that the prosecution of these cases are [*sic*] biased or undertaken for any reason other than to secure the ends of justice. From the very moment the alleged riot occurred on the night of January 20, 2000, the ILA has desperately tried to divert attention from the tragic events of that evening. The first target of the diversionary tactics were the police on the scene that night. . . . But the ILA did not stop with criticizing the police. The union turned is focus on me, again, with the aim of diverting attention.

Condon reiterated the charges from Savage and others that he was prosecuting for political reasons. Condon denied them unequivocally, saying that "when these prosecutions were initiated, I had no intention of running for governor." Then he listed the salient facts again as he saw them and continued:

> Despite this independent, objective evidence regarding the seriousness of these charges and this matter, powerful political pressure in Charleston continues to be mounted in an effort to minimize these events and to discredit me. Recently, Mayor Riley of Charleston attempted to call me and then wrote me about this issue. I believe such contact was totally inappropriate. . . . In addition, I have been contacted by a member of the Charleston City Council who informed my Office that the Council intended to pass a resolution condemning the prosecution of these cases.[12]

WALTER BAILEY WAS A REPUBLICAN, and even voted for Charlie Condon for governor, but he didn't believe in letting politics interfere with prosecution.[13] When Condon contacted Bailey, he told him it was because Ralph Hoisington, who was by then the solicitor in Charleston County, had a conflict of interest. Bailey was willing to take on what he saw was a righteous case.

He immediately contacted local law enforcement and started preparing for trial. He scheduled meetings with SLED to get the report on their investigation, and he scheduled time to view the videotapes, but it wasn't long before he received word from the State Ports Authority and the higher levels of law enforcement that this case needed to be resolved.

"After the riot took place, they wanted the thing to go away," he explained later. "They didn't want to see it prosecuted; they didn't want any adverse publicity over it." Officials from the port made it clear—and Bailey already knew from living in the Low Country—that Charleston faced competition from the Port of Savannah, less than a hundred miles south, and didn't need a high-profile trial of "rioting longshoremen" to tarnish its reputation as a port.

He also found the police department's take on the case unusual. "The upper echelons of the Charleston Police Department, I guess because of politics and its relationship with the State Ports Authority, wanted it to go away, too," he said. "So you didn't have the usual push for it. Usually when you have law enforcement injured in the line of duty, you get a call from the agency saying, 'This defendant hurt my officer, I want you to go after them.'"

The motions hearing was two days away. Bailey would watch and advise the two young attorneys Cranshaw and Avant, who had been working the case for eighteen months. More important, it would give him a chance to see what the defense had to offer.

THE COURTROOM WAS PACKED for the October 12 hearing in front of Judge Rawl. It seemed every lawyer and half of Charleston's citizenry was squeezed into the room. Walter Bailey, Brad Cranshaw, and David Avant appeared for the prosecution. At the defense table sat Peter Wilborn, Lionel Lofton, Andy Savage, and legal heavyweights Armand Derfner and Michael Tigar.

Andy Savage went first. His job would be to lay out the facts of the case for removing the attorney general from prosecution and dismissing the charges. First, Charlie Condon was guilty of prosecutorial misconduct. He had used his position as attorney general for personal political gain, referring to the "union riot" in paid ads for the campaign he co-chaired for George Bush, and Condon was now running for governor. He issued pronouncements that would bias the public against the defendants, hurting their right to be presumed innocent and muddying the pool of county grand jury members of more than a year ago. And just this month, he compared the longshoremen to the terrorists who had flown planes into the World Trade Center, an immensely provocative analogy about an event that was still traumatizing America.

Savage cited a judge scolding the prosecutor in a 1935 case: "The [prosecutor] is the representative not of an ordinary party to a controversy, but of a sovereignty whose obligation to govern impartially is as compelling as its obligation to govern at all; and whose interest, therefore, in a criminal prosecution is not that it shall win a case, but that justice shall be done."[14]

Savage punctuated his presentation with courtroom theatrics he had honed over the years, playing to the judge and the crowd when Charlie Condon didn't appear for the hearing. (The prosecution had filed its responses to the motion to dismiss the attorney general just the day before, but a meeting with the judge before the hearing had allowed the defense attorneys to see that Condon had removed himself from the case.)

"Where are you, Charlie?" Savage would periodically yell behind him to the crowd.[15] As to the prosecution changing attorneys, Savage urged the judge to tell Condon, "You can't quit. You're fired!"[16]

Savage then argued his second point: Condon's intimidation of the grand jury. Savage asserted that the grand jury is supposed to act as a barrier between the citizen and the overzealous prosecutor.[17] He quoted a Supreme Court decision from 1981:

A grand jury is not a prosecutor's plaything and the awesome power of the State should not be abused but should be used deliberately, not in haste. A prosecutor should at all times avoid the appearance or reality of a conflict of interest with respect with his official duties.

Savage said this case applied perfectly to Condon when he dismissed the local magistrate's decision to drop the charges and convened a grand jury.

"As opposed to the grand jury functioning as a separate arm of justice," he told the court, "it was used as the next weapon in the attorney general's arsenal."

When Savage was done, Avant defended his boss to the court. "The attorney general does not have to be trampled on," he said.[18] "The statements complained of by the defendants in this case cannot be viewed in a vacuum. They must be viewed in light of public posture of the case, much of which was created independent of any action on the part of the Office of the Attorney General and, in fact, on behalf of the defendants."[19]

As for Condon's role with the grand jury, Avant had his own list of legal precedents showing the attorney general's authority to convene and enter the grand jury room. Not only does statute and case law *not* limit the role of the attorney general, Avant argued, but it *expands* it beyond that of county solicitors. In fact, the grand jury's job is to hear "evidence on behalf of the prosecution."[20]

Finally, Avant argued that Condon had already removed himself from the case, so the issue of removal for prosecutorial conduct was moot.

The most substantive arguments were still to be heard. The very constitutionality of South Carolina's riot statute was in question, and the defense was well aware of the long list of cases that had challenged it before and lost.

Here Michael Tigar took over. His reputation preceded him. This was the man whose defense of Oklahoma City bombing conspirator Terry Nichols led to an acquittal of the murder charges against him, the man whose rapport with that case's jurors allowed him to shed tears during his closing argument as he told them, "This is my brother, and he's in your hands."[21]

Tigar lived up to his reputation that day in Charleston as he took Judge Rawl, the prosecution, and the packed courtroom through the maze of two centuries of case law as if he were giving a tour of his own home.

First Tigar reminded the court of the incredible breadth of the indictments. Each man was charged that he did unlawfully and willingly "unite, combine, conspire, confederate, agree, have tacit understanding, or otherwise participate in a combination" for the unlawful purpose, that being "instigating, aiding or participating in riot, as defined in Count II of the indictment."

Count II charged them with "participating in . . . a tumultuous disturbance of the peace, by three or more persons assembled together, of their own authority, with the intent mutually to assist each other against anyone who shall oppose them, and putting their design into execution in a terrific and violent manner, whether the object was lawful or not." Then he facetiously referred to the end of the indictment as having "two multiple choice clauses" or what might be considered a laundry list of possible crimes.

"The purpose of the assembly, or of the acts done or threatened or intended by the persons engaged, was . . . to resist the enforcement of a statute of this state, or the United States; or obstruct a public officer to this state, or of the United States, in serving or executing any process or other mandate of a court of competent jurisdiction, or in the performance of any other duty; or the offender carried, at the time of the riot, firearms, or any other dangerous weapon or was disguised."[22]

In other words, Tigar argued, the state had thrown the book at these men, and had never bothered to tell them what page they were on. Tigar explained one case after the other that spoke to a defendant's right to know the specific charges against him. He then moved on to explain why the riot statute, adopted in 1968, was itself "suspect." It allows people to be convicted for showing up or being present at a riot without any proof of involvement. Finally, he argued that the statute was unconstitutional because it applied to events where both lawful and unlawful behavior could occur, and one couldn't tell which one the person charged had been involved in.

Anticipating the prosecution's argument with the Abernathy case, Tigar explained the limits of that case. It didn't address the definition of "rioter" and it didn't involve applying the rioting charge to both protected (lawful) and unprotected behaviors.[23]

"The South Carolina riot/rioter framework, therefore, appears to allow punishment of an individual merely because he belongs to a group, some members of which commit acts of violence," Tigar argued. "Not only is the citizen left without guidance, but prosecutors are armed with excessive discretion." In fact, this case was proof of that, he said, because while local police charged the men with trespass, the attorney general upped the charges to riot on all of them in a day, with no indication that he knew anything more about them than that they had been present.

Armand Derfner, replete with colorful disheveled clothes and a magnifying glass on a lanyard around his neck, alternately hunched, reading and sifting through piles of paper, and stood to finish off the motions and summarize for the defense. Having him in the courtroom lent an auspiciousness to the occasion. As he cited one case after another, it became obvious that if he hadn't been directly involved in a case he was citing from thirty-six years ago, he had been sitting in the courtroom, and if not in the courtroom, then later discussing it over a glass of wine with the attorney who *had* argued it. He, Tigar, Lofton, and Savage stood on solid legal ground, but Derfner and Tigar could make the ground sway with their eloquence.

Young Peter Wilborn sat in awe, watching his superheroes perform right there, just for him. Indeed, it was more of a performance *for* attorneys *by* attorneys.

"It was dramatic if you knew all the details," Derfner modestly admitted later. "It was dramatic in the way Shakespeare can be dramatic if you know English and you've read the play."[24] But the end goal was always in sight: free their clients.

JUDGE RAWL TOOK THE MOTIONS UNDER ADVISEMENT, meaning he would not rule that day. The defense had put up an impressive case. There was no doubt Bailey could show the violence of that night and put up a good case for conviction, but what severity of conviction? And at what risk? If this big-time lawyer from Washington helped them win the constitutionality argument over South Carolina's 1968 riot statute it would shake loose forty years of legal precedent. Additionally, they clearly planned to make the indictments themselves look silly in front of a jury.

And finally, the defense had more than argument in their repertoire, they had evidence. Although no one had mentioned it, there was the undercurrent, the silent presence, of the damning video footage that only attorneys, police, and Ken Riley had as yet seen, showing the incontrovertible evidence of disciplined police forming up and then running toward the retreating longshoremen to get within shooting range. The white checker taking a bullet to the leg that sent him airborne, the extra troops marching in long after the longshoremen were standing peaceably in their parking lot—the video made it clear that the police had not acted in self-defense. They could have used that claim if they had shot at the men as they threw stones, or in the interest of crowd control, but the crowd was gone by then. Nor could they say they were protecting port property, since the men were on the public right of way by the time the shooting started.

With hundreds of subpoenaed documents showing the intricate preparations for the evening, the defense could argue that police had planned to arrest two hundred people and had only arrested five people by the time the longshoremen walked away. It would be easy to argue that the police needed to shoot off some weapons and pick up a few more arrests so their half-million-dollar show of force wouldn't look like an overreaction by a bunch of hick cops, an image Chief Reuben Greenberg so detested. Perhaps that was why the chief refused to cooperate with the prosecution.

Bailey believed the case was a good one and that the men deserved to be convicted. But this prosecution was outside his usual jurisdiction. He didn't know the subtleties of relationships between law enforcement, longshoremen, politicians, lawyers, and judges in Charleston the way he knew them in his own circuit.

What had not been subtle that day was the message Bailey received directly from Judge Rawl. In the judge's conference with attorneys before the hearing and another right after it, he made it clear he wanted the case settled, and at least for now, he was putting the burden of compromise on the prosecution.

Between pressure from the judge and what he had seen of the case so far, Bailey knew what he had to do. While he continued to move forward in preparation for trial, meeting with SLED, even asking the attorney general's office to pay for a title examination to determine the State Ports Authority property line and the video verification he needed, he also opened up negotiations with Lofton and Savage.[25] It was time to put this case to bed.

12

Victory!

In the face of global capital, labor cannot be set aside by country, but by culture, by language. But in order to unite we need these stories that can move people. It doesn't matter if you're old, it doesn't matter if you're young. Some people say young people won't support unions because they don't feel passionate. I don't think so. It's because we don't give young people stories that touch them to the core.
— Chang Hsu-Chung, president, Taiwan Telecom Workers[1]

Two days after the motions hearing, the *Boston Globe* published a long feature story about the Charleston 5.[2]

"Any effort to break a union anywhere is going to draw the attention of maritime workers all over the world," College of Charleston history professor George Hopkins told reporter Jennifer Graham. "I'm not sure how many Charlestonians are aware of how significant this trial is going to be. This will no doubt attract international attention."

Indeed. The IDC and the ITF had already called for aggressive "industrial action" for the first day of the trial, now set for November 14. On October 16, the AFL-CIO's John Sweeney followed suit by sending word to affiliates nationwide encouraging them to organize a National Day of Action for that day.[3]

Meanwhile, Brett Bursey of the South Carolina Progressive Network had contacted Judge Rawl and asked if his courtroom could accommodate 1,500 to 2,000 people. The organizer then asked if he could get a live feed to the property next to the courthouse in Charleston. He had rented the property and a large circus tent, and was planning to show the trial on televisions to the spillover crowd. He had already reserved the power poles in case the trial ran into the evening hours and was lining up speakers and even an art display. "'Circus' comes to mind," said a smiling Bursey when he described it later.[4]

To help mobilize people for the trial, state senator Robert Ford sent out a flier on his senate letterhead announcing that the trial would begin at 9 a.m. November 14 and telling constituents, "Your presence is urgently needed! The Charleston 5 are residents of my Senate District. I am asking that you come out and urge others to come out and support these hardworking men."[5]

THE LAWYERS WERE ALREADY NEGOTIATING a settlement when Walter Bailey and Andy Savage received a letter from the Maritime Association of the Port of Charleston.[6] President John Hassell III explained that the Maritime Association was a nonprofit, industry association with 157 members including vessel owners and agents, tug and towing operators, freight forwarders, private terminals, terminal operators and stevedores, railroads and more.

"After a review and careful considering of the subject cases, the Maritime Association hereby encourages all parties to actively pursue an expeditious resolution of the cases," he wrote. "It is our opinion that to do otherwise is not in the best interests of our community, state or nation."

Less than a week later, political commentator Jim Hightower made the Charleston 5 the subject of his syndicated radio show. Never one to mince words, the Texan let Condon have it.[7]

"Look up 'Neanderthal' in your dictionary and you'll see his picture," Hightower proclaimed. "Charlie is a political opportunist and full-blown gooberhead who presently is South Carolina's attorney general. He's also running for governor, so to kiss the butt of the state's business establishment ol' Charlie got a secret grand jury to indict the five dockworkers."

Letters, faxes, and phone calls flew among negotiating attorneys between October 25 and November 6. Savage checked with his clients Ken Jefferson and Jason Edgerton. Lofton checked with his clients Elijah Ford, Peter Washington, and Ricky Simmons. Then there were the calls back and forth to Bailey, and back and forth to Derfner and Wilborn. The prosecutor was willing to reduce the rioting charges (to a lesser charge of rioting) so long as the men made a public apology and the union conducted a blood drive and fundraising effort for World Trade Center victims. The Five turned down the offer.

"I am not a big fan of last minute settlements," Bailey told the two attorneys. "Once I have prepared a case for trial, I want to try it."[8] The prosecutor set a deadline for the end of negotiations, the date the cases would go forward no matter what.

Savage, Lofton, Derfner, and Wilborn were in regular contact. Wilborn was conveying everything to Riley and Dewitt, and acting as the voice of the Charleston 5 campaign in meetings with the attorneys. He was also acting as the voice of the attorneys with the campaign, and not one the organizers necessarily welcomed. Attorneys and campaign leaders had discussed many times what they "could live with" if the prosecutor ever made an offer. Now the prosecution was doing just that.

But the campaign had grown far beyond the prosecution. Around the world, dockworkers were willing to strike, risk losing their jobs, risk bankrupting their unions, risk police violence for these five men—or more accurately, for what these five men represented. The ante had been kicked up so high that declaring victory was getting more and more difficult without a complete acquittal, free and clear, of any and all charges. That, the attorneys agreed, was not going to happen.

The events of September 11, 2001 were complicating the case. The Port and Maritime Security Act of 2001 (S.1214) working its way through the terrorism-terrified U.S. Congress named a lengthy inventory of crimes that would exclude people from future work on the Charleston waterfront or any other U.S. port. These included a list of felonies including "willful destruction of property," "aggravated assault," as well as conspiracy to commit a felony. If any of these men were convicted or pleaded guilty to any of these charges, they'd never work as longshoremen again. They had to be careful of plea bargaining.

September 11 and what the Bush administration was making of it politically did nothing good on the campaign's side of the operation either. Suddenly the AFL-CIO leadership was nervous about any kind of activity that might appear un-American, unpatriotic, or something the new conservative administration could make out to be aid to terrorists. The president had starkly stated that everyone in the world was "with us or against us." It would not be auspicious for labor to invite the title of being against the United States. That meant that the timorous AFL-CIO was less likely than ever to support work stoppages at the ports. Even if port action was successful, there was little chance a traumatized American public would look upon it sympathetically.

Image aside, port shutdowns around the world would still have the economic impact the campaign hoped for, but the entire threat was much more of a gamble in this new black-and-white world of a war on terrorism. The attorneys still held the police brutality video that could sway a jury, but juries are always a gamble. The attorneys knew, despite what the campaign had so effectively communicated, that the men they represented were not heroes; they were just regular working-class guys who woke up every morning and walked into the day with more than their share of the damage an imperfect and sometimes desperate life inflicts on a person. They were not saints and the other side would be sure to magnify that fact. This would be a good case to settle the way it had started, on misdemeanor charges that, with good behavior, would eventually disappear from their records.

Meanwhile, the lawsuit against the local by Perry Collins and his nonunion stevedoring firm WSI was still percolating along. On October 29, Judge David C. Norton scheduled a June 1, 2002, jury trial to decide if Perry Collins could claim the $2.5 million in compensation from the union. Defense attorneys had to be sure that if these five men pleaded to a particular charge in this case they would not then become defendants in the WSI one.

By the end of October everyone closely involved believed the cases would be settled short of trial. It was just a matter of how. Bailey was negotiating sometimes separately and sometimes simultaneously with Savage and Lofton. Campaign lawyers Wilborn and Derfner were at the mercy of the criminal defense attorneys whose first interest had to be their clients, and the labor lawyers heard only secondhand about informal maneuvers and negotiations, which were moving quickly between November 1 and 7. They kept Riley, Dewitt, and others in the campaign up to date as best they could, with multiple phone calls every day.

Finally, when Lofton saw a deal Ricky Simmons and Peter Washington could live with, he took it. When Wilborn heard about it, he was furious. Lofton's third client, Elijah Ford, unhappy with the offer, asked Wilborn to represent him in the final negotiations. Ford was willing to take his case to a jury. Meanwhile Andy Savage was still working to get the "riot" language out of any settlement offer so he could settle Jason Edgerton's and Ken Jefferson's cases. A few days later, Savage also took the deal when he saw it, and only later contacted Derfner and Wilborn, leaving the union's attorneys to break it to the campaign organizers that in the end the defense attorneys had acted to cut deals for their clients without consulting the campaign.

It was November 13, a day before dozens of ports around the world had promised to shut down, stopping millions, perhaps billions, of dollars in commerce for the sake of five men from South Carolina, when the last three men pleaded no contest to misdemeanor charges. The pleas were not an admission of guilt. The felony charges were gone. None of the Five would serve any time. Bailey had confirmed that they would not become part of the WSI case. The statute they pleaded to included the word *riot* but their pleas would be limited to the term *affray* which removed the issue of premeditation, and removed from the public eye the most inflammatory word in the case.

Each defendant would pay a $100 fine and their files would eventually be expunged. The language and level of their pleas ensured that they would not have to worry about losing their jobs in the future because of port security legislation. Finally, they were free. Their cases were closed. Then the writing and re-writing of history began.

The West Coast longshoremen in the ILWU, which had played such a large part in the victory, announced victory the day the first two of the Five accepted Bailey's offer.[9] The AFL-CIO waited until all five were settled before it issued a press release on November 13 boasting of the settlement.[10] Within a week, the ITF issued the news in its online newsletter.[11] Not until more than six months later did the ILA in New York publish a major feature story in its union newspaper reviewing the Charleston campaign, including initiatives the campaign organizers had never known about or even suspected, and some they would simply never believe. The article said:

> ILA President John Bowers brought the issue of the Charleston 5 to the national and international labor stage. He secured a pledge of full support from AFL-CIO President John Sweeney who dedicated key staff members to work in Charleston with the ILA to help secure the release of the Charleston 5. The AFL-CIO got Royce Adams of the Coalition of Black Trade Unionists and Bill Fletcher of the AFL-CIO's Civil Rights Department to work with Kenneth Riley and the ILA, locally in Charleston. . . .
>
> ILA President John Bowers made repeated calls to U.S. Secretary of Labor Elaine L. Chao, a personal and longtime friend of the ILA leader, asking her

to use the weight of her office to encourage Attorney General Condon to settle the matter. President Bowers instructed the ILA's Legislative and
Government Affairs office in Washington to continually lobby South Carolina
Senator Earnest 'Fritz' Hollings and Charleston Congressman James Clyburn
to help gain the Charleston 5's freedom.[12]

EVERYONE FROM THE DEFENDANTS' ATTORNEYS to the Charleston 5 campaign,
from ILA's John Bowers to community activists to overseas longshoremen of
the IDC and the ITF took credit for the resolution of the case. But Charlie
Condon was what one political operative referred to as "a man who makes
headlines without making headway." Many in Charleston, especially in the
legal community, said the case took its natural course, and in hindsight, ended
up just as it should have from the start. Condon's antics only caused some
delay, and the campaign didn't necessarily affect the legal case. But many others look at a legal and historical landscape littered with "rioting" black workers, the power of the state's business community, the overwhelmingly antiunion sentiment of organized conservative Christians and politicians, wide-
spread institutional and individual racism, the disproportionate numbers of
convictions of black citizens, the overwhelming economic power of global
logistics on local communities, and white professionals' underlying resentment of black longshoremen making better wages and conclude that only the
campaign could have saved the case.

The numbers support the latter position. Data on container cargo shipped
through the Port of Charleston show the only drop in container traffic at the
port in at least five years occurring at the height of the campaign, in 2001. In
2000, before the Charleston 5 story hit the world stage, 1,246,181 twenty-
foot equivalent units (TEUs—a standard measure of volume of container
freight) came through the port. In 2001, that dropped 7 percent to 1,158,751
and didn't recover completely until three years after the event, in 2003, when
the number reached 1,249,770, slightly above the 2000 volume. Actual metric tons shipped through the port confirm Charleston's plunge, one not suffered by any other nearby port during that time. Records show that
10,735,445 metric tons came through Charleston in 2000 and then plummet-
ed to 9,887,521—8 percent—and had still not recovered by 2003 when the
figure reached 10,146,149 metric tons.[13]

Native son Charlie Condon had proven to be bad business for South Carolina.

THE DAY BEFORE the Charleston 5's victory party, ILA 1422 dedicated its new union headquarters. It was designed by African American architect Harvey Gant, a former mayor of Charlotte, North Carolina, who was born and raised in Charleston. It was more than a union hall; it was a community center. The union had made the conscious decision to add space so that the entire community could enjoy the building, using it for weddings, rallies, graduation parties, and family reunions.

The next day, March 2, 2002, Charleston 5 supporters filled the hall. Longshoremen from both coasts, local politicians, and other supporters looked on as Julian Garcia, now head of the International Dockworkers Council, presented Ken Riley with a plaque that contained a copy of the letter the Spanish dockworkers had handed to the Nordana captain in Barcelona and Valencia. Evelina Alarcon from Los Angeles presented the local with a Cesar Chavez poster signed by the farmworker's widow. Teamsters from the Overnight organizing campaign in Atlanta presented a plaque.

John Bowers and Benny Holland of the ILA attended the celebration as well. Bowers committed to releasing the funds the ILA in New York had collected for the Charleston longshoremen, though he wasn't specific about the amount. ILWU president Jim Spinosa, on the other hand, gave Riley a check for $167,000 to cover legal expenses and pledged his support through the end of the legal battle with WSI.[14]

That week, ILA 1422 hosted the first-ever general assembly of the International Dockworkers Council, the meeting at which the ILWU finally officially joined the group. (Local 1422 had joined at the Tenerife meeting.) The ILWU was facing the threat of a massive lockout by the Pacific Maritime Association, the West Coast counterpart to USMX, the East Coast employer group. Just two weeks earlier, a half million workers in Barcelona had hit the streets, and two weeks later, two million Italian workers would demonstrate for union rights in Rome.

The time seemed ripe to face off with global capital to shape it into something more humane, something less abstract and more concrete, something that kept local economies healthy and workers safe and respected. And for the moment, the members of ILA 1422 were the stars of the show, victors in a long history of struggle and loss.

13

The Battle to Come

For the first time in our history, ideology and theology hold a monopoly of power in Washington. Theology asserts propositions that cannot be proven true; ideologues hold stoutly to a world view despite being contradicted by what is generally accepted as reality. When ideology and theology couple, their offspring are not always bad but they are always blind. And there is the danger: voters and politicians alike, oblivious to the facts.

—Journalist Bill Moyers[1]

IN FEBRUARY 2006, more than five hundred labor activists and academic researchers from fifty-five countries gathered at the Crowne Plaza Hotel on Times Square in New York. The three-day conference was held in multiple languages, simultaneously translated by women in booths at the back of the room.

It had been eleven years since the sacking of the five hundred Liverpool dockers and their subsequent failed attempt to build international pressure against their company, a strike that fell like the proverbial tree in the forest; only few had heard. And it had been five years since the Charleston 5 longshoremen won their international campaign to keep their jobs union, a fight much more akin to a tremor in the ocean.

Attempts to bring labor and the academy together were common during the late 1990s and early 2000s but this was by far the most successful to date. What had changed? The event, three years in the making, was organized by Kate Bronfenbrenner, a Cornell labor studies professor who had gained a reputation for her pragmatic program of research on corporations that helped American labor build its case against what it experienced as a bullying and manipulative management consultant industry, and against a government that had rigged the union election process to the point where 10,000 worksite activists were fired per year in efforts to intimidate workers from voting for a union.

In July 2005, unions representing almost forty percent of the AFL-CIO left the fifty-year-old federation and formed their own coalition called Change to Win. The fractured AFL-CIO threw what was left of itself behind the Cornell professor's effort, as did the new Change to Win coalition.

Individual unions helped fund travel for union leaders from Taiwan, Brazil, Nigeria, but funding wasn't always enough. Of the forty visas that conference organizers requested, thirty-five were approved by the Bush State Department, and many of those only after such intense haggling that State issued a personal apology to Bronfenbrenner after the fact. (In some cases, the country of origin was the cause of visa denials, such as the one denied for the Turkish union leader.) Most notable was the support of the global union federations, or GUFs, umbrella groups representing worldwide coalitions based on industries such as transportation, food, and other sectors of the global economy. These groups, and *their* umbrella, the International Confederation of Free Trade Unions, contained the infrastructure for a worldwide worker mobilization. What they had lacked until now was the vision.

This meeting was marked by one overriding characteristic: urgency. After decades of watching capital go global, after organizing hundreds of thousands to disrupt the Seattle WTO meeting in 1999 only to see business go on as usual, after watching one after another third world country become, at a fraction of the wage costs, the industrial park that had once been the center of major U.S. metro areas, the American labor movement was reaching out, from the belly of the beast, Bronfenbrenner would admit, to its brothers and sisters around the world. American unions needed all the help they could get from wherever they could get it. As it seems it had always been, it was a time of crisis, but not one single crisis by one single union or a tiny group of workers. This was a long-term crisis of worldwide proportions, and even if the millions of workers represented by the heavy hitters assembled in that Times Square hotel that weekend didn't know it, labor was taking a monumental step forward to face that crisis.

Only one American labor celebrity addressed the group, Rich Trumka, secretary-treasurer of the AFL-CIO. His speech lacked the energy and vibrancy of his early days in national office. It lacked the passion he was known for when he led the Mineworkers Union. Perhaps he toned it down on purpose, knowing that this was not a group of striking workers needing a boost, but a group of thinkers and doers with an immense task in front of them.

"Whatever flag may fly at corporate headquarters," he said, in a line common since the 1990s, "the fact is these companies show no allegiance to any country." He called on the world labor movement represented there to reverse neoliberal policies, learn from each other to build capacity, and find more effective ways to connect with academic allies and one another.

In stark contrast, Harris Raynor, international vice-president and director of the southern regional joint board of UNITE! HERE, a Change to Win coalition member, wasted no time pointing his finger at himself and every other union leader who had failed to see what was coming.

"This happened on my watch," he said of the drop in union density, "on *my* watch." He could have been talking to his own children about global warming, crime and war, apologizing and accepting responsibility for what he had been unable to stop. It was that kind of candor that set the tone for the rest of the meeting.

With a $350 registration fee and $200 per night hotel rooms, the sheer expense of the conference culled the group to those motivated people who had the resources, and those who didn't have the resources but had been invited and financed by conference organizers because of what they could bring to such a discussion. There was little room for ultra-left activists who are often long on Marxist-Leninist analysis but short on funding—though the union leader from South Africa, for one, minced no words about being a communist.

On the other hand, the conference attracted leaders of international federations who have been faulted in the past and, like Raynor, faulted themselves now for being little more than letterhead institutions with no actual power to mobilize workers to bolster any threat federation leaders might make. The statement these men made during those three days can not be understated. They were products of the Cold War and for most of their formative years in the labor movement their target for destruction was socialism, not capitalism. Employers maintained a firm but somewhat distant second place as the enemy on the world stage. It is not insignificant that the leader of the International

Confederation of Free Trade Unions announced the culmination of three years of work, a November 2006 gathering at which, he said, "the divisions of nearly a century will disappear."

American longshoremen were there. The West Coast's ILWU was a co-sponsor of the event. They funded a study of SSA Marine, the fifth-largest logistics company in the world and a major player in the union's lockout struggles in 2002 that shut down the West Coast for ten days. (The same SSA had lost the Nordana work in South Carolina.) Such studies, also done on Alcoa, Exxon-Mobil, Kraft Foods, Siemens, and others global companies, were the centerpiece of the conference, offering a standard research model that would help academics provide the kind of information unions need to contend with global employers and giving unionists an opportunity to see how useful academics can be when they try.

The ILA was there, too, but sent no one from its national office, located right there in Manhattan. Ken Riley flew up from Charleston, encouraging Vincent Cameron the longshoreman president from Jacksonville as well as Tony Perlstein, a young activist from the docks in New Jersey to attend. The next generation was doing its homework.

Riley scanned the SSA report for information about the Southeast. He had just been appointed an international vice president, replacing his longtime opponent from Charleston, Ben Flowers, now physically incapacitated by old age and illness, as representative of his region at the national level. But it had not been automatic or easy. He listened intently to the professors from California that the ILWU had enlisted to get the facts on one of the worst union employers in the industry.

The ILWU has been doing its homework for some time. Another report the union commissioned stated that between 1980 and 2000 the container volume going through West Coast ports grew 181 percent. Growth in employment throughout the whole supply chain went from 190,000 to 290,000, yet employment in the most highly organized sectors—rail and ports—was practically stagnant. The ILWU is tracking a crucial trend in the industry. The work is going to inland warehouses and production centers that pay low wages to workers to rearrange cargo, or "stuff and strip" containers as it's called, that come through ports and are put on trains without stopping. In other words, low-wage and often vulnerable immigrant laborers are doing ILWU members' work sometimes thousands of miles from the port for thousands less per year. Peter Olney, ILWU director of organizing, referred both wryly and angrily to "the port of Kansas City" and to "desert ports" in California that are growing exponentially due to this kind of work being moved inland. This was not a joke. The plan is to open a new port just south of the U.S. border, unload containers with low-wage Mexican longshoremen, put the containers on trains and take them to warehouses in Kansas City, a low-wage region of the United States that will become a freight hub for the global movement of merchandise.

"The longshoremen need to follow the container and keep that work," said Lawrence Thibeaux, former president of ILWU Local 10, and by the time of the conference, a member of the union's legislative action committee.

The ILWU is ahead of its East Coast counterpart in other ways, too. For example, the union has built coalitions with environmentalists—a traditional enemy—to demand higher air-quality standards for the thousands of trucks operating in and out of the port every day. Ships are major contributors to port pollution as well.

"That's our air," Thibeaux said. "That's our neighborhood. Longshore-men and their families are the first ones to suffer from those trucks going by." So the union developed a "Growing the Ports/Greening the Ports" initiative in West Oakland to address the needs of port workers and community mem-bers, who are often one in the same. It includes millions toward retrofitting trucks with filters that will reduce emissions by 89 percent, Thibeaux said. Later, a much larger "Saving Lives Campaign" driven by the ILWU in Los Angeles and Long Beach focused on ship stack emissions in the highly con-gested port. Joe Radisich, ILWU international vice president in 2007 and a port commissioner, used the union's leverage to pressure shipping companies to reduce those emissions.

This might seem strange to East Coast longshoremen in the ILA, especial-ly those in Philadelphia, for example, who in 2005 and 2006 waged a signifi-cant battle to dredge an additional five feet, a difference that would keep the port competitive as the industry moves to larger ships that draw more water. The battle pitted Pennsylvania's governor Ed Rendell against acting New Jersey governor Richard Codey, who, backed by environmentalists, refused to agree to the dredging. Rendell, who chaired the board of the bi-state port authority, held up the budget for months into the new year and threatened to disband the authority if New Jersey didn't agree to the dredging.

The Delaware River Port Authority responded in January 2006 with the announcement of a $5 billion project to develop fifty miles of New Jersey waterfront to spur, it claimed, "thousands of jobs, new housing and improved ports" but no dredging.[2] In a significant battle for the U.S. Senate, the ILA endorsed the ultraconservative incumbent Pennsylvania Republican Rick Santorum over the Democratic challenger Bob Casey Jr., who won the election by a landslide. Union leaders told the media that Santorum had promised the funds needed for the dredging.

In the fall of 1999 the South Carolina Ports Authority's plans to expand to nearby Daniel Island became public. A larger port translates into more longshore jobs, so ILA 1422 certainly wasn't going to oppose it. But environmentalists, and some say the force behind them, real estate developers, fought back the powerful SPA and the project was eventually scrapped. Daniel Island is now the latest, greatest planned community, home to technology firm Blackbaud—but no port.

The ILA was millions of miles behind their brothers and sisters in the ILWU when it came to building such strategic alliances or gaining this kind of knowledge about employers. At one point in the conference in New York, an ILWU and an ILA member were talking in the hall. They were asked if the ILA has this kind of research on employers, and the ILWU member guffawed and said, "The ILA *is* the employer!" The joke was in reference to the ILA's close, and reputedly crooked, relationships with many employers in the ports of New York and New Jersey.

Ken Riley connected with a Rutgers University professor looking for community allies on the East Coast to support his research on global companies and the ports. By then Riley as a member of the ILA executive board hoped he could use his position to convince other board members to back research that could help the union keep jobs.

But Cameron from Jacksonville, new to this kind of gathering, asked frankly in a workshop how he was expected to get his members involved in something that seemed so abstract and far away. That was the question in the back of every unionist's mind: Once we have the research and know where we need to go, how will we ever get our members to do what they must to leverage meaningful threats?

This meeting was not called to address in any detail that most basic issue of power. There was other work to be done, that had to be done, before that question became relevant.

Workplace power is still defined by the workplace, by its employees' relationships among themselves, with their union, and with their employer. That is another immense challenge the union movement must face, almost simultaneously, at the local level, but that would not happen here in New York.

This meeting faced the global issues, with many of the global players—federation leaders who must learn new ways, affiliated unions that must be willing to give some real power to the federations to which they belong, academics who must refocus their research to be relevant and practical, and union leaders who need the research that will give unions organizing and bargaining power. For now it was enough that unions could put their resources toward organizing an event such as this and toward fostering the international relationships they would need in the future.

Guy Ryder, general secretary of the 155-million-member ICFTU understood the daunting work ahead of his audience.

"We recognize the need for fundamental change in the international labor movement," he said. "Cross-boarder trade union solidarity has to become an everyday part of union activity. It has to be an internationalism that moves the public policy agenda that is so badly stacked against working people today."

SSA, THE STEVEDORING FIRM that lost fifty longshoremen jobs when Nordana went nonunion in 2000, had grown to one of the top five terminal operating companies in the world by 2004.[3] Through joint ventures and partnerships the company has established a presence in Canada, New Zealand, South Africa, Namibia, India, Vietnam, and Thailand, not to mention most of South America.[4] SSA was awarded a $4.8 million contract at the port of Umm Qasr in Iraq right after the American invasion. By 2005, SSA was in every major U.S. regional market as well. In Mexico, it took just three years to get established throughout the country's ports, handling an estimated 28 percent of all Mexican cargo. While ILWU members would suffer from a Mexican port just miles south of Los Angeles, SSA, showing no allegiance to any country, as Trumka said, stood to gain.

"The state of Missouri and Kansas City Southern Railway believe that an efficient new terminal and improved rail link between Lazaro Cardenas and Kansas City could provide a competitive alternative to the congested ports of Los Angeles/Long Beach for U.S. bound imports from Asia," according to the research report released at the conference.[5]

IN THE SOUTHEAST, SSA was starting its own war between the states. It had approached the South Carolina Ports Authority about building a port in Jasper County, just across the state border from Savannah, Georgia. The 1,800 of acres, located in South Carolina but owned by the state of Georgia, are full of silt that Georgia has been dumping for years from its dredging operations in the Port of Savannah. When SSA promised to build a $600 million facility on the land, Jasper County began condemnation proceedings over the property. Not to be left out of the fray, the South Carolina State Ports Authority went to court to win the power to supersede Jasper County's rights to condemnation with its own condemnation. It succeeded.

Near retirement in 2006, Charleston SSA's Lee Tigner explained the negotiations:

> When we first came up with this idea, the State Ports Authority said, "That is the silliest thing we ever heard of in our life. That is a terrible place to build a port." We said "Okay, butt out. We'll build it."[6]

SSA wants 500 acres to build a "megaterminal," Tigner explained. "When you do that the surrounding land then gets bought up by people wanting to establish port-related interests." He said the infrastructure for a terminal there would be very easy since it is close to highways and railroads, just what a terminal operator needs to move cargo inland. As for aesthetics, Tigner said, "There's only one ugly place on the inland waterway and it's this place. *Anything* you do to that place would make it better."

Of course, the Georgia Ports Authority is fighting the deal, which would become direct competition for Savannah. The South Carolina Ports Authority is fighting it because the agency wouldn't control the privately owned Jasper County site. Then, to secure a union-free environment in case it did win its case, the SPA board voted in September 2005 to ban any landlord-tenant operations in South Carolina ports, a move designed to maintain its control over all port property and operations. That meant the owner of the port could not lease it to another agency to operate it.

With that control, the SPA would hire all employees to operate the cranes and perform other functions, and state employees in South Carolina are banned by law from belonging to unions. As if operating below a political equator where everything spins in the opposite direction, the port is fighting privatization because the board sees private port operators as "union" operators. Ken Riley supports privatization for the same reason.

Tigner, who boasts being from a "union-hating family," said the port is a dangerous place to work and that the union is important in the efficient operations there. "The labor force has to be dependable," he said. "You have to have a central hiring hall. You have to have fixed times to start and stop a vessel. You have to pay people enough so they're clamoring to get the jobs. You can't have stragglers coming in, pulling these trucks through this obstacle course that is our terminal. You have to have qualified labor."

Besides, it's good for the economy, Tigner said. "If you're an auto dealer in South Carolina, do you want a guy making $8 an hour or $23 an hour? He can't buy your car if he's only making $8 an hour."

SSA bids its jobs on a cost-plus basis, meaning that it calculates its profits on a percentage of total costs. When labor costs are high, as they are under the ILA contract, each percentage point rakes in higher profits for the company.

But as port space in Charleston became scarce, stevedores and port companies moved some of their operations inland. What the companies lost in the efficiency of proximity, they more than made up for in labor costs. Example: It takes a Ports Authority crane operator to move the box from the ship to the chassis it will sit on for a truck to move it to the right place on the port. It takes longshoremen to connect the containers to the crane and to latch them onto the truck, to drive them to their specified place in the port, and to make sure the right boxes go to the right place so they can be found when it's time to move them again. It takes longshoremen to stuff and strip the boxes—putting the content of mixed containers into the proper containers for truck or train transport.

But what if that crane operator puts the boxes directly onto a train that pulls them to someplace twenty miles from the port? Though the ILA contract claims all work within fifty miles of the port is under its jurisdiction, Tigner said that's "passé" and his distribution centers, run under an SSA subsidiary called Trans-Hold, are nonunion.

SSA has four such centers now in the Charleston area, but is building a 315,000-square-feet center to consolidate them. Workers there cost the company $14 per hour, (including any benefits, taxes, and worker's compensation costs. In other words, take-home wages are likely close to $8 per hour) instead of the almost $50 per hour the longshoremen cost, according to Tigner. With no union to keep the playing field high and level, distribution center owners and operators can keep wages low and profit margins high. So much for a guy buying a car in South Carolina.

Tigner lived through the most radical changes of the past century in the shipping industry. "Back in the early days every single government had a steamship line," he said. "The Peruvians, the Bolivians, the Venezuelans, Brazilians, in South America alone in the '80s there were forty steamship lines, some private, some government ones. Today there are probably four." Today the consolidation of steamship lines is almost complete.

Ryan Walsh and Cooper T. Smith, the companies Tigner so feared in the early '80s, are now part of the same company he is (hence the Cooper in SSA Cooper in the Southeast.) Sometimes Lee Tigner, with his affable Deep South way, sounds like a man who has outlived his time.

"You cultivate all these friendships and the next thing you know they've sold that business to somebody else and all those guys you've been fooling with all these years are either fired or down at the bottom of the totem pole again," he said. "Instead of dealin' with that good ol' boy from New Orleans you've known since you went into the business, you've got some Kraut from Hamburg you never met."

It MAY HAVE BEEN A SAD COINCIDENCE, or a statement of infinite optimism, but the street on which the fired Liverpool dockers chose to locate their building is called Hope. Their home, which they've dubbed CASA, in honor of its former identity as the Casablanca Club, houses a pub at the front of the main floor, meeting space with another bar in back, and office space with a full complement of computers upstairs. In September 2005 it was the hub of the activities surrounding the tenth anniversary of the dockers' struggle, launched when five hundred men were fired for honoring another union's picket line. The anniversary event alternated between farewell party and memorial service.

These workers, their thinning gray hair and thickening paunches betraying their years off the docks, weren't celebrating being sacked, the ruddy-faced dockers' president Jimmy Nolan said repeatedly. No one celebrates that. Instead, the Liverpool dockers had invited more than four dozen of their friends from across the globe to thank them for their unwavering support for the last decade. The next two days would prove Nolan wrong, though, as dockworkers from Spain, Sweden, Australia, Japan, the United States,

Ireland, Belgium, Italy, and Canada left their unions' daily struggles to fly to this northern English port town not to receive thanks but to give it.

The main day of the event, sandwiched between two nights of festivities at the union hall, opened with jokes about Guinness and bleary eyes. About a hundred people gathered in the local community college a few blocks from CASA for a day of remembering and saying good-bye.

"They've come here to pay their respects," Terry Teague, Liverpool docker, said of the dozen leaders waiting on the stage to speak. But in echoing what would become the theme, "the defeat that turned to hope," Teague also spoke of the IDC. "That is without a doubt the greatest legacy to come out of the Liverpool dockworkers—twenty-one countries, thirty-five unions, 60,000 members."

The Lord Mayor of Liverpool was one of the first speakers, as was Doreen McNally, who had organized the Women of the Waterfront. Then one dockworker after the next rose to the podium.

"Neptune-Jade, Patrick's dispute in Australia, the Charleston 5, Jorge Silva Beron bleeding in the streets . . . all of these actions spring from the Liverpool situation," said ILWU president Jim Spinosa, looking very composed in his clean gray suit and tie. But at the end of his remarks, as he handed Jim Nolan a plaque, his voice cracked. "We love you all . . . and our table is set," he said before hugging the old Englishman.

Swedish dockworker Bjorn Borg reminded Teague, sitting on the stage, of his frequent comment that the Liverpool workers are no longer "real" dockworkers.

"Being a docker is much more than doing the physical work on the docks," he said, looking him straight in the eye. "It's very much a frame of mind, and you are some of the best dockers in the world."

Julian Garcia, current general coordinator of the IDC, assured the crowd that "ideas do not die," and added, "We're here because the workers of Liverpool are our friends, our companions; they are friends who have given us unforgettable experiences for the rest of our lives."

Canadian longshoreman Pat Riley heaped high praise on the Liverpool workers in yet another emotional speech. "You were our heroes in 1995, you are our heroes in 2005, and you will be our heroes forevermore," he said.

But the day was more than one of praise and gifts—it was an opportunity to move forward. One of the most noticeable speakers on the agenda was

Jimmy Kelly, recently elected president of the British Transport and General Workers Union, which had left the dockworkers out to dry ten years before.

"I be sayin' as the first Irishman to be elected president of the TGWU," Kelly said, "we won't be repeatin' what was done to the Liverpool dockworkers." The place erupted in applause.

Then it was time to make amends at the international level. First Frank Leys, the new secretary of the Dockers' Section of the ITF, stood to speak. The room suddenly turned chilly.

"We can't change the past," he said plainly. "We were not there. But staying silent has never brought workers forward." He then addressed the ports directive, a move to privatize docks in the EU that caused EU dockers to shut down Europe for a day. In every line he emphasized unity.

When Australian dockworker Paddy Crumlin stood to speak, conversations in the hallways stopped and the back of the room filled with people who had been waiting outside to hear him. Crumlin had been recently elected to replace John Bowers as head of the ITF's Dockers Section, and his union was not affiliated to the IDC like the others in the room. More than one of the IDC's founders had expressed pleasant surprise that Crumlin had come at all, and one Canadian longshoreman had used Crumlin's name on the agenda to prove to his union president that the event was worth the time away from work.

Crumlin prefaced his remarks by saying he was officially speaking as a representative of his union, the Maritime Union of Australia, (MUA), then quickly launched into his critique of the ITF.

"Dockworkers can't afford to be defeated," he said in a booming voice. "If we do, then the global forces, the Cato Institutes in the U.S. and others will replicate our defeats and take them elsewhere." He was straightforward about the failure of the ITF in the Liverpool situation.

"ITF should've played a stronger role," he said. "The international transportation system to which we are all linked wouldn't have had the confidence to take the MUA on if they hadn't won in Liverpool.

"We learned from Liverpool, too. We need a multifaceted strategy—a political strategy, engaging with government. You've got to have a legal strategy so that you don't get bankrupted; you got to have an industrial strategy so you're prepared to break laws; and you've got to have a community and media strategy so you don't separate yourself from your community.

"'The fight is never over," he continued. "The think tanks, the neoliberal forces—all they do is study where they went wrong and come back and have another go at it, and another go and another go.

"We're organizing internationally because the employer is organizing internationally. If we don't organize shipping and if we don't organize road and rail, we'll become small pockets with very good conditions—and *very* vulnerable."

Crumlin finished by saying he had sent thirty of his fellow Australians to support the ILWU in the U.S.'s West Coast lockout in 2003.

"I was called an economic terrorist!" he said. "We are a threat to what they are doing to our own societies—and I'm proud of that!"

Then Ken Riley stood to speak, the last in a long line. His longshoreman father had died just a few days earlier after struggling for years with the after-effects of a stroke. He told the dockers how his family had scheduled the funeral around his trip so he could get to Liverpool and "see where the strength of this movement comes from." And so he buried his father and got on a plane. "We mourn for the dead and fight like hell for the living," he said, quoting the old labor organizer Mother Jones. "We come from the American South where labor is oppressed. We continue to win because losing is not an option. We must win because of what losing would have meant. Workers who believed in us would have been in jail twenty years. You showed us the way."

Riley and his second officer, Robert Ford, were the only members of ILA at the conference. (By contrast, the ILWU had brought more than a dozen people twice the distance.) At that very moment, on the other side of the Atlantic Ocean, half of the ILA's executive officers were sitting in a courtroom facing federal racketeering charges and the end of an era. Some things hadn't changed.

"The night we were on the streets getting beat by the cops," Riley continued, "most of our executive board was a hundred miles down the road. If it weren't for other dockers we wouldn't have made it." He looked out across a sea of dockworkers from around the world and smiled.

"Thank God there were people like you who knew what struggle was."

14

Not Just Another Labor Story

One must know the enemy's purpose before adopting a strategy to undermine it.
—Nelson Mandela[1]

THE EVENTS THAT USHERED IN the twenty-first century on the Charleston docks were a confluence of global forces. Class warfare rose to a new level when capital fueled by neoconservatives gained control of the U.S. government in the form of George W. Bush and the global economic system in the form of the WTO, the World Bank, and the IMF. How did it happen? And how were working people complicit in it?

First, how it happened. The massive, global leap in technology contributed to the whole: the development of container technology for shipping; speed-of-light global communications; international flows of capital; internationalization of manufacturing; plus the maturation and operation of the World Bank, International Monetary Fund, and World Trade Organization that forced many national economies to participate in the market institutions of the neoliberal revolution.

Working people became complicit in their own devastation through economic displacement and their desire to seek security in religion. An orchestrated right-wing movement grafted politics onto religion, exploited racial divisions and fears, used regional and historical insecurities, manufactured a cultural revolution to make these developments seem natural and inevitable, manipulated the press to make right-wing religious and political efforts seem mainstream, and won elections for corporate stand-ins who then used government to enhance these processes.

In the wake of "neoliberal" policies imposed on countries around the world, the impersonal forces of "markets" displaced the authority of elders and kin.[2] Instead of living off their own land, people were forced off the land, their families and communities ripped apart as many were compelled to seek work in factories in an American-dominated system that weaves the economic, the political, and the religious into a seamless web of government policy and corporate activity.[3] The events on the Charleston docks on that evening in January 2000 were a response to the probes of one company, a small survivor moving with the giants of the logistics industry—a key element in moving the goods through the global economy.

Condon's response was one tiny event in another global movement, one to gain corporate control of local and national economic and political systems. The movement achieved this by engineering legislative and executive branch victories for corporate front men through campaigns that manufactured a culture in which it all seems natural, inevitable, and ordained by God. Developed over years of grassroots organizing, corporate funding, "think-tank" propaganda, press manipulation, and savvy strategizing, these forces were an ingredient in every national debate, every executive branch policy imposed on a government agency, from the Food and Drug Administration to the Environmental Protection Agency, and practically every decision made in every newsroom and publishing house in the country. This political formula became the "winning recipe" for politicians like Condon to employ in attempts at higher office.

RILEY AND CONDON WERE BOTH boys growing up in Charleston when Southern whites started to leave the Democratic Party in 1964, after Lyndon Johnson aligned it with the civil rights movement. Fundamentalists worldwide fear colonization, foreign influence, traditional science, and sex. Inside the U.S., the American version of colonization is federal power. Few Americans felt more colonized than Southerners did a hundred years after the Civil War when the federal government began to enforce civil rights laws. The Old South is the "heritage" Confederate flag supporters celebrate.

Senator Barry Goldwater of Arizona was one of Johnson's most vocal opponents. The popularity of Goldwater's opposition to the Civil Rights Act fueled his run for the presidency and southern whites turned eagerly to Goldwater's platform of "barely disguised racism in the Deep South vein."[4] Goldwater's proclamation that "the moral fiber of the American people is beset by rot and decay"[5] set the course for the New Right, the results of which we still feel today. We heard the echoes of this in Condon's mantra of how "mob violence . . . ought not to be allowed to succeed in South Carolina."

After the Democratic landslide, President Lyndon Johnson and a Democratic Congress passed the Voting Rights Act in 1965. Blacks began to vote and stand for office as Democrats while South Carolina's Senator Strom Thurmond led the white backlash and the defection to the Republican Party.

The success of Goldwater's extremist positions in the South in 1964 encouraged young Republican activists to learn from those experiences to build a movement that would eventually give America presidents Ronald Reagan, Bush I, and Bush II and fuel a reactionary cultural revolution across America.

In 1968 Alabama's segregationist George Wallace focused on white Southerners' resentments, and only Thurmond's support of Nixon's Republicans carried South Carolina against Wallace's third party in the national election.[6] The Republicans appropriated Wallace's segregationism in Nixon's "Southern Strategy," by which they first courted then rewarded Southern politicians. In the 1972 election, Nixon swept the South.

Meanwhile, erstwhile Goldwater activists were playing an increasing role in the Republican Party. "We are radicals, working to overturn the present power structure in this country," remarked Paul Weyrich, a young conservative at the time.[7] To create room for their ideology and make it seem mainstream and credible to the press and public, they formed the Heritage Foundation. This "foundation" hired economists with PhD's to produce "studies" that legitimized the corporate ideologies of their sponsors, such as privatizing public services and Social Security, attacking health and safety standards, and opposing minimum and prevailing wage laws. Thirty years later these policy issues had become conventional, even centrist. Their cultural revolution was complete and their message more sophisticated than ever. It's an amazing and dangerous leap to go from workers organizing unions getting killed by police and intimidated by company thugs to a world of right-to-work states where politicians make hay by passing laws that strengthen "the right *not* to belong to a union, without fear of intimidation or coercion."

These new ways of framing the issue did not come out of nowhere. By 1974 the radical right began an orchestrated advertising attack on pro-labor incumbents by fanning racial hatred with racist code words such as "states' rights," "federal interference," "crime," "school vouchers," "freedom of choice," and "welfare queens."[8]

It worked.

"We can elect Mickey Mouse to the Senate," bragged Terry Dolan, head of the National Conservative Political Action Committee. "People will vote against the liberal candidate and not remember why."[9]

By the time these message manipulators were done, black and union in the South were the most dangerous things to be in America.

ABOUT THE SAME TIME, this radical right began to appeal to blue-collar workers through emotional issues such as gun control, taxes, and crime. During the 1970s Paul Weyrich saw the potential to expand this base among white, blue-collar fundamentalists by grafting his political radicalism onto religion.

Fundamentalist religions with their doctrines of inerrancy, that religious texts are correct representations of realities and are the literal truth, can define roles clearly in a murky, confusing, and rapidly changing world.[10] They provide a way to play to the insecurities of men who are threatened by changing gender roles and assertive women by opposing newly visible gays, gun control, and women's choice about abortion.[11]

These deeply personal matters moved many ordinary working people to support fundamentalism, and the political messengers of the extreme right molded their messages to resonate with it through the Moral Majority, which became a significant force in 1980 when it delivered the presidency to Ronald Reagan.[12] Now wearing the mask of religion, the right could disguise its corporate agenda as morality. And with the ear of powerful politicians, fundamentalists had a new avenue to strut their agenda. The fundamentalists and the politicians rewarded each other handsomely. South Carolina led the nation in becoming one of the fertile centers for this exchange in a two-pronged attack on unions from the church and state.

The late Jerry Falwell was one popular preacher who railed against unions, but he wasn't alone. "Unions are one of the organizations leading the world to wickedness," Tim La Haye told his growing number of followers.[13] And Pat Robertson harnessed his powerful Christian Coalition to a corporate agenda. "Christians have a responsibility to submit to the authority of their employers since they are designated as part of God's plan for the exercise of authority on the earth by man," he preached.[14] Supporting a union, by extension, was irresponsible and ungodly.

"In truth, a lot of people who voted for the Republican candidates positively despise the party," Weyrich admitted. "These voters were drawn into the political process because of their beliefs in certain issues which overrode their party preference. Of these, the three most effective for us in unseating liberal incumbent senators have been the Right-to-Life, Right-to-Work, and Gun Control groups."[15] Republican operative Ralph Reed elucidated this strategy when he said that issues such as school prayer and abortion are "the bridge that gets you to constituencies that aren't with you on the economic issues."[16]

Blue-collar workers vote for the radical right because it feeds an emotional need, such as in their opposition to gun control ("the right to defend my home") or a woman's control over her own reproductive health ("if white women keep having abortions, pretty soon we'll be in the minority in this country"). But the radical right supports the corporate interests that support it and corporate interests are opposed to those of the blue-collar workers. The more working people vote for the right, the worse their economic situation becomes. The worse their situation becomes, the angrier they become and the more they support fundamentalists and the right.[17]

Black longshoremen never suffered from this delusion because they were always alienated from a racist political and social system, were able to isolate their good fortune in the union, and, for the more entrepreneurial longshoremen, the social networks that help them build their own small businesses. They are buoyed by churches that more often than not preach community over individuality. Ken Riley, Anthony Shine, Leonard Riley, and others knew exactly who their friends were, even if they were a bit unclear about the range of enemies arrayed against them.

Whereas the religious right cannot be painted with too broad a brush, just as black churches cannot, certain figureheads and organizations keep making return engagements on the stage of world politics. These are the same people and organizations, the Christian Coalition and others, to which

Condon turned for support in his run for the Republican nomination for governor in 2000. They are the glue that holds international politics and commerce together to become such a driving combined force in South Carolina politics.

The Moral Majority's and Christian Coalition's national presence have diminished but their legacy lives on in the megachurch movement.[18] It constitutes more than three hundred and fifty churches and two million parishioners.[19] Seacoast Church, based in Mt. Pleasant just across the bridge from ILA Local 1422, is a well-funded, well-articulated, and calculating part of this nationwide and worldwide movement of modern marketing. More sophisticated and subtle than its predecessors, its stealth political agenda includes conservative interpretations of the Bible. The Seacoast Statement of Faith places them in the Dominionist camp, the latest and most dangerous group endorsing biblical inerrancy. "The sole basis for our belief is the Bible, which is uniquely God-inspired, without error, and the final authority on all matters on which it speaks," the statement says.

"I bet you—and this is total speculation on my part—I bet you [Seacoast pastor] Greg Surratt has not done four sermons in four years that have touched on political issues," Baptist pastor Flowers, a confessed liberal commented. "But if he did, they'd be far-right wing."[20]

CHARLIE CONDON STILL LIVES on Sullivan's Island. In 2002, as he prosecuted the Charleston 5, he received only 16 percent of the vote in the gubernatorial primary, coming in third in a seven-way race.

After leaving the attorney general's office, he went to work as vice president and general counsel for Palmetto Surety Corp., a Mt. Pleasant-based insurance company.[21] In 2004, he ran for the Republican nomination for U.S. Senate against five others.

"He's got a following," Republican policy analyst Neil Thigpen told the *Post and Courier.* "The Christian conservative network goes all over the state, and he's always been right on their issues."[22]

Condon said he planned to tone down some of the provocative rhetoric of his earlier campaigns, but at least one of his most avid supporters preferred Condon just as he had always been.

"If you are an ultra-conservative charter member of the vast right-wing conspiracy, one of the 'little people' who pays taxes, owns a gun and believes the holy trinity consists of Jesus, Jefferson Davis and Robert E. Lee, you have to relish this Republican primary as much as I do," wrote Bill Schleuning of Myrtle Beach, in a letter to the editor.[23]

"Condon's campaign rocks the boat with every politically incorrect initiative in the book: being pro-life; backing sweeping tax reform; downsizing government; supporting the National Rifle Association; placing the responsibility for crime back on the criminal; backing immigration control; and supporting Israel, Southern heritage groups and domestic violence victims."

It would seem Condon hadn't changed his spots much since the Charleston 5 prosecution. If the rest of Schleuning's list doesn't give it away, the mention of Israel, spliced almost awkwardly between the domestic issues of immigration control and Southern heritage, does. Israel enters Condon's campaign rhetoric because it's part of a worldview that Israel must be protected as a biblical land in order for Christ to return. This worldview belongs to Dominionists.[24]

Dominionism is a new militant Christian political movement, a hybrid of Pentecostals, Southern Baptists, conservative Catholics, Charismatics, and Evangelicals who believe that America is destined to become a Christian nation led by Christian men. They believe that Jesus has directed them to build the kingdom of God here and now. America is an agent of God and all opponents are agents of Satan. Dominionists will return the United States to a legal system based on the Ten Commandments and base education on creationism. The federal government will proselytize, protect property rights, and secure the homeland. Are these Dominionists just another fringe group? First, look who's backing them:

- Amway founder Rich DeVos, a supporter of James Kennedy, a Republican contender for governor of Michigan. $5 million.

- Jean Case, wife of former AOL chief Steve Case. $8 million.

- Tom Monaghan, founder of Domino's Pizza, a supporter of Focus on the Family, a mega-ministry that works with Kennedy to eliminate all public schools.[25]

James Dobson, founder and chairman of Focus on the Family, is the most powerful of the Dominionists. He delivered the Christian vote for George W. Bush in 2004. His movement is centered in Colorado Springs where 1,300 employees send out four million pieces of mail a month and broadcast to a radio audience of 200 million in ninety-nine countries. In the States he appears on one hundred television stations every day. He has put the Bush administration on notice that if the White House does not support his anti-homosexual, anti-stem cell research, anti-abortion, anti-public school program, Bush will lose his support, and Dobson has a media machine that can make or break a president.

The decades-old dream that Pat Robertson and other radical Christian rightists had of a new political religion that would take control of America's institutions to transform them into a global Christian empire is all too close to being realized by these Dominionists running powerful mega-churches. They are sophisticated. They are insidious. What some call a return of fascism others see only as open, welcoming communities of faith providing spiritual support to the mobile, rootless workers of the new economy.

In 2000, Ken Riley and his men were facing an international network that no single Website, email, or magazine article could expose. Corporations and governments brought more than ideology and profits to the fight Riley and his friends would wage; they would bring millions in donations toward a Christian mission to colonize countries while simultaneously wiping out unions—the greatest threat and often the only organized response to corporate repression anywhere.

Within two years of the Charleston 5 victory the Bush II administration and its neoconservative corporate and religious allies invaded Iraq under the pretense of removing the "tyrant" Saddam Hussein, a man American policymakers didn't consider a tyrant when the United States backed his invasion of Kuwait only a few years earlier. The American occupiers set up permanent military bases and wiped out every single law of the land—except one: Hussein's law prohibiting workers from organizing into unions. That certainly helped SSA maximize its profits as it opened its port operations in Iraq just weeks after the invasion. It also laid "business-friendly" groundwork for every multinational corporation salivating at the chance to move into Iraq once the hostilities subside, should such a day ever arrive.

And though the religious right and its powerful corporate underwriters continue their expansion into one of the most powerful political machines in the world, organized labor—a named enemy along with the devil and the Antichrist—continues to relive the same situations over and over again. This is the frustration union leaders like Ken Riley face every day. Yet he and others have a vision for change, a new strategy that with the right resources and the right leadership, can begin to take down, brick by brick, this formidable wall of wealth and power built over the last four decades.

But Condon lost the 2004 primary, too. Maybe his extremist positions and provocative statements had gone by the political wayside, much like the Christian Coalition had. He moved his office down the road, to a new space on Johnny Dodds Highway to launch his private law practice. The building he now occupies has a large, almost defiant, sign on its face for the benefit of the heavy commuter traffic: "Charlie M. Condon, Attorney-at-Law."

The advertising must have worked. In early 2007, Governor Mark Sanford nominated Condon to the South Carolina State Ports Authority Board.

"Some political appointments are so boneheaded, so out of touch, so shamelessly arrogant that they can only make you gasp," one Charleston journalist wrote of the appointment.[26]

Dewitt and Riley quickly mustered their respective resources—financial, political, and legislative. Within weeks, and after intense lobbying at the state capitol and crucial support from their old friend Senator Robert Ford, the nomination disappeared.

But by 2007, Local 1422's union hall was packed to the rafters with local residents coming to hear 2008 presidential hopefuls John Edwards and Hillary Clinton speak. It was a place for memorial services and weddings. It was where local legislators held forums to connect with their constituents. It even hosted an event supporting gay marriage. And in June of that year, it was command central for firefighters struggling with their greatest loss since 9/11—nine firefighters killed while battling a warehouse fire in Charleston. The hall had become the community center that members had envisioned in 2000 when they made tough decisions about building an extra space.

Whoever wins the next presidential election, Riley and his fellow dockers still face the same problems the Liverpool dockers faced a decade before. First, decades of policy stacked against them. And second, the intransigence of their own overarching union organizations. The summer of 2005 AFL-CIO split caused by the defection of the coalition of unions called Change to Win pitted Sweeney's own SEIU and the Teamsters against those who remained with the old federation, including the ILWU and the ILA. Because ILA 1422 is the most powerful union local in South Carolina, the national split didn't affect it much. In fact, after the split, the ILA still leased office space to Teamster organizers for a time.

Meanwhile, Riley continues to promote his ideas to the ILA in New York but with little success. When Wal-Mart established a terminal in Charleston, Riley started organizing its workers, until Wal-Mart threatened to move to Savannah and take its more than 200,000 containers per year with it. If ILA locals worked together, that would make no difference, because Savannah would threaten the same organizing drive, as would Jacksonville and Tampa, and so on. But they aren't working together. Still fearful of reform, the local presidents of powerful New York and New Jersey ports maintain control over the union even though 80 percent of the East Coast trade now comes through the South. Many say these men have been handed their jobs through "appointment or anointment"; they did not earn their leadership positions through organizing their locals, running campaigns, and holding open and honest elections that indicate a majority of support for them. Therefore they don't owe their members anything; they owe only the people who got them where they are. As long as that power structure is in place, the ILA will be slow to reallocate resources to organizing to protect and grow its membership.

Facing a moribund international union, a divided labor movement, and a political-corporate assault on unions, Riley remains patient, even optimistic, about the possibilities offered by the IDC's federation of dockers' locals. He's also optimistic that age and time will catch up with even the worst union leaders and that soon Leonard and Eddie McBride's efforts with the Longshore Workers Coalition reform group will come to fruition. They continue to organize, one longshoreman at a time, in ports up and down the East Coast, for the day they hope will come soon: when the ILA constitution changes the election process from its current system of delegates voting for international union officers to one member, one vote.

CONDON AND RILEY could never have known how southern heritage, Dominionist Christians, right-wing political operatives, and corporate money could come together to shape commerce, the shipping industry, and the Republican Party and make the events of that night in January 2000 inevitable. Understanding the story as something beyond the docks, beyond Charleston, beyond the individual lives and personalities involved, provides a way to tie together many such events, in the past and in the future, to make a pattern we can see and affect if we so choose. It is a story we are bound to relive in cities and rural communities, around the country and around the world, until we learn to organize a response. The Campaign to Free the Charleston 5 provides a window into that story and pieces of a solution.

But this much is truer today than ever: No city is safe from the damage unchecked global commerce can do. No region is immune from its devastating effects. And only an organized, collective response can force global players to redefine their priorities and treat local communities with the dignity and respect that builds healthy societies.

Afterword

CAN ONE VIOLENT CONFRONTATION of longshoremen and police on the Charleston docks, a protracted legal battle and a worldwide organizing campaign have anything to say to our country eight years after it happened?

Yes. Today the political, social and religious climate of South Carolina is just one degree hotter than the rest of our country. South Carolina resembles a third world country in many ways, and the United States increasingly shares that resemblance. White South Carolina's plantation attitude hasn't cooled off—it's just that the forty-year strategic campaign by the American Right has made the rest of our country so conservative that South Carolina doesn't seem so extreme anymore.

Strange as it may seem to Northerners, South Carolina is the bellwether for the rest of the country. Where in our land do we *not* live with, tolerate, and promulgate the racist assumptions that keep black people from achieving better lives at the same pace as whites? Where in our country have conservative Christians *not* made inroads (and sometimes superhighways) into our political debate, media, and education systems to dispute scholarship and equality and inculcate the public with oversimplified ideas of right and wrong to the detriment of reason and our democracy? What part of our country has escaped the assault on science, tolerance, and peace that right-wing radicals have engineered with the help of religious fundamentalists?

Where does Wal-Mart not rule with its relentless logic of the race to the bottom—paying workers less so you can buy stuff for less so you won't need to be paid more? What industry has escaped the assault on workers' rights?

Where in our land, or in the rest of the world, has there been greater inequality of any kind? America, the shining light of prosperity and democracy, under the assault of the Right, has become a second-rate nation that lives on myths instead of dreams. All measures of inequality have increased and all measures of quality of life have declined.

Where in our land do our households, communities, and commerce *not* rely on foreign goods made by people we will never see or know under conditions we dare not inquire too carefully about?

These are the goods that fuel our consumer economy. These are the goods that longshoremen move on and off massive ships in our country's ports every day and night. South Carolina, its black longshoremen, and the campaign of a small group of dedicated people waged to free five wrongly charged men have much to tell us.

Suzan

Ken Riley had already become famous among labor activists around the world when we met him in 2003. The story I had remembered from 2000 when I threw some money in a bucket passed at a Charleston 5 fundraiser was inaccurate, but later I learned I wasn't alone in walking away with the facts muddled.

I remembered some kind of riot on the Charleston docks when 660 police confronted a few hundred longshoremen. Videotape showed workers throwing rocks and railroad ties, jumping over police cars, and tearing down temporary light poles. Yet workers who were there called it a "police riot." Why?

There were not five black men, as many thought, but four black and one white, charged with felonies that could destroy their lives and imprison them up to five years.

Workers were not striking but picketing a shipping line that had decided, after more than twenty years of calling at the port of Charleston, to use nonunion labor. Longshoremen had picketed every ship in that line that called in Charleston—a picket once every two weeks for more than three months. Each picket escalated the provocation.

What was at stake was more than just five guys on rigged charges. The prosecution of these five men, none of them particularly active or exemplary union members, could have a chilling effect on union activity for decades to come in a state already so anti-union that only 3 percent of its workforce worked under the protection of union contracts. These five men were not heroes, but the campaign to free them was nothing short of heroic.

Second-generation longshoreman Ken Riley was not one of the Charleston 5; he was the president of the local union that represented the four black men (the white Jason Edgerton was a member of local 1771, clerks and checkers). He became the main spokesperson who traveled the world on their behalf as they sat under house arrest for twenty-two months awaiting trial. He and his officers—all college educated on longshoremen's wages—had been elected less than three years earlier. They were native Charlestonians, had worked on the docks all their lives, knew few people outside of their community and their union, and, faced with the intense media coverage and prosecution by a nationally known attorney general, were woefully ill-equipped to defend the members caught up in the dragnet that night.

Like many people I had spoken to since the 2000–2001 "Free the Charleston 5" campaign, I wasn't clear if they had won a true victory or a pyrrhic one.

In 2004, Samantha Clark, a union sister from the National Writers Union, emailed me to say she had just been to the South Carolina state AFL-CIO meeting and met the most amazing man with the most incredible story.

"The Charleston 5?" I said to myself as I read on about the longshoreman who had become a legend. She had told Ken I was the one to write his story, and she connected us.

Ken and I eventually met in a hamburger joint in Myrtle Beach. I sat across from this solidly built, dark-skinned longshoreman from a part of the country and a culture foreign to me. But his bright eyes were kind and his smile quick and calming. He wore a baseball cap over his closely cropped hair, a cap like the one he wore the night he took the blow to the head that gave him twelve stitches. There, facing this modest man and pleasantly articulate union leader, I suddenly felt about three inches tall. He could tell this story better than I could any time, any day.

"The truth is, Ken, I feel a bit intimidated by the entire project," I told him.

"Why?" he asked innocently.

"Well, I'm a *white, Yankee girl* who's never been a longshoreman," I said, emphasizing each word for its own devastating weakening effect. "What do I know about what you've been through?"

He smiled. "You'll do just fine. I think you're just what we need."

It is that kind of faith that characterized most of our dealings, including when I introduced Ken to my husband, Paul, who would be contributing his anthropological experience to the project.

Paul

Wherever we anthropologists ply our trade, do fieldwork, and live with people around the world to understand their lifeways and wisdom, we see the effects of the global system. We see it as factories replace the rice, corn, and wheat fields where peasants used to grow their own food. We see it in increasing rates of misery around the world. We see the households that used to feed themselves begging for work in factories or for handouts in overcrowded cities.

Some say it's better for folks to have a low-paying job under bad conditions than no job at all. Anthropologists wonder why that situation arose. How did it happen that folks who used to grow their own food are displaced from their land and livelihood? The many moving works by anthropologists offer testimony to these facts and how they are connected to larger global flows of capital and communications. We have documented the baneful effects of NAFTA, the WTO, the IMF, and the World Bank.

But every stitch the people in the factories make, every rivet they drive, every mold they fill is part of the same global system of finance and commerce. All of that stuff moves in containers to and fro around the planet at the beck of a computer. And sooner or later longshoremen have to take the containers off the ships and put them back on.

A Matter of Perspective

While we both enjoy telling a good labor victory story, this would not be the *Worker's Vanguard* version of the Charleston 5, with the shining, faultless heroes and the lone wicked villain the Left would have us believe made up the entire saga. Nor would it be the *New York Times*, slicing and hacking away at people's reticence, using quotes out of context or meeting up with secret informants who would pass along anonymous tips.

That's what we *didn't* want to do. But we couldn't quite say exactly what we *did* want to do, except that we wanted it to be true. Such a vague approach did nothing to settle the nerves of Local 1422's lawyer Peter Wilborn, an absolute pit bull of an attorney when it comes to protecting his client from any perceived threat.

We set out to tell a story from as many perspectives as possible, and to respect the varied points of view of longshoremen, prosecutors, police, defense attorneys, local businesses, global logistics companies, and activists worldwide. To get these perspectives we traveled to Charleston numerous times to interview all of the principals and others to get background information on the logistics industry and the Charleston waterfront. We traveled to Liverpool to commemorate the tenth anniversary of the Liverpool dockers' fight, a worldwide campaign that had galvanized dockworkers for the first time in recent history and laid the groundwork for the subject of this book, and to interview Spanish, Australian, and Swedish dockers who had roles in the story. We went to a conference in New York to learn more about the logistics industry. We rode around the docks of Charleston and Vancouver to get a better sense of the scale of the machinery longshoremen work with. We talked to archivists and searched libraries in Charleston. We went to church services and interviewed clergy in Charleston. We visited the S.C. Chamber of Commerce and interviewed a number of legislators. Finally, we went over the details time after time to be sure we had them right.

We believed that when these perspectives converged in the telling, as they had in real life, that very convergence would tell the story for us. We also knew that the long racist history of South Carolina, the complex and divisive religious terrain, the unique dependence a longshoreman unloading cargo in Spain has on the longshoreman who loaded it in Charleston, the power of collective action on both small and grand scales, and the immense and complex global system were critical dimensions to this story. These were dimensions that no one inside the story would have recognized with more than a shrug, if only because these are the atmosphere, the very air that surrounds every person involved. To them these details are not worth mentioning.

But it is those details that make this story much bigger than some individual case study or nostalgic labor victory from days of yore to be told to console people in the face of today's defeats. They make it a lesson in American history. They show why these events had to happen, that the story was inevitable. They call out a warning to every American community for today and the future as if to say: You can demand that global commerce be humane, allow people to retain their dignity, and respect the law of the land. If you are smart in your strategy and courageous in your tactics, you will change the balance of power and keep your communities healthy and strong. And if you do not heed the morals of this story, you and your communities will lose whatever purchase on the global system you have as well as your very dignity.

The Charleston 5 story gives us an opportunity to learn from some brilliant and lucky people who banded together under tough circumstances to bring their story to the world. Lo and behold, the world listened and its response rocked our shores. There's also a cautionary story because the larger union structures, the ones that should have responded, did not. The workers had to rediscover union activism, reinvent it, and they became radicalized by that process.

You didn't hear about it? No surprise there. But we have no doubt that the victory of the Charleston 5 created a blueprint for a future where commerce, having torn down national boundaries in its neoliberal-driven, greed-driven gallop across the globe, is forced to stop and negotiate humanity, decency, and respect not with statesmen and diplomats but with the lowest members in the hierarchy: the workers who move its goods and the local communities in which they live.

We said we set out to report all perspectives, but readers of our early drafts made it clear that we were being unkind to our audience: the story was little more than a cacophony of voices and details. So in the interest of telling a more focused story, we have had to trim, but we have documented extensively so those of you who'd like more of the story can find it.

Two important perspectives that eluded us throughout our research represent the two almost mythical sides of this battle: Charlie Condon, the S.C. attorney general, and the Charleston 5. We decided that if Condon would not, after our repeated and tenacious attempts to contact him, make himself available, we would not take extraordinary measures to contact the Five, either. Their lives had gone in new directions, as had Condon's, some were not willing to speak of these events at all, and none was in the position to speak for everyone. Ultimately, we realized that they all deserve to retain their largely symbolic places in this battle. Any representations we made of these six men come from previously published accounts, the relevant legal files we were able to attain, including those from the attorney general's office, and interviews with witnesses to the events, press accounts and press releases. Condon speaks for himself.

Despite our best efforts to present all sides equally, the president of Local 1422 still became the protagonist in this complicated story. Honestly, it's hard to find a more fitting hero in real life, and we are fortunate to have met him. But Ken Riley, first-term local union president, Charleston native, car hobbyist, husband and father of three in 1999 was not the same Ken Riley, worldwide celebrity, confident spokesperson, savvy strategist and rising star in one of the world's most powerful transportation unions we met in 2005 when we started this project. We hope we conveyed that in the telling of this story.

Finally, there are details in this book that never came out in the television, magazine, and extensive Web coverage of the almost two-year battle of the Charleston 5. CNN viewers and *New York Times* readers saw flying railroad ties and gravel, riot shields and clubs . . . because that was the story that terrified—and notably—mostly white reporters decided to tell. Subscribers to the leftist *People's Weekly World* and *The Internationalist* saw the same photos, but interpreted them differently. No published photo of the event tells the story like the police videotape recovered from that night tells it. That's why we described those details here.

In the end, the astounding events that ended that evening's altercation were not provoked by anything but a single command given by the man least suspected of it. Only the attorneys knew these details, and to this day only they and a handful of people know what happened in the immediate aftermath. Ken Riley, who had already left the scene at the terminal gate to get treated in the emergency room, learned the details as the attorneys prepared him in the days leading up to trial. Ironically, it was not until September 11, 2001, that he saw for himself just how, as one of his boyhood friends told him when he fetched Riley from the hospital, "it got worse."

To the credit of the many people we interviewed on every side, these details did not become evident to us until our last research trip to Charleston when we gained access, finally, after a long and frustrating search, to the attorney general's files and the entire videotape. These details shed light on today's America, the America we thought—we hoped—we had outgrown long ago. The fact that the black men present that evening never bothered to describe the violent details before now speaks volumes. In the memorable words of state representative Gilda Cobb-Hunter, "Black folk are just frankly tired of it. 'I don't wanna talk about it because nothing changes. We'll have this vigil, and sing Kum Bah Ya and the next day it's the same thing.'" Perhaps history will

show us that the Free the Charleston 5 campaign was not only a way to force
the process of globalization onto new terrain, but a way to bring us as a nation,
the *entire* nation, one step closer to the ideals for which we strive—the pursuit
of happiness and liberty and justice for all.

Notes

Chapter 1: The Provocation

1. Epigraph: Pilcher, Willie, *The Portland Longshoremen; A Dispersed Urban Community,* Holt, Rinehart and Winston, New York, 1972, p. 12.

2. Knight Ridder News Service, "Protesters March for Removal of Confederate Flag from S.C. Statehouse," 17 January 2000.

3. Will Moredock, *Banana Republic: A Year in the Heart of Myrtle Beach* (Charleston: Frontline Press, 2003).

4. Buster Edwards, interview with authors, 5 May 2005, corroborated by Ken Riley.

5. James Hammond, "Getting Plant Took Personal Touches," *Greenville News,* 9 June 2003, online edition.

6. Brett Bursey, "Picketing Longshore Workers Face Felony Charges, Jail," *The Point,* June 2001.

7. Gary Tillman, "Briefing the Troops," transcript of police videotape, 19 January 2000.

8. Susan Hill Smith, "Kenneth Riley, ILA President Dedicated to Keeping Union Progressive," *Post and Courier* (Charleston, SC) 19 December 1998.

9. Center for Economic Forecasting, "Economic Impact of the South Carolina State Ports Authority," School of Business, Charleston Southern University, 30.

10. The account of this night is taken from CCPD videotape plus interviews by the authors with eyewitnesses Tony Bartleme, Reuben Greenberg, Ken Riley, Bill Davis, Marion Green, Charles Brave, Leonard Riley, Johnny Alvanos, and Tony Hill.

11. J. Ruopoli and T. Brown, "State Ports Authority Supplementary Report," 20 January 2000, SPA-170 in *WSI v. ILA 1422.*

12. CCPD videotape, 19 January 2000. Charleston City Police Department videos made available to authors through a Freedom of Information Act request. Video stored at the Dorchester County Solicitor's office, Summerville, S.C. in a box marked "Charleston V."

13. J. Ruopoli, "Charleston City Police Department Supplemental Report," 23 January 2000, Charleston City Police-310 in *WSI v. ILA 1422.*

14. CCPD videotape from 19 January 2000. In terms of union and many other demonstrations, none of these actions are out of the ordinary for civil protest—ordinary members of a group and another bunch of designated "marshals" do their best to let people protest while also keeping it from getting out of hand.

15. Leonard Riley, interview with authors, 7 February 2005.

16. "CCPD Witness Statement of Sgt. Lawrence Boudolf, Employed by the State Ports Authority," 27 January 2000, case no. 0001396, attorney general's case preparation files, Summerville SC.

17. CCPD videotape, 19 January 2000.

18. In another example of culture clash, the 911 operator tells the longshoreman, who is speaking over the sound of a helicopter, voices, and vehicles, not to "yell" at her. Video shows he is speaking to her quite calmly though firmly about the situation.

19. Reuben Greenberg, interview with authors 12 May 2005.

20. Robert New, interview with authors, 12 May 2005.

21. Ken Riley, interview with authors, 7 February 2005.

22. Bartleme, interview with authors, 9 February 2005; Bill Davis, interview with authors, 13 June 2005.

23. Hack Green, interview with authors, 13 June 2005.

24. Daniel Riccio, Charleston Police Department, supplemental incident report, 20 January 2000.

25. CCPD, "Warning One" prepared by Charleston City Police Department.

26. Reuben Greenberg did not supply this portion of the videotape to the authors, and by the time they discovered it he had retired and was unavailable for comment. Evidence and interviews point to Chief Greenberg as the man who gave the order to shoot at the retreating longshoremen, even though until then his approach had been one of restraint. Charleston defense attorneys and others resisted the idea that Greenberg gave the order for the same reasons. Yet in the videotape he is standing next to the troopers who are firing. He is the commanding officer that night. An internal note of the South Carolina Highway Patrol from Reginald Gosnell to Ralph Mobley, the day before the event clarifies that "the Patrol has been tasked to provide assistance and support to the Charleston City Police Department...." Finally, Condon himself confirmed the chain of command when, while defending against the charge that the prosecution was racist, said "a black police chief (Greenberg) was in charge of the event." Tony Bartelme, "Indicted longshoremen adopted as union crusade," *Post and Courier* (Charleston SC), 3 September 2001.

27. "Activities Surrounding Nordana Vessel Call, January 19, 2000," SPA-0042 in *WSI vs. ILA 1422*. No author cited; document appears to have been prepared by SPA VP Anne Moise or Capt. Lindy Rinaldi.

28. Larry Young, interview with authors, 11 February 2005.

29. Charlie Condon's reputation for avoiding media interviews proved true for the authors. Information related to Condon is taken from press releases issued by his office, newspaper reports, interviews of colleagues and supporters, professed religious beliefs, and his actions.

30. South Carolina Chamber of Commerce, "Legislative, Regulatory and Union Update, 2005." This sentiment is recorded in almost every publication from the chamber.

Chapter 2: Storm Rising

1. Epigraph: Bernard Groseclose, "Public Input Valuable to Permitting Process," *Port News,* Port of Charleston, Charleston, S.C., December 1999, 4.

2. The shippers organized themselves into the Container Carriers Corp., later named USMX, in the 1980s because the frequency of ILA strikes caused by negotiating individual contracts was slowing down cargo and hurting the industry.

3. Stella Hopkins, "Charleston Braces for Protest on Waterfront," *The State* (Columbia, SC), 23 January 2000, B1.

4. Steen Obst to Claes Rechnitzer, email, 3 October 1999.

5. Obst to Rechnitzer, email, 7 October 1999.

6. Ben Brazil, "N. Charleston Port Idea Fizzles," *Post and Courier* (Charleston), 22 December 2000, 1.

7. Kaj Brodersen and Claes Rechnitzer to numerous Nordana officials, email, 15 October 1999, WSI 2546.

8. Tony Bartleme, "Another Player Entering the Terminal Picture," *Post and Courier* (Charleston), 15 January 2000, 1-A.

9. Kaj Brodersen and Claes Rechnitzer, to Nordana colleagues, email, 15 October 1999.

10. Claes Rechnitzer, deposition, *WSI vs. ILA 1422,* 10 April 2002, 213.

11. Brodersen and Rechnitzer to Nordana colleagues email, 15 October 1999.

12. Ken Riley, interview with authors, June 2006.

13. Douglas Feiden, "The Fat Cats on the Waterfront: How Bosses Load Up on Pay Despite Their Ever-Shrinking Union," *New York Daily News,* 3 January 2004.

14. John Bowers, letter to ILA membership, 28 March 2001.

15. The union's position is that ILA 1422 could not and did not organize, endorse, or participate in the events that followed as an organization, though its rank and file members may have.

16. Ports Authority Police Department, statement of Sgt. Cishek (unsigned), 26 November 1999.

17. Lindy Rinaldi to Anne Moise, SPA, memorandum re: After Action Report/Nordana Line/Vsl Schakenborg, 6 December 1999.

18. Summary of Capt. Rinaldi's report 11/30/99–12/1/99, Nordana Vessel Schakenborg, Berth 2, 10:20 p.m.

19. Riley, interview, June 2006; and Rechnitzer deposition, 9 April 2002, 168.

20. Lindy Rinaldi to Anne Moise, SPA, memorandum, re: SPA Police, 14 December 1999.

21. Claes Rechnitzer to Duane Grantham, "SPA Operations and George Young, SPA Marketing and Sales," email, 14 December 1999.

22. George Young, vice president, Marketing and Sales, SPA, to Claes Rechnitzer and Kaj Brodersen, email, 15 December 1999.

23. Melanie Fore, South Carolina State Ports Authority Police Department, Incident Report Complaint: 1/02/00, 19:15 hours.

24. Rinaldi to Moise, memorandum, 5 January 2000.

25. Claes Rechnitzer to Lars Rasmussen, Re: non-ila, 10 January 2000, WSI-2330, *WSI vs. ILA 1422.* Another racist signal to the longshoremen is the "they all look alike" attitude that is inextricably tied to the "crime" of simply being black and present, all of which is implied in Collins' attempt to prosecute the workers as a group, based on no individual identifying information.

26. Rinaldi to Moise, memorandum, 5 January 2000.

27. Rinaldi to Moise, memorandum, 11 January 2000, SPA 0037. *WSI vs. ILA 1422.*

28. Moise to Rinaldi, email, 18 January, 2000, SPA 0040 in *WSI vs. ILA 1422.*

29. Claes Rechnitzer to Ditlev Wedell-Wedellsborg, Lars Rasmussen, and Steen Obst, email, 20 January 2000, WSI-2167 in *WSI vs. ILA 1422.*

30. Ibid.

Chapter 3: Condon and the "Christians"

1. Epigraph: Reverend Joseph Darby, interview with the authors, 10 June 2005.

2. Gilda Cobb-Hunter, interview with authors, 10 May 2005.

3. Oran P. Smith, *South Carolina as a Southern State: Religion, Race and Republicanism*, in *South Carolina Government: A Policy Perspective*, ed. Charlie B. Tyer (Columbia, S.C.: Institute for Public Service and Policy Research, University of South Carolina, 2003).

4. Herb Silverman, "Inerrancy Turned Political," in *The Fundamentals of Extremism: The Christian Right in America*. Kimberly Blaker, editor. New Boston, MI. New Aboston Books. 2003. 174–208.

5. Larry Young, authors' interview. 11 February 2005. Young was in high school with Condon.

6. Lee Bandy, "Condon Relies on Faith," *The State* (Columbia, S.C.), 28 May 2002.

7. Aaron Sheinin, "Election May Widen Condon, Hodges Rift," *Knight Ridder/Tribune News Service*, 30 July 2001.

8. Bill Schleuning, Myrtle Beach, S.C.; posted on SC Hotline, available at http://www. schotline. com/letters0608.htm.

9. Editorial, "Unconstitutional Policy," *Winston-Salem Journal*, 27 March 2001, A8.

10. Bill Robinson, "South Carolina Attorney General Objects to Sexual Education Materials," *Knight Ridder-Tribune Business News*, 28 August 2000.

11. Sybil Fix, "Citadel Concedes, Accepts VMI ruling to Admit Women," *Post and Courier*, 27 June 1996.

12. Bruce Miller, former head of the local Christian Coalition, said that the Coalition has room for everyone, but political science professor Bill Moore at the College of Charleston doesn't necessarily agree. He referred us to the Bob Jones University materials that still called Catholicism "a cult."

13. Lee Bandy, "Use of Faith May Backfire in November," *The State* (Columbia, S.C.), 9 June 2002.

14. Don Flowers, interview with authors, 7 June 2006.

15. *Close Encounters with the Religious Right: Journeys into the Twilight Zone of Religion and Politics. Robert Boston.* New York. Prometheus Books. 2000. 78–83.

16. Ibid., 76. Reed would become George W. Bush's liaison to the religious right. From there he would chair the Georgia Republican Party and run for that state's lieutenant governor post, a race he lost in July 2006 due to his close association with convicted lobbyist Jack Abramoff.

17. Silverman, "Inerrancy Turned Political," 196.

18. Close Encounters, 77.

19. Kimberly Blaker, "The Social Implications of Armageddon," in *The Fundamentals of Extremism: The Christian Right in America*, ed. Kimberly Blaker (New Boston, Mich.: New Boston Books, 2003), 114–53, 123. Heston, while blunt, is not alone in his thinking. There is a continuing relationship between modern-day racism and fundamentalism in organizations such as the Aryan Nation and the Christian Identity movement. Some Dominionists, such as the founder of the Chalcedon Institute, R. J. Rushdooney, even favor slavery. Dominionist James Dobson for example, the next generation, has a powerful hold over the airwaves and niche publishing industry with his popular radio show Focus on the Family and numerous bestselling books. Perhaps the most notorious example is South Carolina's Bob Jones University, which lost its tax-exempt status in 1982 because of its policy banning interracial dating and marriage. The university's attorney argued that separation of races was a religious belief because "God intends

the races to be separate." Bob Jones Sr. was himself associated with the Ku Klux Klan. Yet Black Baptist churches commonly preach social justice and responsibility, love and mercy.

20. Ibid., 120–23.

21. Bandy, "Condon Relies on Faith."

Chapter 4: Taking up Positions

1. Epigraph: Mayor Joe Riley, on-air remarks, Live Five, WCSC Charleston, 20 January 2000.

2. Ken Riley, interview with authors 13 June 2005.

3. Ibid. David Tolan explained in May 2006 that he and all USMX executives had been advised not to talk to the authors because of a pending civil RICO suit brought by the U.S. government against the ILA suit pending in federal court.

4. Jack Heyman, interview with authors, 9 March 2006.

5. Tony Bartelme, "Riot on the Waterfront," *Post and Courier* (Charleston), 10 January 2000.

6. Stella Hopkins, "Nonunion Labor Triggers Unrest," *The State* (Columbia. S.C.), 21 January 2000, 1A.

7. S.C. Attorney General's Office, press release, "Condon Says Union Rioters Who Attack Police Will Be Put 'Under the Jail,' " 20 January 2000.

8. Hopkins, "Nonunion Labor Triggers Unrest."

9. Richard Green, "8 Dock Riot Charges Tossed," *Post and Courier* (Charleston), 1 February 2000.

10. S.C. Attorney General's Office, press release, "Statement of Attorney General Charlie Condon on Magistrate's Decision to Dismiss Dock Riot Charges," 1 February 2000.

11. Schuyler Kropf, "Charged Words May Color Condon Campaign," *Post and Courier* (Charleston), 11 February 2001.

12. Lyn Riddle, "S.C. Posts a Controversy," *Atlanta Journal-Constitution,* 12 August 1998.

13. "It's basically a black union and racism certainly plays a role in the politics of the state, though more subtle than in the past, so you have a state that is strongly anti-union and a state that is still very much affected by race so it certainly would be a win-win proposition as far as that particular issue is concerned." Bill Moore, interview with authors, 13 June 2006. Moore, College of Charleston political science professor, is an expert on extremist groups.

14. "There was a theology that was a fundamentalist theology that took root in the late 70s early 80s that did not like the ambiguity of life. That wanted everything to be black and white, right and wrong. There is no gray." Don Flowers, interview with authors, 7 June 2006.

15. Schuyler Kropf, "Condon and Miles to Run for Governor in 2002," *Post and Courier* (Charleston), 6 February 2001, 1.

16. Dave L'Heureux, "S.C. House Approves Anti-Union Measure," *The State,* 3 February 2000.

17. Sam Gresock, "Unions Gain 321 Members at Six Companies in 1999," *The State,* 29 January 2000.

18. N.A., "Labor Activity in 1999 Set Record for Decade," *Post and Courier* (Charleston), 7 February 2000.

19. Dave L'Heureux, "Panel OKs Ban of Labor Representatives on the State Ports Board," *The State,* 17 February 2000.

20. Wilbert Lee Jenkins, *Chaos, conflict and control: The responses of the newly-freed slaves in Charleston, South Carolina to Emancipation and Reconstruction, 1865–1877.* Ph.D. diss. Michigan State University, 1990, 135.

21. Reuben Greenberg, interview with authors, 12 May 2005.

22. Ted Reed, "Union Leader Balances Camps, Friends Say," *The State,* 4 Sept. 2000.

23. Claes Rechnitzer, deposition, plaintiff's exhibit 41, WSI–3634, *WSI vs. ILA 1422,* 10 April 2002.

24. Claes Rechnitzer to Stephen Cotton, letter, WSI–3636, *WSI vs. ILA 1422,* 30 January 2000.

25. "Perry Collins will bring materials which prove his stevedores hourly salary is average 12 US$." Kaj Brodersen to George Young (SPA), email, WSI–3006, *WSI vs. ILA 1422,* 7 February 2000.

26. "He virtually broke my attitude down. He probably, at that time, had a more cool mind than I had myself, and he was solely concerned about his business and nothing else. So he reminded me of the real scope of this." Rechnitzer, deposition, 290.

27. Eli Poliakoff, *Against the Grain in the Palmetto State: The Improbable Political Influence of Organized Labor in Charleston, South Carolina,* B.A. thesis, Dept. of Government, Harvard College, March 2000, 51–55.

28. Lawrence Thibeaux to Ken Riley, letter, 27 January 2000.

Chapter 5: On the Waterfront

1. Epigraph: Jamie McAlister, "The World's Ocean Ro-Ro Specialists Join Forces: Wallenius Wilhelmsen," *Port News,* Port of Charleston, November 1999, 19.

2. Skip Johnson, "Author Calls Book on State Ports 'Historical Fraud,'" *Post and Courier* (Charleston), 17 August 1991.

3. Ibid.

4. The authors' tour guide in Charleston said he had received a 94 percent grade on his tour guide exam.

5. Timothy Ward, "South Carolina's Ports, A Valuable Asset to Economic Prosperity," Greater Columbia Business Monthly, June 2005, 46.

6. Gini Beyer, comp., Charleston Regional Business Journal, Market Facts Book of Lists, Directory of U.S. Exporters (Charleston: Commonwealth Business Media Inc., 2006).

7. Andrew Herod, *Toward a Labor Geography: The Production of Space and the Politics of Scale in the East Coast Longshore Industry 1953–1990,* Ph.D. diss., Rutgers University, 1992. Quote cites the affidavit of Nester Sanjuro, president of Twin Express, in NLRB Case Nos. 22-CC-541 et al., National Labor Relations Board, Washington D.C.

8. Ibid., citing NLRB Case Nos. 2-CC-1364.

9. Perry Collins, interview with authors, 7 June 2005.

Chapter 6: Nordana Bows to Global Pressure

1. Epigraph: Rhonda Evans and Jason McNichol, "SSA Marine Strategic Corporate Research Report," Univ. of California, presented at the Global Unions Conference, New York, 9–11 February 2006, 4.

2. Claes Rechnitzer to Coleman Marine Supply, email, 26 January 2000.

3. Christy Hunt to Steen Obst, email, WSI 2177, Plaintiff's Exhibit 38, 20 January 2000.

4. Claes Rechnitzer to SKOCPT, email, 26 January 2000. See also Dave Munday, "All Quiet on the Waterfront; Police Stand Guard For Ship's Unloading," *Post and Courier* (Charleston), 24 January 2000.

5. Claes Rechnitzer and Kaj Brodersen to Lars Rasmussen, Ditlev Wedell-Wedellsborg, Jens Viggo Jensen and Steen Obst, email, Subject: Non ILA, 2 February 2000.

6. Ibid.

7. Union longshoremen seldom if ever negotiate directly with shipping companies. The stevedoring firms are responsible for finding business and competing against each other, with the union's master agreement acting as a constant among all bids for service.

8. Kaj Broderson to Lars Rasmussen et al., email, "Non ILA Charleston update," 5 February 2000.

9. Claes Rechnitzer, deposition, *WSI vs. ILA 1422*, 10 April 2002, 270–72. The letter from the consulate was referred to but not provided during the deposition.

10. Wayne Pinkleton, "Stevedore Responds," Letter to the Editor, *Post and Courier* (Charleston), n.d., posted at www.ibpatdc5.org/Charlston.htm.

11. Pauline Bradley and Chris Knight, eds., *Another World Is Possible, How the Liverpool Dockers Launched a Global Movement London,* Radical Anthropology Group and Haringey Trades Union Council, 2004), 36.

12. Jack Heyman to International Dockworkers Council, email, 13 February 2000.

13. Julian Garcia, interview with authors, 23 September 2005.

14. Ibid. Padraig Crumlin confirmed this in an interview with authors, 24 September 2005.

15. Paco Rivero, WECO agent in Spain, to Claes Rechnitzer, Kaj Brodersen, Ditlev Wedell-Wedellsborg, and Lars Rasmussen, WSI 2679, 10 April 2000.

16. Julian Garcia, interview with authors.

17. Paco Rivera to Claes Rechnitzer, email, 10 April 2000; Rechnitzer, deposition, 10 April 2002, 266.

18. Ken Riley, interview with authors, 12 June 2005.

19. Ibid.

20. Bill Fletcher, interview with authors, 29 June 2005. Ken Riley confirmed this exchange.

Chapter 7: Black Longshoremen: When Race and Class Collide

1. Epigraph: Henry Eichel, S.C. Focus of Unions, *The State,* (Columbia, SC) for Knight Ridder Newspapers, F1. 8 July 2001.

2. Since then, many neo-Confederates have pointed to these pro-Confederate blacks as proof that the evils of slavery were simply a Northern excuse to invade the South.

3. O'Neill, Stephen. *From the Shadow of Slavery: The Civil Rights Years in Charleston,* Ph.D. diss., (University of Virginia, 1994), 51.

4. O'Neill, 50–51. This brown elite used its economic resources to gain the approval of whites and to show the whites that they were different from the blacks.

5. Wilbert Lee Jenkins, "Chaos, Conflict and Control: The Responses of the Newly Freed Slaves in *Charleston, South Carolina, to Emancipation and Reconstruction,* 1865–1877,"

Ph.D. diss., Michigan State University, 1990. Later published as *Seizing the New Day: African-Americans in Post-Civil War Charleston* (Bloomington: Indiana University Press, 1998); Edward Powers Jr., *Black Charlestonians: A Social History 1822–1885* (Fayetteville: University of Arkansas Press, 1994); O'Neill, "From the Shadow of Slavery: The Civil Rights Years in Charleston."

6. O'Neill, "From the Shadow of Slavery," 67.

7. Long after slavery ended, and into the twenty-first century, blacks still derogatorily referred to advantaged light-skinned brothers, or any other black who would go along to get along, as "house Negroes." This emphasized the contrast to themselves, the "field Negroes" who bore the brunt of physical labor.

8. Powers, *Black Charlestonians,* 126.

9. Charleston Daily News, 5, 7, 9 January 1867 and 25 February 1868, quoted in Sterling D. Spero and Abram L. Harris, *The Black Worker, The Negro and the Labor Movement* (New York: Columbia University Press, 1931), 182–83.

10. Ibid., 183.

11. Eli Poliakoff, *Against the Grain in the Palmetto State: The Improbable Political Influence of Organized Labor in Charleston, South Carolina,* B.A. thesis, Dept. of Government, Harvard College, March 2000, 57.

12. Ibid.

13. Jim Campbell, interview with the authors, 8 June 2006. Campbell was collecting oral histories of ILA retirees. After World War II, the Charleston longshoremen officially affiliated with the International Longshoremen's Association (ILA). Campbell said that one retiree reported that when the union men from New York came to Charleston to negotiate, they demanded that German be permitted to join them at the table, and he did.

14. Millicent Ellison Brown, *Civil Rights Activism in Charleston, South Carolina, 1940–1970,* Ph.D. diss., Department of History, Florida State University, 1977, 189–92.

15. W. K. Pillow Jr., "NAACP President Endorses Picketing," News and Courier, 24 March 1969. Information about the 1969 strike was found in clips collected and kept by Mayor Palmer Gaillard Jr. and donated to Charleston Public Library.

16. Ralph D. Abernathy et al., *Appellants v. John F. Conroy et al.,* No. 13933, U.S. Court of Appeals, Fourth Circuit, argued 4 May 1970, decided 21 July 1970.

17. This announcement, coming through an AFL-CIO representative stationed in Charleston for the strike, was met with surprise by local ILA members, suggesting that the decision was made in New York and was the result of 1199 pressure on the AFL-CIO and the New York leadership of the ILA.

18. N.A., Federal Service 'Was Invaluable' Nixon Aide Says," *News and Courier,* 28 June 1969.

19. O'Neill, "From the Shadow of Slavery," 3–5.

20. Brown, "Civil Rights Activism in Charleston," 119–212.

21. In 2004, for example, unemployment was 6.8 percent, about 140,000 people, and almost three times that many had given up looking for work, putting real unemployment closer to 20 percent. U.S. Dept. of Commerce, Bureau of Economic Analysis, 27 September 2005.

22. U.S. Dept. of Commerce, Bureau of Economic Analysis, "Personal Income Grows In Second Quarter 2005," 28 September 2005.

23. South Carolina Dept. of Commerce, "Labor Availability," 2005, 9.

24. Figure based on $70,000/year, an estimated average based on full-time work plus royalties.

25. South Carolina Chamber of Commerce Annual Report, 2005. In 2005 alone, the chamber successfully lobbied to move $68 million to the highway fund to provide the vital infrastructure business needs, but on the taxpayer's tab, and another $51 million into its governmental arm, the Department of Commerce, to continue promoting the state. But business pays taxes, right? Not exactly. The chamber successfully won an astounding $835 million in tax cuts for South Carolina businesses in the same legislative session.

26. Jay Hancock, "S.C. Pays Dearly For Added Jobs," *Baltimore Sun,* 12 October 1999.

27. Howard Hunter, interview with authors, 9 June 2005. Hunter explained that the chamber later commissioned a study of its pro-business approach in 2003 which would radically alter its strategy:

"We were holding ourselves out to be the cheap place to do business, labor wise, business cost wise, and what that study showed us is that we'll never win that war. There are too many others who can provide cheap labor." Instead, the state needed to offer a better educated, more productive workforce. "Not longer hours or harder, but smarter," he said, "creating a workforce that's more highly skilled, tying the universities into the private sector with the research they're doing, and leveraging that."

Two of the movers and shakers on this front, Clemson University president Jim Barker and Wall Street financier and native Darla Moore, who donated $25 million to Clemson, had already seen the writing on the wall. In 2003 they struck a deal with the state and BMW to build an International Center for Automotive Research in Greenville. South Carolina, would provide a workforce educated by taxpayers and fine-tuned for BMW. "I think this is as significant as the Port of Charleston in its time, as significant as the original BMW announcement," said Harry Lightsey III, president of BellSouth's South Carolina operations, at the time. Rudolph Bell, "Auto Park Hailed As Economic Milestone," *Greenville News,* 9 October 2003.

28. Hancock, "S.C. Pays Dearly For Added Jobs."

29. Will Moredock, *Banana Republic: A Year in the Heart of Myrtle Beach* (Charleston: Frontline Press, 2003), 278.

30. Ibid., 279.

31. Ibid., 285.

Chapter 8: Condon and Riley Launch Their Campaigns

1. Epigraph: Clement Eaton, *The Freedom-of-Thought Struggle in the Old South* (New York: Harper Torchbooks, 1964), 146.

2. Future governor and U.S. senator, respectively.

3. Blease Graham, interview with authors, 8 June 2005. Graham is a professor of political scientist at the University of South Carolina.

4. Lee Bandy, "S.C. Attorney General Backs Elizabeth Dole For President," Knight Ridder-Tribune News Service, 11 February 1999.

5. Frank Bruni, "Bush Attacks McCain on Finance Plan," *New York Times,* 10 February 2000.

6. Richard L. Berke, "Why Certain Political Symbols Stick," *New York Times,* 27 February 2000.

7. Ibid.

8. Ibid.

9. Craig Hines, R. G. Ratcliffe, and Clay Robison, "Campaign 2000; Bush Notches a Win in S. Carolina; Rival McCain Loses Momentum," *Houston Chronicle,* 20 February 2000, 1.

10. Oran P. Smith, "South Carolina as a Southern State: Religion, Race and Republican-ism," in *South Carolina Government: A Policy Perspective,* ed. Charlie B. Tyer (Columbia: University of South Carolina, Institute for Public Service and Policy Research, 2003), 333. Special thanks to Bill Moore for pointing out this essay.

11. Hines et al., "Campaign 2000."

12. San Francisco Labor TV interview Steve Zeltzer, "Labor on the Job Presents Charleston Longshoremen Battle Union Busting & Confederate Flag," on *Flashpoints,* TCI San Francisco, 12 May 2000.

13. Bill Fletcher, Donna Dewitt, and Gilda Cobb-Hunter, interviews with authors, 2005–6.

14. Because of questions about properly allocating and receiving funds, a separate "Campaign for Workers' Rights" formed to receive funds for the defense.

15. Ken Riley to John Bowers and Benny Holland, letter, 9 December 1999.

16. Ibid., 17 April 2000.

17. "It was clear to me that they thought that I was pretty much out of my mind. Let's say there was a lack of engagement around it." Bill Fletcher interview with authors, 25 June 2005.

18. Schuyler Kropf, "Greenberg Backs Condon for Senate," *Post and Courier* (Charleston), 18 February 2004).

19. Donna Dewitt, interview with authors, 20 April 2005. Union membership is in fact spread pretty evenly across the state even sixty years after the uprising.

20. Ibid. Chances are, given polling statistics, that these white union members also vote Republican.

21. Ken Riley seldom loses his composure, but when this discussion arose he was clearly angry and frustrated over the issue of the union hall construction.

22. Patrick T. Riley, business agent, ILA Local 273, Saint John, NB, Canada, to Ken Riley, letter, 17 March 2000.

23. "The Black Radical Congress was important in terms of getting black activists in different parts of the country to start to get engaged," Fletcher said later. "Some members didn't quite see the relevance. Some people looked at it as a 'labor struggle.' They weren't initially convinced it wasn't more than a labor struggle and even so, there might not be enough cross over with black community."

   Donna Dewitt found a similar problem among her ranks: "Before we even tried to do defense committees, we were trying to make South Carolina members understand. A lot saw it as a racial issue, not something labor should be involved in. It's civil rights, and I had to do a lot of convincing that this is about jobs and keeping union jobs in the port, and that we're all about civil rights. It became a real contention—conservative members were saying this is a bunch of renegade members that had got out of hand, and we shouldn't support them."

24. IDC, "New International Trade Union for Dockworkers Is Born," press release, 6 July 2000. http://www.labournet.net/docks2/0007/idc1.htm.

25. Attorney General Charlie Condon's Office, "Condon Comments on Supreme Court's Upholding of Miranda," press release, 26 June 2000.

26. Jonathan Maze, "Despite Local Union's Victory, Labor Divisions Remain," *Post and Courier* (Charleston), 4 September 2000.

27. ILWU International Executive Board, resolution, "ILWU Policy on Charleston," 2–13 December 2000.

28. Attorney General Charlie Condon's Office, "Condon Says Public Funds Cannot Be Donated to a Labor Union," press release, 18 December 2000.

29. Andy Savage, interview with authors, June 2006.

Chapter 9: The Tide Starts to Turn

1. Epigraph: *A Trade Union Guide to Mobilization,* published by International Confederation of Free Trade Unions, Belgium, Second Edition, November 2004, 81.

2. Evelina Alarcon, "South Carolina Dockers on the Frontline for Democracy and Jobs," *People's Weekly World,* 24 March 2001.

3. Brad Cranshaw to Charlie Condon, email re: Charleston Riot Update, Charleston V files, Dorchester County Solicitor's Office, 24 and 25 January 2001. The name Hethington is misspelled throughout the correspondence.

4. Schuyler Kropf, "Condon and Miles to Run for Governor in 2002," (Charleston) *Post and Courier,* 6 February 2001, 1.

5. Aaron Sheinin, "Election May Widen Condon, Hodges Rift," *Knight Ridder/Tribune News Service,* 30 July 2001.

6. Jack Heyman, "Charleston Longshore Workers' Tour Takes Bay Area By Storm—$13,640 Raised for the Dockworkers' Defense," http://www.ilwu19.com/global/ charleston/tour.htm.

7. Herb Kaye, "S.C. Dockers Appeal for Support in Bay Area," *People's Weekly World,* 1 March 2001, posted to [BRC–DISC] Charleston Dockers, Document C. City Police 11, *WSI vs. ILA 1422.*

8. Steve Stallone, "Charleston Campaign Update," 13 February 2001, http://www.labournet.net/docks2/0102/charles1.htm.

9. Riley, Ken, interview with authors 15 March 2007.

10 Ken Riley, work calendar, "Charleston 5-related speaking engagements, July 2000– September 2001." Special thanks to Fran Shuler for unearthing this document.

11. Stallone, "Charleston Campaign Update."

12. Benny Holland to All Local Union Presidents South Atlantic & Gulf Coast District, ILA, letter, 14 March 2001.

13. John Bowers to ILA presidents, letter, 30 March 2001.

14. Padraig Crumlin, interview with authors, 23 September 2005.

15. Stallone, Steve interview with authors, 12 March 2007.

16. Kees Marges, ITF Dockers' Section Secretary, to all ITF affiliates, "ITF Reaction, Charleston: A Clear Case of Union-Busting," letter, 5 April 2001, repr. in ILA Newsletter 18/3 (Summer 2000): 5. Available at: http://www.ilaunion.org/news/nlp_char_page05.htm.

17. Peter Wilborn, interview with authors, 14 June 2006.

18. Claes Rechnitzer, deposition, WSI of the Southeast LLC v. ILA Local 1422, Kenneth Riley et al., 9 April 2002, 162–69. Videotaped deposition taken at Quality Hotel Marina, Vedbaek, Denmark, by Shirley Ann Tanner.

19. Rechnitzer, deposition, 10 April 2002, 317.

20. Riley, work calendar.

21. Donna Dewitt, interview with authors, 9 March 2006.

22. Jack Heyman, "Eyewitness Report on Charleston 5 Rally," 21 June 2001, http://www.labournet.net/docks2/0106/charls15.htm.

23. Brad Cranshaw to Charlie Condon, email re: Charleston Riot, 29 May 2001. If the assistant attorney general's working files are an accurate indication, Charlie Condon did not leave much of a paper correspondence trail.

24. SC Progressive Network, "June 9 Rally for Workers Rights in Columbia to Target Attorney General and State Legislators," press release, 31 May 2001.

25. Office of the Attorney General, "Condon Responds to Charges by S.C. Progressive Network Concerning the Five Defendants Indicted for Riot in Charleston," press release, 31 May 2001.

26. David Avant to Charlie Condon, email re: Riot Case, 1 June 2001.

27. Ibid.

28. Center for Responsive Politics, "President-elect George Bush, The new administration," http://www.opensecrets.org/2000elect/other/bush/transitioncmtes2.asp, 2 January 2001.

Chapter 10: Free the Charleston 5!

1. Epigraph: Marc Levinson, *The Box: How the Shipping Container Made the World Smaller and the World Economy Bigger* (Princeton, N.J.: Princeton University Press, 2006), 26.

2. Estimates range from 4,000 to 9,000 marchers. The authors have erred on the side of caution.

3. Jack Heyman, "Eyewitness Report on Charleston 5 Rally, 21 June 2001; http://www.labournet.net/docks2/0106/charls15.htm.

4. Lee Sustar, "Why You Should Defend the Charleston Five," Center for Economic Research and Social Change, 2001.

5. Text from http://www.iacenter.org/daewoo_ch5.htm

6. Lowery is a legend, a cofounder of the Southern Christian Leadership Conference, a world-renowned civil rights leader. A short biography is available at http://pewforum.org/events/0605/lowerybio.htm.

7. Bill Fletcher to 14 members of the steering committee, email re: Suggestions and Questions Regarding Next Steps, 11 June 2001.

8. Henry Eichel and Kate Derringer, "Charleston Five Case Spotlights S.C. Union," *Charlotte Observer*, 24 June 2001.

9. Schuyler Kropf, "Condon and Miles to Run for Governor in 2002," *Post and Courier* (Charleston), 6 February 2001, 1.

10. Henry Eichel and Kate Derringer, "Charleston Five case spotlights S.C. union," *The Charlotte Observer*, 24 June 2001..

11. Charlie Condon, "S.C. Must Bring Families Together," Charlie Condon, *Post and Courier* (Charleston), 28 June 2001, 15.

12. Bob Jones University listing of Greenville Area Churches, available at http://www.bju.edu/about/community/churches.html.

13. Aaron Sheinin, "Election May Widen Condon, Hodges Rift," *Knight Ridder/Tribune News Service*, 30 July 2001.

14. Lee Bandy, "Attorney General Launches Probe of Allegations of Racial Discrimination," *Knight-Ridder News Service*, 6 August 2001.

15. Jimmy Hyde, interview with authors, 31 May 2006. John Cox had suffered a stroke and was still recovering at this writing.

16. Lindsay Barenz to Ken Riley and Bill Fletcher, email, 25 June 2001.

17. William Rasberry, "On the Waterfront," *Washington Post,* 23 July 2001.

18. Steve Stallone to Bill Fletcher, email re: Report on Last Week's Work in LA with Ken Riley, 20 August 2001. Also, Steve Stallone interview with authors, 12 March 2007.

19. Ken Morgan, Local 6 ILWU, and Kees Marges, ITF Dockers' Section Secretary, online posts, 29–30 August 2001; http://www.labournet/docks2/0108/charls9.htm.

20. "If you'd asked ten prosecutors who they'd rather have, Cottingham or Rawl, eleven would've picked Cottingham." Andy Savage, interview with authors, 9 June 2006. This explained the attorney general's earlier effort to get the case in front of Cottingham.

21. Andy Savage to Armand Derfner, Peter Wilborn, and Lionel Lofton, letter, 16 July 2001.

Chapter 11: Countdown to Trial

1. Epigraph: Andy Brack, interview with authors, 5 June 2006.

2. Tony Bartelme, "Indicted longshoremen adopted as union crusade," *Post and Courier* (Charleston SC), 3 September 2001.

3. Andy Savage to Brad Cranshaw and Lionel Lofton, letter, 12 September 2001.

4. Mayor Joe Riley to Charlie Condon, letter, 24 September 2001.

5. Ibid.

6. Brad Cranshaw to Charlie Condon, email re: Charleston Riot, 25 September 2001.

7. Defendants' Motion to Quash the Indictment or to Disqualify the Attorney General, *State of South Carolina v. Kenneth Jefferson and Jason Newman Edgerton,* filed 2 October 2001.

8. Charlie Condon, Live Five Talk Back, transcribed by Ray Swartz & Associates, Charleston, S.C., 3 October 2001.

9. Brad Cranshaw to Charlie Condon, email, 4 October 2001.

10. Brad Cranshaw to Monique Ferguson, copied to Johanna Ferguson, Office of the City Prosecutor, email, 4 October 2001.

11. Ralph D. Abernathy et al. v. John F. Conroy et al., citation 429 F.2d 1170.

12. Charlie Condon to Walter Bailey, letter, 10 October 2001.

13. Walter Bailey, interview with authors, 13 June 2005.

14. Berger v. United States, 295 U.S. 78, 88 (1935), cited in *State of South Carolina v. Ken Jefferson and Jason Newman Edgerton, Defendants' Motion to Quash the Indictment or to Disqualify the Attorney General,* filed 2 October 2001.

15. Andy Savage, interview with authors, 9 June 2006.

16. "Tony Bartelme, Charleston Five Lawyers Attack Motives in Case," *Post and Courier* (Charleston), 12 October 2001, 1.

17. Defendant's Motion to Quash the Indictment, filed 2 October 2001.

18. Bartleme, "Charleston Five Lawyers Attack Motives in Case."

19. State's Memorandum in Opposition to Defendant's Motion to Quash the Indictment or to Disqualify the Attorney General and Supplement, *State of South Carolina v. Ken Jefferson and Jason Newman Edgerton,* filed 11 October 2001.

20. Ibid.

21. Phil Ponce, "The Jury Shall Decide," *NewsHour*, 17 December 1997; transcript available at: http://www.pbs.org/newshour/bb/law/july-dec97/nichols_12-17.html.

22. Defendant's Motion to Quash the Indictment, filed 28 September 2001.

23. The authors have pared down the arguments made in the hearing.

24. Armand Derfner, interview with authors, 14 June 2006.

25. Walter Bailey to Charlie Condon, Re: *State of South Carolina v. Jason Edgerton, Elijah Ford, Ricky Simmons, Kenneth Jefferson, and Peter Washington Jr.*, letter, 2 November 2001.

Chapter 12: Victory!

1. Epigraph: Chang Hsu-Chung, speech at the Global Unions Conference, Feb. 2006.

2. Jennifer Graham, "Violent Clash Stirs Union Passions," *Boston Globe,* 14 October 2001.

3. John J. Sweeney, memo to principal officers of state federations and principal officers of central labor councils, Re: Charleston Five Defense Committees, 16 October 2001.

4. Brett Bursey, interview with authors, 6 June 2006.

5. "Support the Charleston Five," flier, n.d., found in prosecutor's files.

6. John Hassell III to the Honorable Walter Bailey Jr. and Andrew Savage III, Esq., letter re: The Charleston 5 Cases, 24 October 2001.

7. Francine Thompson to L. Barenz et al. (22 others), email, Subject: Jim Hightower's Commentary, http://www.jimhightower.com/air/archive.asp, 30 October 2001.

8. Walter Bailey to Andrew Savage and Lionel Lofton, letter Re: State of South Carolina vs. Jason Edgerton, Elijah Ford, Ricky Simmons, Kenneth Jefferson and Peter Washington Jr., 25 October 2001.

9. ILWU Pres. Jim Spinosa to all ILWU locals, memo Re: Victory and Vindication for the Charleston Five, www.labournet.net/docks2/0111/charls4.htm., 9 November 2001.

10. "Freedom Here for Charleston Five," AFL-CIO News for Working Families, http://www. afl-cio.org/aboutus/ns11102001.cfm?elink.

11. n.a., Charleston Five Victory, ITF News On Line, no. 32 (21 November 2001); http://www.itf.org.uk/itfweb/online/english/Body_211101.htm.

12. n.a., Charleston 5 Update: ILA's Charleston Five Grateful for Labor's Support; Proud to Defend Workers' Rights, ILA Newsletter 19/1 (Summer 2002), 18.

13. Report, "U.S. Waterborne Foreign Container Trade by U.S. Custom Ports," U.S. Department of Transportation, Maritime Administration, 2001. Additional proof of the drop in Charleston's traffic during that time shows up three years later in a port-published article, "Charleston's Peak Season?" Ingrid Torlay, Port Charleston, Sept.–Oct. 2004.

14. This account relies heavily on Jack Heyman's "Report on a Victory Celebration: The Charleston Longshore Victory . . . and Beyond," *Labor Standard,* 25 March 2002.

Chapter 13: The Battle to Come

1. Moyers, Bill, Acceptance speech, Center for Health and the Global Environment at Harvard Medical School fourth annual Global Environment Citizen, 1 December 2004 http://chge. med.harvard.edu/events/documents/Moyerstranscript.pdf.

2. Leonard N. Fleming, "Massive N.J. Port Project Proposed: The $5 Billion Renewal of 50 Miles of Waterfront, *Philadelphia Inquirer,* 12 January 2006.

3. Drexler, "Stevedoring Services of America, Inc.," independent research report, (Denver: June 2002) as cited by Rhonda Evans and Jason McNichol, "SSA Marine Strategic Corporate Research Report," Univ. of California, presented at the Global Unions Conference, New York, 9–11 February 2006, 5.

4. Ibid., 7.

5. Ibid., 19.

6. Lee Tigner, interview with authors, 12 June 2006.

Chapter 14: Not Just Another Labor Story

1. Epigraph: Nelson Mandela, "Long Walk to Freedom," quoted in *The Impossible Will Take a Little While: A Citizen's Guide to Hope in a Time of Fear,* ed. Paul Rogat Loeb. (Boston: Back Bay Books, 1995), 73.

2. Sarah Anderson and John Cavanagh with Thea Lee and the Institute for Policy Studies, *Field Guide to the Global Economy* (New York: The New Press, 2000).

3. See, for example, Diane Wolf, *Factory Daughters: Gender, Household Dynamics and Rural Industrialization in Java* (Berkeley: University of California Press, 1992); Mary Beth Mills, *Thai Women in the Global Labor Force: Consuming Desires,* Contested Selves (New Brunswick, N.J.: Rutgers University Press, 1999); Patricia Wilson, *Exports and Local Development: Mexico's New Maquiladoras* (Austin: University of Texas Press, 1992); Eric Wolf, *Europe and the People Without History* (Berkeley: University of California Press, 1982); Ted C. Lewellen, *The Anthropology of Globalization: Cultural Anthropology Enters the 21st Century* (Westport, Conn.: Bergin and Garvey, 2002); Anderson and Cavanagh, *Field Guide to the Global Economy;* George Collier and Elizabeth Lowery Quaraticllo, *Basta! Land & The Zapatista Rebellion in Chiapas* (Oakland, Calif.: Food First Books, 1999).

4. Will Moredock, *Banana Republic: A Year in the Heart of Myrtle Beach* (Charleston: Frontline Press, 2003), 189.

5. Thomas J. McIntyre, *Fear Brokers* (Cleveland: Pilgrim Press, 1979), 55.

6. Moredock, Banana Republic, 190.

7. McIntyre, Fear Brokers, 67.

8. Ibid., 192–93.

9. Joanne Ricca, *Politics in America: The American Right Wing* (2002), 8 available at http://www.wisaflcio.org/political_action/rightwing.htm. Wisconsin State AFL-CIO.

10. Malise Ruthven, *Fundamentalism: The Search for Meaning* (Oxford: Oxford University Press, 2004).

11. Karen Armstrong, *The Battle for God* (New York: Alfred A. Knopf, 2000) 368.

12. Ricca, *Politics in America,* 8.

13. Ibid., 9.

14. "The Right Wing and Labor," UAW Solidarity Magazine, September 1995. Cited in *Politics in America,* 9.

15. Conservative Digest, June 1979; "The Profile Movement and the New Right," America, 13 September, 1980, 108. Cited in *Politics in America,* 7.

16. "Mobilizing the Christian Right," *Campaigns and Elections,* October/November 1993. Cited in *Politics in America,* 10.

17. Thomas Frank, *What's the Matter with Kansas?: How Conservatives Won the Heart of America* (New York: Metropolitan Books, 2004).

18. Jenny B. White, *Islamist Mobilization in Turkey: A Study in Vernacular Politics* (Seattle: University of Washington Press, 2002).

19. Scott Thumma, Exploring the Megachurch Phenomena: Their characteristics and cultural context, 2–4. Taken from his Ph.D. diss. *The Kingdom, the Power, and the Glory: Megachurches In Modern American Society,* Emory Univ. 1996. Updated statistics in Megachurches Today 2000: Summary of data from the Faith Communities Today 2000 Project available at http://www.hartfordinstitute.org/megachurch/faith_megachurches_FACTsummary.html.

20. Don Flowers, interview with authors, 7 June 2006.

21. Schuyler Kropf "Condon Tones Down, Enters Senate Race," *Post and Courier* (Charleston), 27 August 2003.

22. Ibid.

23. Bill Schleuning, "Condon Deserves Chance to Continue S.C. Service," Opinion, *Sun News,* 28 May 2002.

24. Ibid.

25. Bob Moser, "The Crusaders: Christian evangelicals are plotting to remake America in their own image," *Rolling Stone,* http://www.rollingstone.com/politics/story/ 7235393/ the_crusaders, 7 April 2005.

26. Will Moredock, "A Slap in the Face, Condon and Sanford smack down dockworkers," *Charleston City Paper,* 9 May 2007.

Index